How to Save the FMCG Industry

Chris Leach

How to Save the FMCG Industry

A Practical Guide for Building Collaboration between Suppliers and Retailers

Chris Leach
Aytoun Consulting Ltd
York, UK

ISBN 978-3-030-92985-5   ISBN 978-3-030-92986-2 (eBook)
https://doi.org/10.1007/978-3-030-92986-2

© The Editor(s) (if applicable) and The Author(s), under exclusive licence to Springer Nature Switzerland AG 2022
This work is subject to copyright. All rights are solely and exclusively licensed by the Publisher, whether the whole or part of the material is concerned, specifically the rights of translation, reprinting, reuse of illustrations, recitation, broadcasting, reproduction on microfilms or in any other physical way, and transmission or information storage and retrieval, electronic adaptation, computer software, or by similar or dissimilar methodology now known or hereafter developed.
The use of general descriptive names, registered names, trademarks, service marks, etc. in this publication does not imply, even in the absence of a specific statement, that such names are exempt from the relevant protective laws and regulations and therefore free for general use.
The publisher, the authors and the editors are safe to assume that the advice and information in this book are believed to be true and accurate at the date of publication. Neither the publisher nor the authors or the editors give a warranty, expressed or implied, with respect to the material contained herein or for any errors or omissions that may have been made. The publisher remains neutral with regard to jurisdictional claims in published maps and institutional affiliations.

Cover illustration: eStudioCalamar

This Palgrave Macmillan imprint is published by the registered company Springer Nature Switzerland AG.
The registered company address is: Gewerbestrasse 11, 6330 Cham, Switzerland

To my wife Jane, and my daughters Lucy, Katie, and Maisie. Without their love and support I wouldn't be where I am today.

Foreword

Back in the late 1980s I developed what has become an industry standard process for collaboration between retailers and suppliers, namely Category Management. It has been adopted all over the world, by countless business, and has delivered all that I had hoped for. At its centre is a focus on consumer–shopper needs and the creation of mutual value for the retailers and suppliers involved.

However, we are now at a critical point in our industry. We are faced with rapidly changing consumer and shopper needs, the incredible impact of digital shopping on shopper behaviour, and the major consolidation of retailers and suppliers. All of these trends are posing serious challenges to our industry and there is no more important area in need of our attention and re-evaluation than the collaboration between retailer and suppliers.

In recent years, we have seen collaboration be challenged, with many relationships that are focused on the short term and often characterised by tactical demands accompanied by a real lack of trust and commitment to work together. I have noticed this with increased concern, and I believe we now need to re-address this issue. Since I developed Category Management, we have learned that it is only through collaboration that we, as an industry, can create a real focus on the consumer and shopper and, through that, build a better business for all of us.

I have worked with Chris Leach for over twenty years. He has been instrumental in developing and delivering work across the world, with retailers and suppliers—work that has increased their skills and strengthened their capacity to collaborate. This has been especially evident in the area of Category Management. Chris has experienced the 'good, bad and the ugly' of the real world of retailer and supplier joint working. His perspective is thus grounded in the practical realities we face every day.

Chris's research has allowed him to develop up-to-date insights on the current and increasing dominant patterns of our industry. In particular, it shines a new light on what is happening in collaboration and, more importantly, what needs to change. One might say that, with this volume, he is saying out loud things we have only discussed privately and, from there, goes on to challenge us to change the way we work together.

Chris's book builds on the foundation and principles I established decades ago but offers a call to action much needed in our industry today. It invites us in the most compelling of ways to look again at the joint work we do, to deliver the focus on the consumer and shopper, and to rebuild trust and collaboration between retailers and suppliers.

Los Angeles
2022

Brian Harris

Acknowledgements

- Professor Lynette Ryals, OBE, for supervising my PhD and providing incredible guidance and counsel through the research process.
- Dr. Brian Harris for your continued support and sharing in detail the story of category management.
- Ian Hogg, thank you for your support and friendship over the last 25 years.
- Peter Lloyd, Martin Brewis, Kieran Hemsworth, and Dom Speciale for the camaraderie.
- Richard Garcia, for our always inspiring discussions.
- Liz Barlow and Srishti Gupta at Palgrave Macmillan and Rosemary Morrison, for all of your help and expertise in editing the book.
- To the companies and people involved in my research and interviews, you know who you are—thank you; this would not have been possible without your help and support.
- Many people have helped, supported, and inspired me throughout my career. I wanted to recognise you with my thanks (with apologies for those I have missed)
    - Ahmet Basaranoglu, Andy Batchelor, Alex Conrad, Carol Duguid, David Macklin, David Muskett, David Wood, Ferhat Sezer, Frank Grossi, Guy Shepherd, Ian Ainsworth, Ian Ditcham, James Stok, Jo Walsh, John Dye, Julie Watson, Klaas Mantel, Mark Murphy, Milli Ngo, Mike Holcomb, Neal Austin, Neil Stephens, Norman Gibson, Peter Eglin, Peter Leech, Phil Sanders, Renny Hemingway, Roger Jackson, Sarah Miskell, Will Green

About This Book

In *How to Save the FMCG Industry: A Handbook for Successful Collaboration Between Retailers and Suppliers,* Chris Leach draws from his extensive experience in the industry and original research to re-examine what makes for successful collaboration between retailers and suppliers. He outlines a history of the FMCG industry, showing us where we have come from, where we are now, and the problems we face. His analysis is supported by a summary of relevant research theory and how it applies to the current state of the industry.

He then moves on to give us a compelling review of four case studies of suppliers, showing what actually happens in their real-life efforts to collaborate with their retail customers, and what we can learn from their experiences. He brings all of this together to provide new solutions that can transform the way suppliers and retailers collaborate.

He provides practical ideas and tools on how this can be achieved across a number of key areas that have emerged from the theory and his own original research. These are real-world proposals that aim to step change collaboration and provide an even greater focus on meeting consumer and shopper needs, in order to create value for both suppliers and retailers.

Chris Leach has worked in the FMCG industry for over 25 years. He has worked for suppliers in sales and marketing, a retailer in marketing, and as a consultant to both. In 2019, Chris achieved his PhD from Cranfield School of Management. His research investigated how suppliers create and capture value through collaboration with retailers in the UK Grocery Industry.

Contents

1	Introduction: Why Do We Need to Look Again at Collaboration?	1
2	The FMCG Market: Where We've Come From, Where We Are Now, and the Problem We Face	11
3	The Theory, and How It Applies to the FMCG Industry	47
4	Collaboration in Action: Four Case Studies	87
5	Collaboration Under the Microscope: A Cross-Case Analysis	165
6	The New Model of Collaboration	189
7	Summary and Conclusions: Making the Move Towards Real Collaboration	233
Index		239

About the Author

Chris Leach has worked in the FMCG industry for over 25 years. He started as a 'Saturday Boy' stacking shelves in a supermarket at the age of 16. Following a University Degree in Retail Marketing, he worked first for suppliers in sales and marketing, then later as a retailer in marketing, and a consultant to both. His consulting work focuses on the interface between retailers and suppliers. In this capacity, he has worked across the world with all types of business, building their capabilities so that they can better understand their consumers and shoppers, and translate their understanding into action enabled by collaboration. Leach received his PhD in 2019 from Cranfield School of Management, UK. His research investigated how suppliers create and capture value through collaboration with retailers in the UK Grocery Industry.

List of Figures

Fig. 1.1	Triple Win needs. Source: adapted from Shepherd (2014)	2
Fig. 2.1	ECR collaborative model. Source: adapted from ECR Europe (1994)	15
Fig. 2.2	The 8-step category management model. Source: adapted from ECR Europe (1994)	16
Fig. 2.3	World's largest FMCG companies buying their way to growth—% $ Growth 2017. Source: adapted from Consultancy UK/OC&C	20
Fig. 2.4	Global to local approach high level	21
Fig. 2.5	Channel value growth projections—UK (2021). Source: adapted from IGD (2021)	23
Fig. 2.6	Margin pressures in online grocery retail—estimated margin per order %. Source: adapted from Conti et al. (2021)	24
Fig. 2.7	Vanishing economic profit in grocery retail (2012–2017). Source: adapted from Kuijpers et al. (2017, 2019) (Economic Value Add $bn)	31
Fig. 2.8	The consumer-shopper doom loop	33
Fig. 2.9	The shift away from non-traditional grocery shopping in North America and Western Europe. Source: adapted from Kuijpers et al. (2017, 2019) (Grocery retail sales $bn)	34
Fig. 3.1	Relationship quality factors. (Source: Adapted from Jiang et al. 2016)	50
Fig. 3.2	Power benefit matrix in an inter-firm relationship. (Source: Adapted from Cowan et al. 2015)	54
Fig. 3.3	Types of value in BTB exchange. (Source: Adapted from Pardo et al. 2006)	59
Fig. 3.4	Basic value strategies in business-to-business marketing. (Source: Adapted from Möller 2006)	61

Fig. 3.5	Customer business development team model. (Source: Adapted from Gruen and Hofstetter 2010)	66
Fig. 3.6	Tradition supplier-customer relationship model. (Source: Adapted from Gruen and Hofstetter 2010)	67
Fig. 3.7	Resource-based KAM framework. (Source: Adapted from Guesalaga et al. 2018)	68
Fig. 3.8	Competition Commission retailer power abuses instances reported. (Source: Adapted from HMRC Competition Commission Report—Appendix 9.8 2008)	71
Fig. 4.1	Alpha commercial team structure	89
Fig. 4.2	Alpha customer prioritisation	94
Fig. 4.3	Customer survey feedback	95
Fig. 4.4	Beta commercial team structure	110
Fig. 4.5	Beta strategy document	115
Fig. 4.6	Beta commercial strategy document	116
Fig. 4.7	Beta Customer Team meeting objectives	119
Fig. 4.8	Beta sales strategy document	121
Fig. 4.9	Beta sales strategy document detail	122
Fig. 4.10	Beta commercial strategy document	125
Fig. 4.11	Gamma commercial team structure	129
Fig. 4.12	Gamma corporate strategy document	132
Fig. 4.13	Gamma category captain report	137
Fig. 4.14	Delta Customer Team structure	150
Fig. 4.15	Delta customer feedback	157
Fig. 5.1	Cross-case comparison—company facts and KAM structure	167
Fig. 5.2	Cross-case research comparison	169
Fig. 6.1	Triple Win needs. (Source: Adapted from Shepherd 2014)	190
Fig. 6.2	Foundation principles	192
Fig. 6.3	Opportunities for growth	193
Fig. 6.4	The new model of collaboration	197
Fig. 6.5	Consumer and shopper journey overview. (Source: Adapted from ECR Europe, CS&J Framework 2011)	199
Fig. 6.6	Consumer and shopper journey opportunity mapping. (Source: Adapted from ECR Europe, CS&J Framework 2011)	200
Fig. 6.7	Consumer and shopper journey activation mapping. (Source: Adapted from ECR Europe, CS&J Framework 2011)	200
Fig. 6.8	Partner segmentation	204
Fig. 6.9	Mastering power matrix. (Source: Adapted from Cowan et al. 2015)	206
Fig. 6.10	Mastering power—proposed collaboration × power status	207
Fig. 6.11	Category-centred selling approach	215
Fig. 6.12	Commercial structure high level	217
Fig. 6.13	Golden thread category-centred selling	218
Fig. 6.14	Global to local organisation	219
Fig. 6.15	Commercial skills development	220

List of Tables

Table 3.1	Description of factors driving relationship quality	51
Table 3.2	Research framework for case studies	78
Table 3.3	Research instruments objectives	79
Table 4.1	Alpha Customer Team roles and responsibilities	90
Table 4.2	Alpha research finding categories and descriptions	91
Table 4.3	Beta Customer Team roles and responsibilities	111
Table 4.4	Beta research finding categories and descriptions	112
Table 4.5	Gamma Customer Team roles and responsibilities	130
Table 4.6	Gamma research finding categories and descriptions	131
Table 4.7	Gamma commercial strategy summary	134
Table 4.8	Delta Customer Team roles and responsibilities	150
Table 4.9	Delta research finding categories and descriptions	151
Table 5.1	Alpha findings: collaboration purpose and choices	168
Table 5.2	Alpha findings: collaboration work	172
Table 5.3	Alpha findings: non-collaboration work	172
Table 5.4	Alpha findings: collaboration barriers	173
Table 5.5	Alpha findings: power	173
Table 5.6	Alpha findings: value creation	173
Table 5.7	Alpha findings: value capture	174
Table 5.8	Beta findings: collaboration purpose and choices	175
Table 5.9	Beta findings: collaboration work	175
Table 5.10	Beta findings: collaboration purpose and choices	175
Table 5.11	Beta findings: value creation	176
Table 5.12	Beta findings: value capture	177
Table 5.13	Gamma findings: collaboration purpose and choices	177
Table 5.14	Gamma findings: collaboration work	178
Table 5.15	Gamma findings: non-collaboration Work	178
Table 5.16	Gamma findings: collaboration barriers	179

Table 5.17	Gamma findings: power	179
Table 5.18	Gamma findings: value capture	179
Table 5.19	Delta findings: collaboration purpose and choices	180
Table 5.20	Delta findings: collaboration work	181
Table 5.21	Delta findings: non-collaboration work and collaboration barriers	181
Table 5.22	Delta findings: power	182
Table 5.23	Delta findings: value creation	182
Table 5.24	Delta findings: value capture	182
Table 5.25	Cross-case theme findings	183
Table 6.1	The changing nature of commercial organisations' work and skills	209
Table 6.2	Category management process transformation	212
Table 7.1	Organisational assessment—questions to start your own thinking	236

1

Introduction: Why Do We Need to Look Again at Collaboration?

What we will cover in this chapter:

- Where the Fast-Moving Consumer Goods (FMCG) industry is now, what has changed, and what challenges this has brought to suppliers and retailers?
- Why current ways of working no longer 'fit for purpose' in this new market environment, and what needs to change?

The Fast-Moving Consumer Goods (FMCG) industry is enormous. In the UK alone, it's worth over $150 bn, employing 400,000 people. In the US it's worth over $900 bn, accounting for 6% of its total GDP (Statista 2021). It would not be an exaggeration to say that it plays a vital role in the health and wellbeing of nations, providing for the needs of families, week in week out. We only need to recall the start of the COVID-19 crisis and how incredibly the industry responded to meet the unprecedented challenges it faced to realise its vital importance to our collective health and wellbeing.

At the heart of the industry are two major groups, retailers and suppliers. Both are trying to best meet the needs of the people most important to them, in short, you and me—the consumers and shoppers. Make no mistake about is: retailers and suppliers are incredibly large and powerful businesses. Think of Walmart, with a revenue of $559 bn, or the largest supplier in the world, Nestle, with a revenue of $90 bn.

These businesses have to work together; they need each other to grow their business. The collaboration between each of them is the point at which they exchanged value, and hopefully create it as well in order to meet the needs of their mutual consumers and shoppers (Fig. 1.1).

© The Author(s), under exclusive license to Springer Nature Switzerland AG 2022
C. Leach, *How to Save the FMCG Industry*, https://doi.org/10.1007/978-3-030-92986-2_1

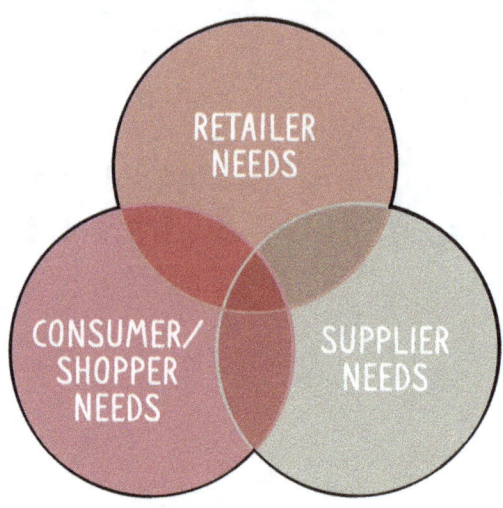

Fig. 1.1 Triple Win needs. Source: adapted from Shepherd (2014)

This is a concept that's well established in the industry. It's often referred to as the 'Triple Win' (Shepherd 2014). This is where each of the three groups needs to see a benefit if an idea, proposal, or tactic is to work. Said differently, we need to show how the retailer, supplier, and, crucially and often missed, the consumer/shopper will benefit from whatever we are proposing to do. Reduce assortments? How do each of the three parties 'win'? If one or more of them doesn't, it's likely not to work.

So, what's the problem? For any industry to grow and develop, it needs strong partnerships. Collaboration that is based upon taking a longer term and a short-term view to building business. But right now, that isn't happening. As those involved in the current FMCG industry know well, the 'norm' is often a confrontational, short-term view, often accompanied by threats of punitive action.

There has been a massive consolidation of retailers and suppliers over the last twenty years, as each buys competitors in order to increase its share and power, in the market. That's a route that's running out of road. What we are seeing is a never-ending discussion on cost reduction and efficiencies, driven by incredibly short-term needs, that I believe is putting the industry itself in a dangerous place.

Why? In the main, this is because the net effect of these trends is that consumers' and shoppers' needs are being left behind. If the discussion is now mostly revolving around lower costs and short-term decisions, there is a real danger that neither side will make the investments needed to innovate and develop the products of the future. They will see that the risks involved are too great when all the discussions they are having with their retail customers is about next week's margin and investment plans.

Such a huge and important industry looking ever inward at its own margins and balance sheet, versus outwards at its consumers and shoppers, is not a good place to be. This is especially true now since, more than ever before, consumers have an unparalleled level of choice in terms of where they can buy and shop. This applies not just to groceries, but to any type of food, drink, or household item.

This is not just a case of deciding which supermarket to shop at or which brands to buy, but it extends even to decision of whether you even want to prepare my meal. In many towns and cities, it's now possible to get my favourite meal delivered to me in less than 30 minutes. With the giant that is Amazon, I can get virtually any item that I can buy in a supermarket (and more) delivered to my house tomorrow. So, while the way we think about buying and shopping is in the midst of this dramatic and dynamic transformation, we have an industry of suppliers and retailers who are often focused on each other in an often conflict-ridden relationship, rather than coming together to examine the wants and needs of their mutual consumers and shoppers.

Collaboration is at the heart of the solution for the FMCG industry. Neither party can do it alone; although the way the behaviour of each side is going, it is easy to believe that they often think they can! Many industries have used collaboration for the good of each side and have transformed the way they work together. They use each other's strengths to grow together, not compete against each other. The opportunity is there for the FMCG industry to develop a fresh approach to collaboration.

Who Am I and Why Am I Writing This Book?

I have worked in the FMCG industry all my life, in suppliers, in a retailer, and as a consultant to both. I have worked in Sales, Marketing, Category Management, for big and small companies, in most of the major world markets. It's been my life. Often enjoyable (well, it would have to be to stay in it for 25+ years), but sometimes frustrating.

It's that frustration that started me on this journey. My first degree was in Retail Marketing in the late 1980s and I have learned a lot from every experience since. Whilst working for two suppliers (Spillers Petfood and RHM Foods) and a retailer (Tesco), I learnt about the industry—both how it worked and how it didn't work. I then worked for a consultancy (The Partnering Group) and gained an even greater understanding of the industry (we will get to that later).

But I was getting increasingly frustrated. Why was the way we worked together (retailers and suppliers) largely the same now as it was 20 years ago? Yes, the retailers and suppliers had become fewer and larger, but the actual way we worked together felt similar. I would talk to friends who worked in the automotive industry, and they described a rapidly changing model of collaboration. So, what was happening in our industry to stop this? The logical way to answer this perhaps wasn't to do a PhD, but that's what I did.

I was fortunate to find Professor Lynette Ryals at Cranfield School of Management, who is a leading researcher in Key Account Management and within that business-to-business collaboration. I entitled my research: *How do grocery suppliers generate and capture value through key account relationships?* I completed it in 2019, and after vowing not to undertake such a large writing task again, here I am.

So why am I here again? First, I have a passion for this industry, and experiences I wanted to share. More than that, I know that my research is the first substantive study in this field and bring new insights and a fact-based foundation to the issues, challenges, and opportunities facing us. Putting those two things together, I felt compelled to offer these insights to a wider audience. I hope to start a new conversation on how we can change the paradigm that guides retailer and supplier relationships in our industry.

My thoughts and proposals come from the heart. It's an industry I passionately care for, one that is important to the many thousands of people employed in it, and the tens of millions of consumers and shoppers that rely on it.

An Industry in Transition

My first proper role in the industry was loading my car with Petfood from a Cash 'n' Carry, and driving around Yorkshire in the UK, 'cold calling' small shops, convincing them to buy my brands.

It involved me in a business-to-business transaction, aiming to show my customer (retailer) the 'value' of my brands and their shoppers, in a simple and as interesting way as possible. To achieve this, I often used data and insights (provided by my head office), and sometimes got involved in collaborative work with the retailer (I physically re-merchandised the shelf so my products could fit on it!). In hindsight, this was a great learning experience; at the time it was hard yards learning direct selling.

1 Introduction: Why Do We Need to Look Again at Collaboration?

So, what's changed since then? Everything and nothing. Everything in terms of the structure of the industry, and everything in terms of the new tools and data that are available. But unfortunately, nothing has changed in terms of the end results for retailers and suppliers. One major change has clearly been the consolidation of retailers.

There are also now more channels of distribution for suppliers to sell in (e.g., the growth in convenience channels, and, of course, online). In addition, suppliers are selling directly to their own consumers (D2C). These trends have brought new opportunities, many challenges, and more complexity and cost to manage for both parties. However, these costs need to be recovered somewhere and that somewhere is often with the supplier. More than that, it's not just the costs that can cause issues, as was fully experienced by P&G in 2013.

> **Hell hath no fury like a retailer scorned—P&G Gets Caught in Rivalry Between Amazon and Target**
>
> In an effort to save P&G and Amazon warehousing and shipment costs, P&G began allowing Amazon to operate within its warehouses to ship items, such as diapers and toiletries, directly to consumers. The move was not received well by other retailers. Target retaliated against the Pampers maker in 2013 after learning about the partnership by moving its products to less prominent spaces in its stores. It also removed the "category captain" status from some P&G brands, meaning it instead worked directly with other suppliers to boost sales of their products, which included ideas like promotions on combined purchases of products.
> Source: Bowman, Motley Fool, Bowman 2015

This example is far from unique, as you will see in my research the use of punitive action by retailers is a common approach to 'collaboration'. I would like to suggest that this is because its 'easy' for powerful retailers to leverage their power, but it also shows a lack of imagination and vision. It often happens due to a clear breakdown in collaboration. Something must be missing between both parties if we reach for drastic measures like this, as opposed to seeking to find solutions that work for everyone.

There have been many changes in the 'tools and process' of collaborative working. For example, the data available to both retailer and supplier has been transformed, in terms of amounts of data, depth of data, and insights tools available. Tesco is a pioneer in this field with its 'Clubcard'. Many have followed and have developed incredibly detailed and sophisticated tools to analyse their customers' buying behaviour. However, most often, this data is not free, but is rather sold to suppliers often as a prerequisite for entering 'collaborative' work with them.

The Value Challenge

What hasn't changed? There does not appear to have been a step change in the value creation and capture between retailer and supplier. Retailers have leveraged their increased power with suppliers for never-ending discussions on cost reductions, whilst suppliers are trying to engage them in collaborating to find new areas for growth. This results in a tension, with the retailer often engaged in a short-term activity (demand for lower cost prices) whilst suppliers' growth plans are more medium term in their delivery of growth. This tension seems to have only one winner.

In the UK, the 'Grocery Codes Adjudicator' Christine Tacon investigated the practices of the industry in 2016. In her report, she gave many examples of the 'collaborative' behaviours of retailers and suppliers.

> It was clear from the evidence that a major focus of the Tesco commercial team during the investigation period was on hitting budgeted margin targets. A percentage margin target was a key element of many of the Joint Business Plans (JBP) which Tesco negotiated with suppliers on a periodic basis. **Payments to maintain the margin target were requested from suppliers by Tesco regardless of whether the planned growth had been achieved and regardless of whether Tesco had delivered on its own JBP commitments.** I found that the direction being given to Tesco's buying team as to the status and enforceability of JBP targets was contradictory and unclear.
> Source: (HM Government Grocery Codes Adjudicator 2016)

Without getting into the detail of this specific example, the text highlighted shows to me that the value equation isn't working, with the retailer demanding their investment/cost reduction regardless of any agreement that was made.

This dynamic was also a central finding in my research, and furthermore, it wasn't very clear what 'value' actually meant in this context. Value is a word we use a lot in life and in business. It's often assumed that we 'know what we mean' when we say value. In this industry, and when it comes to collaboration, my research has shown this isn't the case, not just between retailer and supplier, but within the supplier themselves. I will explore this more deeply in Chap. 3.

For all the advances in data, insights, technology, and in such processes as Category Management, Shopper Marketing, and Revenue Growth Management, we are still aiming to achieve the same things I was doing back in my car selling days in 1991. However, with all the extra levels of sophistication in the ways associated with working, data, tools, and process, the impact on value creation and capture isn't clear.

1 Introduction: Why Do We Need to Look Again at Collaboration?

It's not as if the industry itself hasn't recognised this issue and tried to change it. The Grocery Industry developed the concept of 'Efficient Consumer Response' (ECR) in 1995 to formalise a collaborative approach (Hofstetter 2006). ECR is an industry collaboration framework, developed by retailers and suppliers, that looks at the work deemed important to create collaboration between the two parties. It covers demand-generating and supply activities, and identifies integration and enabling activities, of which collaborative planning is one such activity.

At its inception, the intent of ECR was 'for retailers and suppliers to work together to satisfy the consumers' wishes better, faster and at less cost' (Hofstetter 2006). The ECR approach was intended to offer the suppliers a route to a longer term and a collaborative planning approach with its customers. For retailers, the intent was to gain greater access to their supplier's expertise, creating better value for them and their shoppers.

The motivation for ECR was to improve the collaborative nature of relationships to increase the value developed in the industry and avoid the industry declining into stagnation (Kotzab and Teller 2003). The ECR committee focused this definition on just the issues we are still wrestling with today: *'collaboration … increase the value … avoid … declining into stagnation'*. As we will discuss, we are still facing the same challenges.

Feedback to the government enquiry mentioned earlier and my experience in the industry suggest the end results are often the same as they have always been. In my research, I uncovered many examples of collaborative category management work, a key part of the ECR framework, that were often shut down and stopped by retailers when their short-term demands for cash weren't met. This really questions the value of these activities. If a retailer stops them in order to make demands for short-term investments, doesn't it call into question the approach we are using as an industry?

This focus on the short-term and leveraging scale with suppliers is so common that it's not even hidden from view. When the proposed merger between Sainsbury's and ASDA was underway in 2018, Mike Coupe, CEO of Sainsbury's, stated a key benefit for the merger was 'harmonised buying terms'.

> "Harmonised buying terms"—that is, extracting lower prices from suppliers—will deliver £350 millions of profit to the bottom line of the new business, as well as funding some further unspecified price cuts. That's a great deal of pain for suppliers to take.
> Source: Hipwell, *The Times*, Hipwell 2018

It's Time for Change

We are at a crossroads. There are so many challenges and issues we need to address that doing nothing is no longer an option. If we carry on as we are, my sense is the industry will forever zoom downwards in a spiral of low growth/decline, resulting in ever-increasing pressures on costs passed on to suppliers by ever more powerful retailers.

This could be characterised as the opposite of the 'Triple Win'; in fact it's a 'Triple Loss'! What this means is that if the retailer and supplier reduce investment, focus, and collaboration between each other, the consumer/shopper needs will not be well met, and the destructive cycle will continue and spiral downwards.

For the good of retailers, suppliers, and ultimately the consumer and shopper, the paradigm needs to change. The result of this cost-focussed 'collaboration' will always play out in some way that has a negative impact on shoppers (lower quality/fewer choices/less interesting and relevant experiences). It's time for a change!

What's in Each Chapter?

I have written this book to be a useful tool for anyone in the industry looking for new ideas and thinking about their situation. You may be a student or researcher interested in the case study research and how the industry works. You may be an early-years professional, looking for a sense of where the industry has come from and why we are where we are now. Or you could be a more senior industry leader, looking for inspiration, prompts, and ideas that you can apply to your own organisation.

To help this process, I have added at the end of each chapter both chapter learnings, but also key questions you can ask yourself. These should prompt your thinking and support you in considering how what you have read applies to you and your situation. In the final chapter, you will see a more extensive organisational checklist.

In Chap. 2, I will discuss where we are now as an industry, exploring the key factors affecting retailers and suppliers, and what this means in terms of collaboration. In Chap. 3, I summarise the theory, the literature that applies to retailer supplier collaboration, and the questions it poses for us.

Chapter 4 takes you through my research findings, using four company case studies. Chapter 5 provides an analysis of those cases, which includes my own assessment of what they mean and how they inform the debate on retailer and supplier collaboration.

In Chap. 6, a new model of collaboration is proposed. Based on the research and analysis provided in the earlier chapters, that model outlines practical ways in which we can change the way we work together that will not only prove mutually beneficial but will provide greater value to the consumer. In the final chapter, Chap. 7, I offer both my conclusions and a simple assessment checklist to enable you to understand where your organisation is now and where you could make your own improvements.

References

Bowman, J. (2015) Hell hath no fury like a retailer scorned. *The Motley Fool*. Available at: https://www.fool.com/investing/general/2015/03/06/pg-gets-caught-in-rivalry-between-amazon-and-targe.aspx

Hipwell, D. (2018) Sainsbury's and Asda merger: Suppliers are braced to feel the squeeze. *The Times*, 21 August 2018.

HM Government Grocery Codes Adjudicator—GCA investigation into Tesco Plc—progress towards following GCA recommendations (2016) Accessed at: *https://www.gov.uk/government/news/gca-investigation-into-tesco-plc-progress-towards-following-gca-recommendations*

Hofstetter, J. (2006) Assessing the contribution of ECR. *ECR Journal: International Commerce Review*, 6(1), pp.20-29.

Kotzab, H. and Teller, C. (2003). Value-adding partnerships and co-opetition models in the grocery industry. *International Journal of Physical Distribution and Logistics Management*, 33(3), pp.268-281.

Shepherd, G. (2014) The Importance of Triple Win Thinking. Accessed at: https://www.thepartneringgroup.com/categorymanagement/the-importance-triple-win-thinking/

Statista, (2021). Revenue of the food market worldwide in 2021, by country. Accessed at https://www.statista.com/forecasts/758620/revenue-of-the-food-market-worldwide-by-country

2

The FMCG Market: Where We've Come From, Where We Are Now, and the Problem We Face

'From Triple Win to Triple Loss'

What we will cover in this chapter:

- Collaboration, where have we come from and where are we now?
- The suppliers' landscape and their needs.
- The retailers' landscape and their needs.
- The retailers' view on collaboration.
- What are the questions we need to address?

> To put it bluntly, much of the $5.7 trillion global grocery industry is in trouble. Although it has grown at about 4.5 percent annually over the past decade, that growth has been highly uneven—and has masked deeper problems. For grocers in developed markets, both growth and profitability have been on a downward trajectory due to higher costs, falling productivity, and race-to-the-bottom pricing. One result: a massive decline in publicly listed grocers' economic value.
> Source: Kuijpers, D. Reviving grocery retail: Six imperatives—McKinsey and Company 2018, Kuijpers et al. (2019)

Collaboration: Where Have We Come From?

The modern 'FMCG' industry started with the development of a technology, that being barcodes. Before barcodes, retailers and suppliers had little idea of which *items* were selling well or not. Suppliers sold cases of product to retailers, which were placed on shelves, and the retail relied on manual stocktaking to gain some sense of 'sales' figures. This was a manual process, often done wrong, and one that gave little by the way of accessible data.

That all changed when in 1973 George Laurer, building on the idea of Woodland Silver (Fox), developed the Universal Product Code (UPC), and the era of item-specific tracking was born. Now retailers and suppliers could see the sales of items, and over time see this data split into regions, cities, and stores. Data companies grew in order to merge and chart this data. They could then sell it to suppliers, and ultimately create revenue for not only the retailers and suppliers but also themselves.

This transformed the industry. Now, faced with a 'flood' of data, someone had to make sense of it, and work out how to generate value from it.

In the late 1980s, the retail industry was experiencing several changes. Besides the data challenge, retailers at this time organised their buying teams by supplier. This meant they focussed on the supplier as the organisational construct, not the consumer or shopper. As sales and profits declined, the industry was looking for a new way to unlock growth and looked hard at their organisation and how they could better understand and meet their shoppers' needs.

In the late 1980s a lecturer in Buying and Merchandising at the University of Southern California, Dr. Brian Harris, thought about these questions and the future of the industry. As he explained:

> *We looked at what the biggest asset the retailers were managing, and that was inventory .... how could we better manage that inventory, to lower costs and increase sales?*

Harris's first development was the 'Space Management' software (Apollo). His idea was that all this 'epos' (electronic point of sale) data could better organise physical shelves in a retail store. That meant that products are given a unique place on the shelf, and more or less space, based on what they sold. This move was transformational. In a brief span of time, it actively focused retailers and suppliers on 'the shelf'. This meant they were looking for more and better placement for their brands, at the expense of competitors. The focus was on brands and 'share' at this stage. 'Winning the shelf' became a key strategy for the industry. Retailers and suppliers armed themselves with planogramming software and started collaborating in order to do the detailed work of generating plans.

This work is the foundation of today's collaboration work and still exists at some level. Retailers went through many iterations of how to best do this work, sometimes 'selling' the role of 'lead supplier' to large suppliers, sometimes asking many suppliers to contribute to the planning efforts. Plans became more sophisticated and more granular, and they did increase sales. For Brian Harris, however, something was missing. What he identified was the need for a strategic context to build these plans. There must be more to building a plan that just the past sales of products. What else could they need to develop better performing plans?

These questions led to the development of category management (CM) in 1990. This is a business process that looks at a product category, for example 'Soup', as a discrete business unit and places the consumer and shopper and their needs at the heart of the plan. It recognised for the first time that there were multiple inputs to a plan, and that there were also more tactics than just the shelf that could grow a category. This led to the development of the category management process.

We will review the process shortly, but importantly, it was a process that was developed as a collaborative one from the outset. As Brian said:

> *I based it on the strategic management principles and approach developed by Peter Drucker … how do we apply that level of thinking to a product category?'*

It was a process adopted by retailers in the US such as Schnucks, Wegmans and Walmart, and elsewhere worldwide by the likes of Albert Heijn, Coles, and Woolworths.

Efficient Consumer Response and Category Management

The next step in the change in category management, and in retailer supplier collaboration, occurred when the industry joined to set a standard and way of working together. The Efficient Consumer Response or ECR movement started in the US in 1993, and comprised leading retailers and suppliers, who recognised the need to align around a 'best practice' model for joint working, including efforts associated with category management.

This move transformed category management from a new initiative into one that became the recognised way of working for both sides. From the US in 1993, it was further endorsed and developed in Europe in 1995.

ECR is an industry collaboration framework, developed by retailers and suppliers, that looks at the work deemed important to create collaboration between the two parties. It covers demand generating and supply activities, and also identified integration and enabling activities, of which collaborative planning is one such activity.

At its inception, the intent of ECR was to develop a way 'for retailers and suppliers to work together to satisfy the consumers' wishes better, faster and at less cost' (Hofstetter 2006). The ECR approach would offer the suppliers a route to a longer term and a collaborative planning approach with its customers. For retailers, the intent was to gain greater access to their supplier's expertise, creating better value for themselves and their shoppers.

The primary motivation behind ECR was to improve the collaborative nature of relationships in order to increase the value developed in the industry and prevent the industry from declining into stagnation (Kotzab and Teller 2003).

As seen in Fig. 2.1, the model at a high level contains four areas. The first is the demand management that looks at the activities that can create consumer and shopper demand. There are tactical activities like assortment, promotion, and new products that are developed to generate increased sales in a product category.

The second is supply management that looks at different activities that are important to meet the demand created. In this area, there is also responsive supply (delivering on time in full the product order), integrated demand-driven supply, and operational excellence. These areas focus on both meeting the demand and identifying the cost-reduction opportunities for both parties.

The third and fourth areas are enablers and integrators. Data synchronisation and standardisation are aimed at ensuring a streamlined transfer of data between retailer and supplier. They also identified collaborative planning and forecasting as an integration activity, bringing the retailer and supplier together to build a collaborative value.

Taken as a whole, the model allowed the retailer and suppliers to identify the joint areas of focus and build their business together through the collaborative projects. As an industry body, the ECR movement often started and sponsored such cross-industry initiatives in each of the four areas to create the best practices and standards for the industry to use.

Within ECR, category management (CM) is the process that enables the collaborative shopper's value creation, as shown in the model (Fig. 2.1). It also looks to build the demand-side growth plans in a product category, typically as a collaborative approach between a retailer and key supplier(s). Category management looks to develop a plan for the range, merchandising, price, and promotion of a product category, using the data and also draws on insights between the retailer and supplier.

At its core is the 8-step process developed previously by Dr Brian Harris. Brian had now founded 'The Partnering Group' (TPG) to further develop work with retailers and suppliers. The decision to embed the process in an

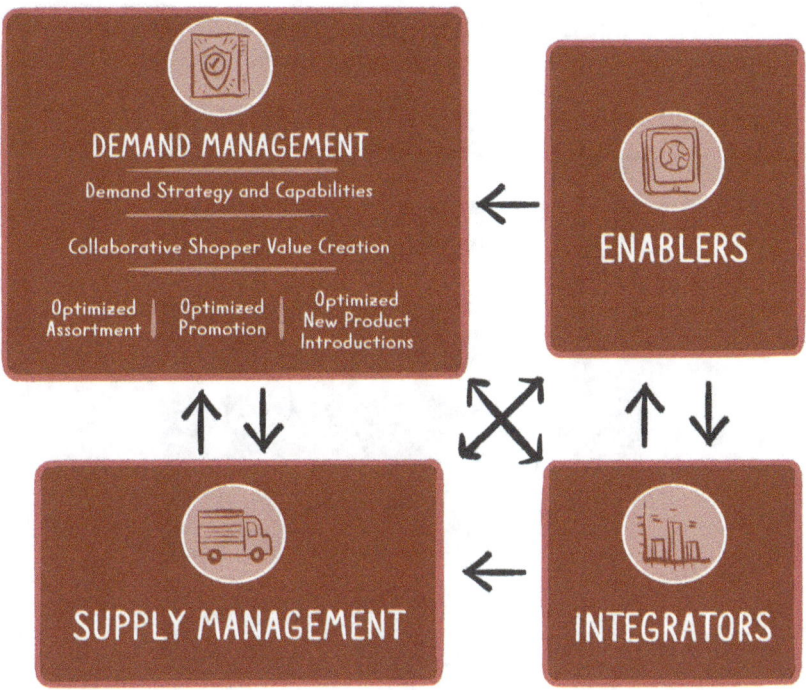

Fig. 2.1 ECR collaborative model. Source: adapted from ECR Europe (1994)

industry-wide initiative (ECR) ensures rapid adoption of this way of working between retailers and suppliers (Fig. 2.2).

In summary, the 8-step process treats individual categories as business units and, through a series of planning steps, develops standalone strategic plans for that category. ECR Europe and TPG designed the process in 1994 as a collaborative model between retailers and suppliers (ECR Europe—TPG, 1994).

At its inception, category management was a standalone process, but retailers have also formalised it, looking to have one supplier act as their lead category management advisor, or 'captain'. One example of this is the 'category captain' concept introduced by Asda-Walmart, and subsequently other retailers.

Category captains are suppliers who take the lead in advising the retailer on the direction and tactics that should grow the retailer's product category. This approach requires the supplier to be prepared to make recommendations to the customer that could offer the supplier no direct benefit but are the best options to grow their customer's business (Desrochers et al. 2003).

When is a category captain relevant? Category captainship emerges when the captain is 'more capable than compared to the retailer, the products are

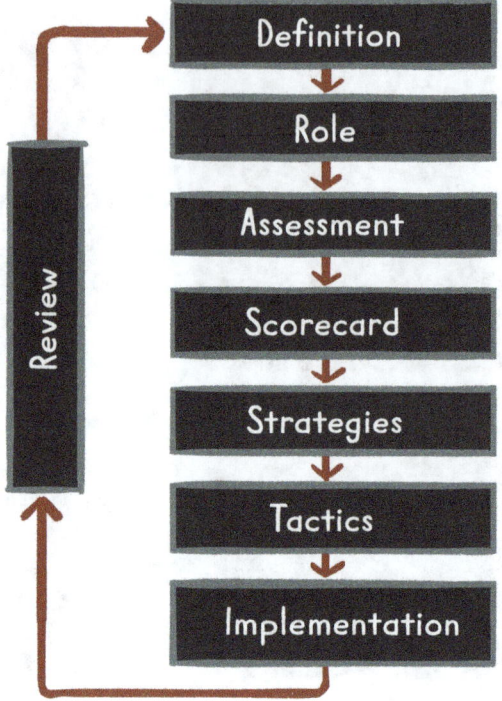

Fig. 2.2 The 8-step category management model. Source: adapted from ECR Europe (1994)

more attractive, and the cost of managing variety, retail margins (relative to suppliers' margins) and competition for captainship are moderate' (Alan et al. 2017, pp. 429).

However, recent research in category captainship has produced differing points of view on its success as a collaborative mechanism. Whilst research has shown evidence that retailers can enhance their performance through suppliers being appointed category captains (Alan et al. 2017), the effectiveness of captains is not as high as theory or best practice would predict (Brusset and Agrell 2017). The reasons for this appear to be on both sides of the collaboration.

Research suggests that the greatest benefit of these types of collaboration is data driven, that is, the power of sharing data for greater consumer insights (Akçura and Ozdemir 2019). However, this conflicts with research that has argued that data sharing mostly benefits the category captain in increasing their sales at that retailer (Alan et al. 2017). We could link this to the characteristics of the supplier and the category. Collaboration that took place in large and highly competitive categories, with little differentiation between brands, was found to help those brands sustain their position and power (Akçura and Ozdemir 2019).

Despite these challenges, some suppliers are seeking to collaborate even more closely with key retailer customers to uncover joint value and integrate their businesses to achieve that value best. This follows the concept of the 'enterprise offering' (Rackham and De Vincentis 1999), which is the idea that 'the customer "buys" the supplier organisation's total value-creating capability' (Rackham and De Vincentis 1999). For example, in the US, Procter & Gamble have created wide-ranging customer business teams, 'to work with the customer to provide joint solutions to problems and joint value for both organisations' (Gruen and Hofstetter 2010, p. 238).

Some in the industry have questioned the overall success of ECR. An interview with Paul Polman in 2006, then CFO of Nestle, conceded 'one of the core challenges is to foster collaboration (with retailers) when in so many areas we are competitors', and further, 'ECR adoption alone does not yield sufficient competitive advantage' (Polman 2006, p. 72).

The overall sense behind ECR is that it has benefits that can accrue for both sides, but these can be costly and difficult to realise: 'the key barriers to ECR are the capability and commitment of involved firms and their collaborative orientation (Aastrup et al. 2007). Further, this was supported by the research of Corsten and Kumar, who found suppliers 'increasingly apathetic about ECR Collaborations' (Corsten and Kumar 2005).

Research into category management as a collaborative mechanism has also questioned its effectiveness, with some arguing that the category management approach as a collaboration process is a mechanism for retailers to exert 'expert power' over suppliers (Dapiran and Hogarth-Scott 2003). In contrast, from a supplier's perspective, research has shown that category management can lead to reduced profitability (Mantrala and Kamran-Disfani 2018). Part of the challenge in the ECR approach could be its attempt to be both collaborative yet involve partners who are competitive (Kotzab and Teller 2003).

Perhaps in reaction to these challenges, and to the changes in the industry since its development in 1995, the category management process was enhanced by the Category Management Association (CMA) (Mantrala and Kamran-Disfani 2018). The CMA (an industry body comprising retailer and suppliers in the US) recognised that changes in the industry needed to be reflected in an updated collaborative model. These changes were the increased power of the retailer, the emergence of multiple new channels for shoppers to consider when buying (so-called Omni-Channel) and the availability of more and more powerful data sets to understand consumers (Mantrala and Kamran-Disfani 2018).

CatMan 2.0 differed from the original category management process (CatMan 1.0) in three areas. First, a new focus on organisation design and development at the outset of the process, secondly the increased focus on shopper facts and insights (from the new data sets available), and finally the addition of shopper marketing as a tactic, recognising that new data and insights can lead to new and more refined targeting of shopper tactics.

Introduced in 2016, it is now about to be replaced by Cat Man 3.0 from the CMA. The stated aim of this new process is 'to provide a playbook for executing wholistic category management across modes (brick-and-mortar, pureplay eCommerce, click-and-collect, 3rd party delivery, etc.), including tactical steps to be completed through an omnichannel lens'. As I will discuss later, I am not convinced there is a need for a new process. I believe the need is more to adapt the questions in the existing process to better reflect the needs of the omni-channel way of shopping that now exists. We will wait to see the impact of the CM's CatMan 3.0 approach.

Recent research is also showing that the challenges in performing category management activities may not just be about the process, but also its work. As consumer and shopper understanding deepens, consumers look not just at single product categories but at groups of interrelated categories when deciding on how to meet their needs. For example, when buying products for breakfast, they will not only consider cereals, but bakery products, yoghurts, fruit, and so on (Mantrala and Kamran-Disfani 2018).

These cross-category interactions increase the complexity of task for collaborations between retailers and suppliers. In a recent study in the Frozen aisle of US retailers, research highlighted that a perceived greater assortment in an adjacent category positively affected the sales of the surrounding categories (Hong et al. 2016). This dynamic has the potential to bring more complexity and challenge to the work of collaboration between the retailer and supplier.

Right now, the work for category management has been placed in the hands of suppliers. As retailers have reduced headcounts, suppliers develop their own 'category visions'. These are strategy documents that show how the supplier believes they can grow the category across the different channels through working with retailers. They look to engage and collaborate with retailers in this work.

This has brought challenges. Which retailers to work with? How to motivate a retailer for what is typically a project-based activity when they have little time or resources. In addition, the benefit of category management initiatives can typically take a long time to realise, when retailers are focussed on results in the short term. Finally, retailers are now using their own technological solutions to manage category management activities, such as range and merchandising tasks.

These dynamics are complicating further the work and benefit of category management work. This is the theme that will be explored further in this chapter.

In summary, the key points are:

- The availability of item level data created the foundation for collaboration between retailers and suppliers.
- Dr. Brian Harris developed the 8-step process to enable consumer-shopper focussed collaboration between retailers and suppliers.
- The ECR movement formalised category management and other work as a cross-industry standard for collaborative work.
- Category management has developed, but its benefits have come into question in recent years, with the supplier taking the burden of the work.

The Supplier Landscape and Their Needs

The landscape for suppliers has changed significantly in recent years. As retailers have been placing ever-increasing pressure on suppliers to reduce costs, suppliers have looked internally at how they can respond and achieve their own cost savings. Two major trends have emerged—the consolidation of suppliers and the emergence of innovative and increasingly powerful small suppliers in many product categories.

Turning first to consolidation, in the last twenty years, we have seen a radical change in the industry's structure, with many major deals driving consolidation of suppliers. Major companies such as Unilever, P&G, and Nestle have made significant purchases of their competitors and complimentary business.

Research by OC&C in 2018 showed that three quarters of growth in the top five CPG's was as a result of acquiring other business, with only 4% of growth being organic (Fig. 2.3).

Certainly, one effect of this consolidation of suppliers is that they have become incredibly large regional or global businesses. For example, suppliers such as Unilever, Procter and Gamble, Nestle, and Kraft have many thousands of people involved in marketing and commercial management teams. What these suppliers have done in order to manage these teams and their work is to standardise this work as much as possible across the world.

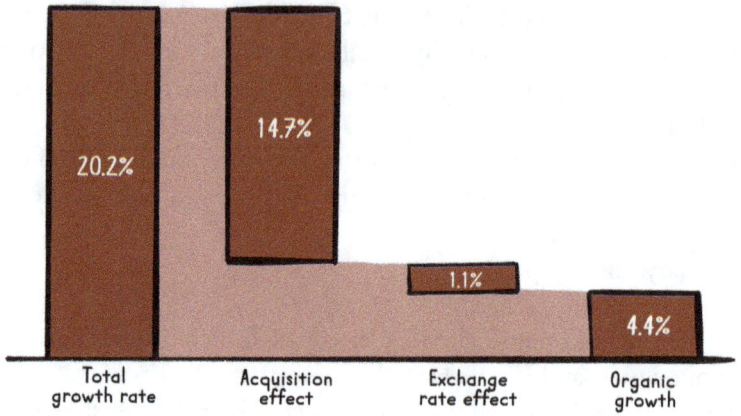

Fig. 2.3 World's largest FMCG companies buying their way to growth—% $ Growth 2017. Source: adapted from Consultancy UK/OC&C

Global to Local Organisations

This has led to the consolidation of manufacturing resources and head office teams, resulting in significant cost savings. One strategy used in streamlining the organisation has been to split their 'go to market' operations into global and regional teams supplying local markets with strategic direction. The global teams are developing strategy and ways of working, and local teams are responsible for delivery, including customer relationship management.

Whist using these strategies and toolkits, the local markets have no room (or resources) to change them. Their focus is on delivery with their customers. They have applied these same principles to develop a global approach to manage their brand portfolio. This means they can also direct local markets on what they want to execute, with which brands, and in which channels and customers (Fig. 2.4).

We know that there is a great focus from suppliers to create category management capabilities that are then used as the primary way of driving collaborative work with their retail customers. To enable this, suppliers will often use a 'Category Vision' toolkit. The Category Vision sets out in one place how the supplier proposes they can grow the category with the retailer. Larger suppliers create global visions, which they then adapt locally to enable the supplier to show retailers how they can work together to grow the category.

So, what has been the impact of this? This approach has undoubted benefits. The operating costs of this model are lower, and it means strategic thinking happens once, centrally, avoiding markets reworking strategies that can

2 The FMCG Market: Where We've Come From, Where We Are Now...   21

Fig. 2.4 Global to local approach high level

cause confusion and conflict. It also means that global brands are being managed centrally, again avoiding local issues.

However, it comes with issues. Firstly, I argue that this has been to the detriment of customer relationships. As suppliers standardise their ways of working and approach, creating central toolkits and ways of working, they are always trying to create a 'one size fits all' solution for all market types across the world. This means that when a customer faces suppliers who are operating in this way, they can run into issues where the supplier has limited flexibility in how well they can meet their needs.

The lack of local adaption and tailoring is an issue. Local customers and consumers are often looking for something from a category that the global brands don't provide and won't provide as it doesn't meet the globally developed strategy. This issue has led to the development of a more agile and focussed competitor, as well as smaller brands that identify and develop the gaps in the market left behind by the global manufacturers.

In the US, small brands grew four times faster than large brands in 2018/19 and as a result, are attractive for investment, with over $18 bn invested in small brands in the last five years (Kopka et al., 2020). The impact of this on large suppliers has been significant.

Where in the past retailers looked to their largest supplier partners for innovation to grow categories, they are looking to these smaller innovative brands for support. These small brands are focussed on being excellent in one area and market position, and they have a high level of organisation commitment to making it a success. What this means is they will be driven to provide the retailer with the help and support they need (including margins/investment) and be very flexible in how they adapt to each retailer's needs. However, this contrasts with the larger suppler who are often slower moving, set on their strategy, and inflexible on adapting to what the retailer wants.

This then shows up as more category support from the retailer for smaller brands (more products listed, more shelf space, etc.), placing even more pressure on the largest brands. As I found in my research, retailers understand that just stocking the same multinational brand, in the same pack size, at the same price, as everyone else, provides little to no competitive advantage to them. Smaller brands offer them a way to differentiate, almost in the same way as own-brands. In response, the reaction of the larger suppliers has been simple, buy out the smaller brands!

As previously explained, research by OC&C in 2017 looked at the performance of the top 50 consumer goods companies globally and highlighted the fact that despite growing value at over 20%, total organic growth was declining, and the reason for the growth was acquisitions. However, with acquisitions as one method of achieving growth, the other major challenge is the difficulty in growing product categories with their traditional customer base of large, 'big box' retailers.

Other channels are emerging and growing fast, and this channel expansion and shift is central to the development of the so-called Omni-Channel challenge. As with lots of new ideas and trends, a lot of confusion and fog exist in this description. At a foundation level, there have always been different channels that businesses sold through to shoppers and consumers. What is different is that many of the new channels that have emerged and become significant, because of their ability to meet shopper and consumer needs in different ways.

Omni-Channel Shopping

Undoubtedly, the largest impact has been that of the online channel, both as a sales channel and as a communication channel with consumers. We know there are now multiple ways shoppers can access most product categories without leaving their home, and these have seen an incredible growth in recent years (and fuelled even more so during the initial 18 months of COVID-19 pandemic). As seen in Fig. 2.5, just in the UK, online now accounts for 22% of the total grocery market and is predicted to grow to a 27% share by 2026.

So, what's the problem, growth is good, right? The first and perhaps most significant challenge is that all this growth is at low to no profit. Research by

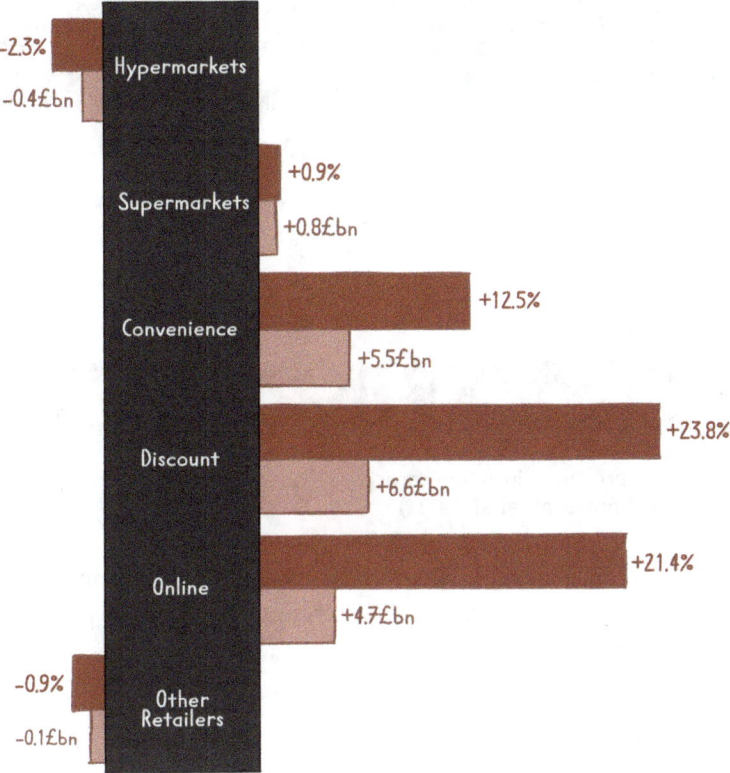

Fig. 2.5 Channel value growth projections—UK (2021). Source: adapted from IGD (2021)

Bain shows that, from a retailer perspective, the only online route to market that they make a profit on is store pick up. The Bain research shows retailers losing money on any other version of home delivery! (Fig. 2.6)

I think this is worth pausing to reflect on for a moment. There is so much energy, effort, noise, and investment in online in FMCG. Yet, the economic model for profit is not yet clear. There is work on automation underway by some retailers that may deliver lower costs and lead to profit, but these are the early days. So, by any measure, this is a major challenge for the industry.

For a supplier, this a challenge that is passed to them. Retailers are looking for partnership with suppliers who can help them 'fix' this profit gap. What is the point of growing a part of your business to lose even more money? However, for suppliers, even if they can provide solutions, this comes at increased costs. The management of online requires additional costly data to

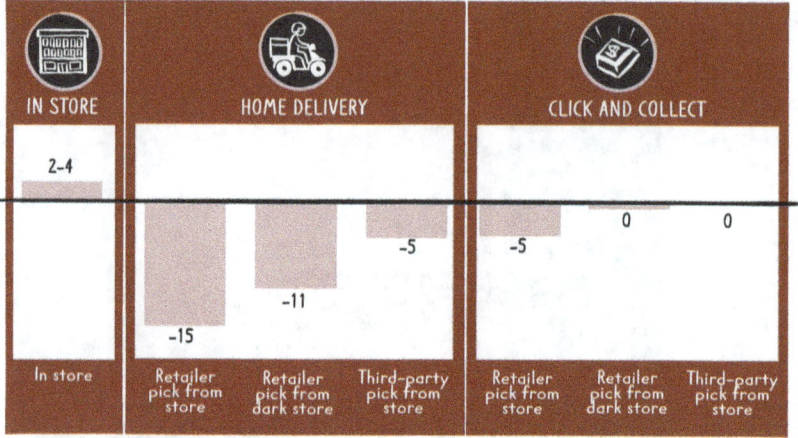

Fig. 2.6 Margin pressures in online grocery retail—estimated margin per order %. Source: adapted from Conti et al. (2021)

understand, and distinct skill sets to understand the channel, and to manage. It's a channel requiring specialisation and resources when the profitability of the channel is yet to become clear.

Direct To Consumer

There are other routes open to the supplier in selling to consumers. They can choose to sell to their own consumers, 'direct to consumer' (DTC). We have seen many examples of this in recent years, such as Gillette in shaving, Nestle with Nespresso, and Mars in pet care. Indeed, Unilever bought a DTC brand, Dollar Shave Club, for $1 bn in 2016, to achieve an immediate presence in that product category. The DTC approach can have undoubted attractions, cutting out a retailer (and its margin), creating a direct relationship with consumers, offering exclusive or added value products that are exclusive to the DTC channel, such as Coca-Cola.

Coca-Cola has launched personalised cans on its DTC site, allowing consumers to design special occasion products with their choice of name and message printed on them.

However, utilising a DTC strategy brings its own issues. First, it's a tiny value opportunity (at the moment) so requires way more resources to set up and run than the return it offers. In addition, it can complicate the retailer relationship. Current retailer partners may ask why can't this level of innovation, tailoring, and new thinking happen in their partnership with the supplier? It can be a potential conflict point for retailer collaboration. It offers brands a direct market relationship with their consumers, enabling them to gather data and communicate in a tailored way with them, and now this appears to be the major benefit, versus the actual sales achieved selling directly to consumers.

Discounters

Discounters now account for 28% share of the UK market (IGD 2021). I am not proposing to cover the history and operating model of discounters here. If you want a recommendation of how Aldi developed and work, 'Bare Essentials: The Aldi Way to Retail Success' (Brandes and Brandes 2015). My aim is to focus on the impact of discounters on suppliers (and later retailers) and what this means for collaboration.

With their limited ranges, low operating cost model, discounters are 'easy' to work for a supplier. They have one approach, and it's easy to understand and operate within. There aren't multiple points of contact, different store formats, large product ranges to analyse and manage, and so on. In my research, I often heard how much of a contrast it was to work with Aldi, for example, in terms of approach versus a major multiple customer. Not that there is deep collaboration with discounters; they don't have the people, or often will, for that approach.

On the downside, for suppliers, there are limited opportunities for brands, with most of their range of own-brands, or a version of their own-brand. Just as important for suppliers is the issue of how to manage the price/pack challenge. For many years, some suppliers refused to sell to discounters, fearing the response from their other customers upon seeing the same brand in the discounter at a cheaper price. This has changed, in part, because the channel is of such as scale it is a lot of potential business to ignore. However, like online, it provides more complexity and challenges to manage.

One-way suppliers have looked to create differentiation is by selling unique packs/pack sizes to discounters. This means they can tailor to the discount shoppers' need for value and have products that aren't as comparable to their products sold to other customers. Again, this is not new. At the start of my career, I was 'car selling' unique packs of petfood to the local store/convenience channel! This approach brings complexity though, and this is a recurrent theme around the omni-channel.

Traditionally, suppliers have succeeded with an operating model of selling largely the same range of products to a few large customers. This volume-base model provides large economies of scale, which are central to the negotiations with those customers, hopefully creating a win-win outcome where both sides see benefits. In addition, the consumer/shopper receives volume or other discounts for buying more (multi buys) so they get a better value, the 'triple win'!

This model is now breaking apart. Multiple different channels of sales are creating unique needs and challenges that need to be managed. This is creating more complexity in supply chains, with suppliers now needing to make unique and specific packs and products per channel. The complexity is now working out how to manage and sell through these channels, and hopefully to make a return for the business in the process! This is creating a demand for more specialised skills, especially in the areas of KAM and category management and, as mentioned earlier, these aren't necessarily profitable channels of business right now.

Supplier Organisation, Work, and Skills

If the traditional supplier model is under pressure, what is the impact of the organisation, work, and skill of those teams? In the final chapter, we will look at the potential solutions, but here I want to outline what I have seen through both my work and research in terms of the challenges suppliers are facing.

In terms of overall organisation, as mentioned, the largest suppliers have looked to organise around global to local models. Their intent is to bring efficiencies and create control over local markets, so that strategic thinking is more effectively executed. Using frameworks and toolkits has been central to this approach, accompanied by learning and development to support the ways of working.

This approach is now in question. First, managing the complexity of the omni-channel is requiring more resources (and costs) when we know growth is very hard to achieve. It's not just costs, there are new skills and capabilities required to understand and develop plans in these new channels. They also generate their own data sets, adding more cost and complexity to the data we expect the supplier to manage.

As we know, the omni-channel is also not just a sales channel, it's a marketing and communication channel. This is questioning the traditional sales and marketing organisational divide. Suppliers' sales teams are being asked to 'act as marketeers' in identifying marketing and product solutions of these new channels, and to work with marketing teams to make them happen. This is happening locally and globally, with supplier teams having relationships at both levels. With a global to local model, there are deliberately fewer resources at the local level.

So, there is the potential for customer frustration as they look for new tailored solutions, which are hard to make happen with a supplier. Some suppliers look to enable this at a global level, developing specific product/pack solutions and marketing activities at a global level, but even in this case, complexity is ramping up.

For example, in my consulting work, I recall a retailer in the UK visiting a global innovation centre for one of their suppliers, where they were discussing recent and upcoming innovations in the product category. They then got into a discussion with the supplier on which of these they found attractive and would like to adapt for their market in the UK. However, after being told that only certain innovations were available in certain markets, as decided by the central team, they could not have the products they were interested in.

Collaboration and Category Management

As we have seen, category management has evolved over the last 30 or so years but is being in question in terms of its relevance for today's challenges. Additionally, we know from research that category management is used by suppliers as THE main way it undertakes collaborating with its retail customers.

We will see from the research that the value of these category management activities is unclear. As well as the research, in my experience, suppliers find it very difficult to attach monetary (transactional) value to the proposals they are making in their category management initiatives. Even when they are using the latest sophisticated tools in areas such as range and space management, which have predictive financial modelling capabilities, they still struggle to make accurate forecasts on the benefits.

If the supplier does provide the predicative value benefits of their proposal, the retailer can be sceptical of the 'theoretical' numbers proposed, often calling them 'consultancy maths'! The suppliers themselves can be afraid of getting into commercial discussions about these numbers, fearing the retailer may use these estimated benefits against them. Their worry is that as they execute the plans, the retailer can demand the benefit shown regardless of whether the plan works.

This fear is genuine. In the report from the Grocery Codes Adjudicator in the UK, they found evidence of Tesco demanding payment for joint business planning activities, regardless of whether the activity delivered the planned effect or even took place at all.

Payments to maintain the margin target were requested from suppliers by Tesco, regardless of whether the planned growth had been achieved and regardless of whether Tesco had delivered on its own JBP commitments (HM Government Grocery Codes Adjudicator 2016).

Despite all the issues and challenges with category management, suppliers are doing more and more of this work. One reason for this is that retailers themselves are reducing headcount significantly across their commercial teams in head offices. In 2016, ASDA alone cut 800 out of 3000 staff (Quinn 2016).

This means that the category management work in areas such as data and reporting, range, and space planning, which they used to do themselves, is being passed along to the supplier. In effect, they are outsourcing the work and passing the cost of this work to suppliers. The suppliers, often in the belief that this is a 'good collaboration with the retailer', are taking on this work even to the extent of placing people in retailers head officers to do the work, be that as a 'category captain' or less formally.

However, this is changing. Category management work in areas such as data and insights development, range, and space management is becoming more and more automated, and the need for people to do this work is declining. Retailers are using these automated tools to bring the work 'in house'. This is also being enabled by them having access and control over their own data and analytics.

Retailers are placing greatest value on the data they generate and own, and suppliers are increasingly 'encouraged' to buy and use this data. The net effect of this is that retailers are challenging data and insights which aren't their own, making proposals more difficult to construct for the supplier. For the supplier, their costs increase further as they buy these additional data sources for each individual retailer. Even Walmart, which once saw data sharing as a key enabler of collaboration, is now moving to a model where they sell their data.

Walmart Has Some Data They'd Like to Sell You

> The earth's biggest retailer is building a Data Ventures unit to monetize what brands largely have gotten for free. ... The potential opportunity is huge. One Walmart and research industry veteran cites a rule of thumb that a retailer can generate $1 million in data and analytics revenue for every $1 billion of sales. For Walmart, that could mean north of $400 million annually in the U.S. alone from its namesake stores and Sam's Club unit.
> Source: Neff 2021

What does all this mean for suppliers? First, that the suppliers' influence may decline, as the need for them to provide resources to do this category management work for the retailer is declining. In addition, if the retailer focuses most on their own data (which the supplier is paying for) what is the need for the wider and deeper data and insights supplier category management teams are generating? This is a short-sighted view; in my experience, the supplier always has wider and deeper insights than the retailer. However, the challenge will be for suppliers to prove the 'value' of this to their customers.

This trend is raising a big question. If category management is THE major mechanism to collaborate with the retailer, and if the retailer can automate many of the tasks of category management, and don't need any extra help from suppliers to do it, what is the role of the supplier in collaboration? If its value isn't clear, then the future of category management as we practise it today must be under question?

Revenue Growth Management (RGM)

We have seen the emergence in recent years of 'revenue growth management' (RGM) work and teams in suppliers. This work looks to understand the value creates levers (price/pack mix/promotion/trade investment) and, through analysis, develops tailored approaches by channel and customer to maximise revenue. What has been the impact of this? In my research and experience, we are still in the early days. Many suppliers are investing in analytic tools to streamline this work, but regardless, it's another area of complexity and cost added. It's also challenging the supplier to consider how to combine this work with that of category management.

With channel complexity comes multiple category management solutions that are required by those channels. Even at its simplest, this means multiple data sources and 4 P recommendations to be created. Again, some businesses are looking to create this capability globally as well as locally, but as discussed earlier, this brings many challenges to meet local needs and adaption to local customer and consumer dynamics.

As growth declines and becomes harder to realise, the category teams are being asked to dig deeper than ever to find growth opportunities for not just themselves but the retailer. Combined with the channel complexity, this is adding work and cost to this area. One outcome of this in my research was that some suppliers are questioning the value of category management. If its costs are increasing, and growth is slowing, what is the value being added?

For some suppliers, the attraction of RGM and its analytics is found in seeing more brand-focussed, ROI-driven analytics that provide more reassurance of where growth can come from. In category management, the proposed benefits of category strategies and tactics are often difficult to forecast accurately and poorly reviewed in terms of their actual performance and ROI. However, for RGM strategies to be achieved successfully, they must deliver a consumer/shopper benefit and a retailer benefit—the triple win! This is the foundation of category management, so these areas need to work seamlessly together if they are to achieve the value growth the supplier expects.

I recall work I did with a supplier in recent years, where they built a complex tailored strategy to offer different sized multipacks to each of its customers. Based on its RGM work, it decided this was the best way to unlock value growth for its brands. Unfortunately, this was built without category team involvement. The result was the proposal had no clear consumer/shopper or retailer benefit. Let's just describe it as a 'hard to sell' to customers, and we know that the less the customer can see the benefit, the more it demands in terms of cost/investment.

However, despite these potential issues, RGM is growing as an area of focus and investment for supplier business. Research by Deloitte (Bazoche et al. 2019) indicates building RGM capability can deliver a 3–5% gross profit benefit, which offers attractive benefits to work towards. It won't be easy, with new data and systems required, and crucially new organisational skills. In research by Kantar into the future of RGM (Bishop et al. 2021), suppliers identified data harmonisation, process, and people as the three key barriers to RGM success.

So, in summary, from a supplier perspective, the challenges they are facing in value creation and capture through collaboration are many. They are

- Slow growth and rising costs are driving acquisitions of competitors.
- Global to local organisation designs have reduced costs, but reduced flexibility and adaption to local needs.
- Smaller and increasingly powerful brands are filling the gaps left by global brand business.
- The omni-channel challenge is driving costs and complexity into the supplier organisation.
- The traditional structure and work of the supplier commercial organisation are under question.
- Category management and Revenue Growth Management work is undergoing significant change and challenge.

The Retailer Landscape and Their Needs

It's not too dramatic to say that right now the FMCG retail industry is experiencing unprecedented change, and, with it, challenges on multiple fronts. These disruptions are from the structure of the industry itself and competition; from the consumer-shopper landscape and their rapidly changing needs and behaviours; and from the wider economy and its impact on retailers' costs. These factors are happening at once and causing dramatic changes in how they are operating.

The rapid growth of the omni-channel is challenging how retailers reach their potential shoppers, in terms of how they communicate with them, sell to them, and who they compete with. There are undoubtedly growth opportunities in selling online, yet this growth appears to come at the expense of profitability.

The effect of these changes has been massive. Research by McKinsey has predicted that grocery retailers could lose $200 billion to $700 billion in revenues if they do not act to address these challenges. For context, the same research showed that between 2014 and 2017 grocery retailer lost 54% of their economic value (Fig. 2.7).

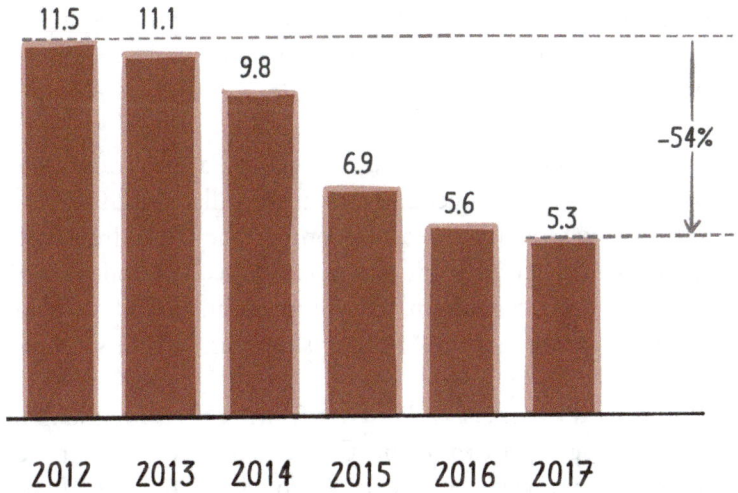

Fig. 2.7 Vanishing economic profit in grocery retail (2012–2017). Source: adapted from Kuijpers et al. (2017, 2019) (Economic Value Add $bn)

Consumers and Shoppers

Consumers and shoppers are experiencing an ever-increasing choice in how they plan and buy their shopping. Many have multiple home delivery options and physical store options to make choices from. They are being offered discounts and loyalty programmes by several retailers. Many of those retailers are making bold promises on the cheapest prices, and these are not only the discounters. For consumers and shoppers, this is both a positive in terms of the choices open to them, but also a challenge in how to navigate the many decisions for them and their families when they're making purchases.

This level of choice is causing confusion, and it's clear in many product categories that are bought regularly, their energy and interest are declining. One-way shoppers manage this amount of choice they face is to revert to 'buying what I have always bought'. As this behaviour increases across other product categories, shoppers become oblivious to the efforts of retailers and suppliers to engage them in interacting with the product categories in different ways.

This is a vicious circle where the consumer spends less time and energy looking at the category, the retailer perceives this as the category being less interesting, so reduces the range, and the opportunity for new items, which reduces supplier activity (new products, promotions), resulting in further reduction in consumer-shopper interest in the category.

It's easy to see that soon, for some product categories, these will almost be automatic reorder items where innovation and new product development will virtually cease. In these cases, shoppers and consumers will search for who can provide them with the cheapest *possible price for the products they want to buy* (Fig. 2.8).

The largest shifts they have seen in recent years are at two ends of the demographic spectrum. At the younger end, so-called Millennials have very different habits to their parents for grocery shopping. They shop frequently, often for meals for tonight/tomorrow, and will look for speed, simplicity, and offers. They have obvious needs for sustainability surrounding their food choices and are increasingly interested in online shopping for its convenience (Barclays 2018).

This group is hard to attract and interest in what they often look on as an 'old fashioned' shopping environment. Convenience stores better meet their needs, as do delivery services, such as Deliveroo and Uber Eats. In addition, they will often blur in home and out-of-home choice together. Dinner tonight

Fig. 2.8 The consumer-shopper doom loop

could be a trip to a local store or ordering a meal on demand from the likes of Deliveroo, or somewhere between, such as subscribing to meal kits delivered to their home.

These factors present tremendous challenges for retailers in meeting their needs, against this very wide competitive set, whilst offering good value and keeping their costs under control. This group is vital to the future of the industry; behaviours set at this stage often carry over into later life stages, when their potential value to retailers is even higher.

At the other end of the spectrum, so-called baby boomers have lots of money to spend relative to other groups but have different needs (Barclays 2018). They look more for increased service in store, have health and wellness concerns, and look for tailored products for their time of life. As with Millennials, they are increasingly using technology, shopping online for bulk items, and using stores for ideas, inspiration, and advice.

For all groups, there is a trend towards out-of-home calories and expenditure growing faster than those bought in supermarkets and cooked or prepared at home. This consumer landscape for retailers is alarming. How do I better meet these needs, compete with out-of-home options, whilst at the same time deliver this in a cost-efficient way? The evidence so far suggests that retailers aren't being that successful in meeting this challenge.

Omni-Channel

We have discussed earlier in the supplier challenges the move to omni-channel shopping. For a retailer, the profit impact is tremendous (Fig. 2.6), and this is a challenge that is forecast to continue. McKinsey research is forecasting that up to $700 bn could shift away from traditional grocery to other formats and channels (including online) by 2026 (Fig. 2.9).

This means a shift not only to convenience, which most retailers are present in, but further growth in online and discounters, where the impact will be much harder to manage. With overall online profitability severely challenged at the moment, grocery retailers are now seeing the 'Big Beast' of Amazon becoming increasingly invested in their market.

Amazon has deployed several strategies as they have entered and developed in the FMCG market. This is seen from their direct selling via Amazon Prime with Morrisons, Amazon Fresh, to now owning and operating their own physical stores with Wholefoods and the Amazon 'Go' convenience format. Their approach to physical retail is to leverage their deep advantage on technology to create differences in shopping experiences versus traditional grocers. These advantages are ones that will be hard and expensive to match.

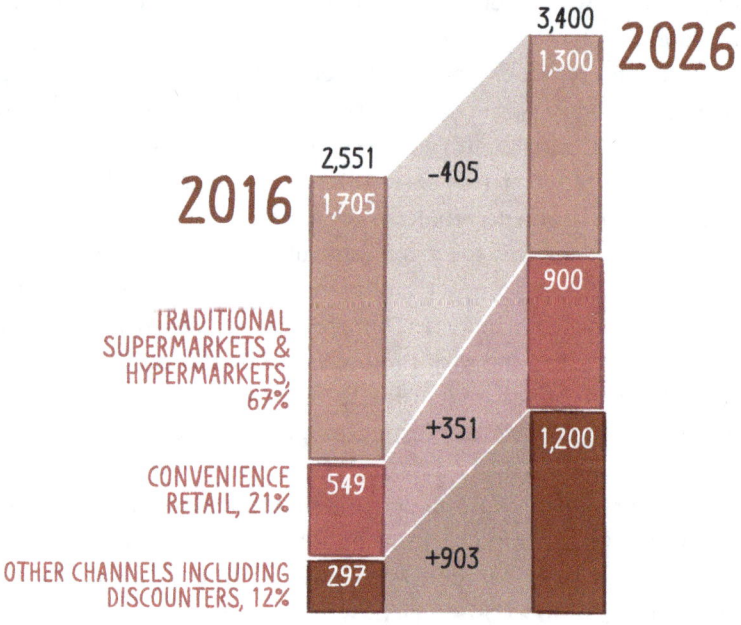

Fig. 2.9 The shift away from non-traditional grocery shopping in North America and Western Europe. Source: adapted from Kuijpers et al. (2017, 2019) (Grocery retail sales $bn)

Further, and perhaps even more challenging, is the Amazon data advantage. Their business encompasses so much of a household's purchasing, they have unprecedented insights into the 'who, what, when, where, and why' of their shoppers. They can mine these insights to refine and target their offer to consumers in a way traditional grocery struggle to match. For Amazon, grocery is such a small percentage of their overall business, so they can afford to take risks and adopt a longer-term view that their competition can't.

Discounters

Discounters in the UK have seen some dramatic growth since 2008. Analysis from Barclays (REF) shows they grew share from around 4% to 13% in the space of 10 years. This has clearly had a big impact on the traditional big four UK retailers. What has been interesting is their response to this challenge and how well (or not) it has worked.

The first obvious response is to match the discounters on price, and all the big four have at various times aimed to do this, with various 'price match' type guarantees. This is usually on a limited basket of comparable goods across the retailers and sees the retailer lose margin to maintain a headline price promise. Whilst this is a logical marketing activity, it doesn't address a couple of key issues on how discounters continue to grow and win in the market.

First, by design discounters have a low-cost operating model, one that is impossible for big four grocer to match. Their business model is just not to set up in the same way. This can only mean margin dilution if they price match, even with supplier funding support. We have seen Aldi and Lidl resist online shopping in grocery until recently, because they know its model carries too high a cost, and they will lose money. Recently, Lidl has moved into this area with a 'click and collect' service, which, as we saw previously, is probably the only version of online grocery shopping that can make a profit right now.

Second, discounters have more appeal to shoppers than just price. Their limited ranges and smaller stores are quicker and easier to shop. Research has shown that this is something highly valued by discount shoppers. The impact on the big four grocers is obvious. They carry way more range and stock and therefore cost, but to what consumer benefit.

The big four retailers have realised this and started significant range reduction programmes in recent years to 're-set' their ranges to more efficient levels. Asda has done this for many years, and recently announced another range reduction initiative, potentially culling 40% of range after its recent purchase by the Issa brothers:

> **Asda Ready to Slash SKUs by up to 40% in End2End Reset Ahead of Issa Brothers' Arrival**
>
> Asda has told suppliers it plans to cut SKUs by up to 40% as a major range review rolls out ahead of the arrival of the Issa brothers.
>
> Stores will move to a new model that is more akin to the discounters, reducing ranges to prioritise availability of key SKUs, alongside innovation in growth areas such as vegan and organic, Asda has promised.
>
> The category transformation programme, dubbed End2End, will also see space handed over to a major rollout of in-store concessions, including partnerships with B&Q, Decathlon, and a raft of food-to-go providers in an 'all under one roof' strategy.
>
> Source: (Quinn, 2021)

This type of approach, which isn't unique to ASDA, poses some fundamental questions. If a shopper faces the same limited assortment everywhere, why go to anywhere but a discounter? Where is the ability to inspire and encourage shoppers with new ideas to encourage them to stay loyal to your store? What about the space that's left behind in these very large supermarkets and hypermarkets? If we reduce range significantly in these types of stores, aren't we in danger of seeing many product categories reduced to 'commodity' status?

One way ASDA is looking to utilise the space released from this range reduction strategy is to offer 'store within a store' offers for their target shoppers. Recently trials were run placing toy departments with the retailer 'The Entertainer', as well as music offers with 'Music Magpie' and fragrance with the retailer 'Per-Cent' (ASDA 2021).

These aren't new ideas, store within a store has been around for many years, and whilst these are trials, it will be interesting to see their impact. Will they drive interest and footfall to the total store? Or will shoppers keep their current behaviour and look unfavourably on reduced ranges among groceries in their main grocery shop?

Own-Brand

One potential beneficiary of the range reduction is own-brand. In the UK, own-brand has long been an important part of the retailer's overall offer, and in many categories, it has been among the most innovative and leading 'brands' for shoppers to choose. As discussed earlier, my research showed that retailers recognise that stocking the same large brands as everyone else isn't a successful strategy for creating a competitive advantage.

Own-brand has the potential to become more important in the environment of reduced ranges. It is unique to that retailer, can be transformed to meet consumers' needs, and offers increased margins to the retailer versus brands. However, it comes at a cost to collaboration. Own-brand suppliers are (by necessity) low-cost producers, driven by retailers to operate that way. They have limited resources and money for the activities that branded suppliers undertake to help retailers grow their category.

This means that the buying and analysis of data, building joint category plans and joint activation initiatives, and so on just will not happen to the same level if retailers continue to remove branded suppliers from product categories. Suppliers in these cases will question hard investing in these collaboration activities if their business is shrinking and under serious threat. This is a theme we will come back to.

Data and Insights

Shopper understanding is the lifeblood of any retailer. Understanding who your shoppers are, their needs, and how their habits are changing is the foundation of creating success. Tesco led the way in this area, launching their Clubcard in 1995, which allowed them to revolutionise their understanding of their shoppers (Humby et al. 2004).

The big four grocers are all now invested in greater understanding of their shoppers. As mentioned, from the initial start by Tesco and Clubcard, even if retailers do not have a loyalty card, there are many and various analytic tools open to them to get a deep understanding of their shoppers and their behaviour. In more recent years, they have streamlined this work through the use of AI and machine learning technologies to enable what was formerly complex and challenging analysis to be done much more easily.

What has been the impact of this? One continuing trend has seen retailers looking to its suppliers to buy and use this data. Recently Morrisons expanded its offer in this area.

> **Morrisons to Share More Data with Suppliers**
>
> Morrisons is to share more operational data with suppliers as part of an ongoing programme to buy and sell more simply and make better decisions.
>
> Morrisons will share more sales, forecasting, waste, stock, and range information through its Morrisons Supplier database and is also offering suppliers the opportunity to see customer data from its More Card.
>
> Morrisons is making the move after listening to suppliers who said that having access to this data would enable them to plan and make the right decisions for Morrisons customers.
>
> Source: FMCG Magazine 2020

We have discussed the supplier's impact on these types of initiatives. For retailers, it appears to be a simple decision in which they can recoup costs from suppliers, and have suppliers spend time and resources providing analysis and recommendations back to the retailer. Even Walmart, who always viewed free data sharing as a bedrock of its collaborative trading approach, has announced they will also sell data to suppliers (Neff 2021).

In 2021, Walmart launched the 'Walmart Connect' product. Their pitch is that when 90% of US shoppers use Walmart, online and in store, they have 150m customers per week. This generates a tremendous amount of data and insights. This can be leveraged by not only selling this data, but also creating a multitude of activation opportunities for brands to buy across the physical and digital Walmart retail offer.

I believe there is a tension developing here. Firstly, retailers are increasingly using and selling more sophisticated data sets to suppliers, yet removing the suppliers ranges from their offer? We will discuss solutions to this in the final chapter, but the increased use of ML and AI appears to be one potential route through streamlining and reducing the cost of this work.

Second, the increased usage of data and analysis is enabling the retailer's ability to target every more finely their customer offer. That targeting can allow physical stores with local assortments, or marketing and online activities, to tailor their offers and communications to shoppers. Whilst this is a logical strategy to follow, it once again increases the cost for the retailer, in terms of the data and analysis required, and the resources to interpret and manage these activities.

Cost Pressures, Consolidation, and Collaboration

The consistent theme of all these trends is increasing costs and complexity for retailers. How have they responded? By cutting costs, on several fronts. They have looked to cut their own headcounts, as analysis by Barclays shows; in the three years to 2018, significant headcount reductions have occurred across the top three UK grocers and this has continued since (Barclays 2018).

I know from personal experience how dramatic this has been. A few years ago, I trained the head office function of one of the top four grocery retailers in category management skills. Over a period of a few months, we trained over 500 people in trading, category management, and insights functions. Today the same team numbers less than 300 people. Clearly, this reduction will cause dramatic changes in the work these teams can do, as their scope of work increases to cover bigger areas.

In addition, retailers have been driven to merge by buying competitors, even in different channels. There are a number of examples including Tesco's purchase of the wholesaler Booker for £3.7 bn in 2017 and Coop acquisition of NISA in 2018. The CMA blocked the proposed merger between Sainsbury's and ASDA in 2020. In their proposals for the merger, they stated the new group 'anticipated cost savings of £500m'. As that deal failed, the ISSA brothers have now bought ASDA, and at the time of writing, the VC company (CDR) takeover of Morrisons is awaiting approval.

Clearly retailers are also turning to suppliers for lower costs. As we will see in the case studies, this is a never ending and continuous 'discussion' between retailer and supplier. It's most often an activity that is confidential, but recent activities from some retailers have emerged into the public domain. For example, Sainsbury's has recently written to all suppliers asking for cost reductions.

> **Sainsbury's asks suppliers for pricing talks after Aldi Price Match move**
>
> Sainsbury's is asking suppliers for "lower prices" following the launch of its Aldi Price Match last month—to "give our customers more of what matters".
>
> In a letter sent to suppliers this week, the Holborn retailer acknowledged that "working together" with its supply base it had "helped to feed the nation" during the pandemic. And as a result of the third national lockdown, it admitted it was in "a strong position".
>
> But Sainsbury's was also "working in a difficult market" it said. "We must continue to adapt and be bold to make sure we keep up this positive momentum and grow volumes further."
>
> Source: Grocer, 2021; Leyland and Quinn 2021

Anecdotal evidence from interviews I undertook with some suppliers showed they were asking for up to 20% reductions in cost prices! As we will discuss later, this is nothing new, nor is it sustainable if we are to address the serious issues the industry faces.

In 2008 the government established the Grocery Codes Adjudicator (GCA), to manage and improve the relationship between the retailer and its suppliers. Its aim was to mitigate some of the worst of the retailer's demands and leveraging of power against suppliers. The GC developed a code of practice for the industry entitled 'Grocery Suppliers Code of Practice' (GSCOP).

Christine Tacon was appointed to run the GCA at its inception and has claimed significant headway in retailers' compliance with its code. However, despite this, the GCA investigated Tesco in 2015 for alleged breaches of the code. The issues involved a demand for short-term payment, withholding payments, and extended payments terms.

More recently, the new adjudicator, Mark White, announced he was to investigate Sainsbury's 'amid claims suppliers have been subjected to short notice delisting's and demands for lump sums as part of its controversial range review' (Quinn, 2021).

It's clear that although improvements have been made, issues still exist with how retailers are looking for suppliers to increase their investments with them, a theme that will become clear in the case study chapters of this book.

In summary:

- The industry structure and consumer and shopper behaviour shifts are fuelling a transformation among FMCG retailers.
- The omni-channel challenge is fuelling increased competition, complexity, and significant cost challenges.
- Online and discounters are proving formidable competitors, causing a strategic reaction that is significant.
- Investments in data and analytic capabilities are increasing and are a potentially significant revenue stream for retailers.
- Cost pressures and their impact on collaboration with suppliers are driving even more short-term, aggressive behaviours by retailers.

Retailer and Supplier Collaboration: Partnership or Partnershaft?

Based on this reality of collaboration, what is the current status of collaboration between retailers and suppliers? The case studies that follow will offer a thorough analysis into specifics. Here I want to outline what I found in interviews with senior leaders in the industry on their viewpoint of the current state of affairs, and potential future direction. What they told me contained some surprises.

All the retailers I talked to recognised that the short-term demands of the business have always caused challenges to collaboration, and this hasn't improved in recent times. There has been a strong move back to costs and price by most of the major retailers, making aggressive demands of up to 20% cost savings with one retailer.

In addition, as we have seen, many retailers are shutting down the opportunity for range reviews and reducing SKUs across product ranges. One retailer told me they had recently cut their range by 25% across one major product area, resulting in 10,000 SKUs delisted. Clearly, this is causing major pressures and strains on the relationship. One person described this to me as a move from 'Partnership to Partnershaft'!

There is clearly a change in the way collaboration works right now. One retailer described it to me as 'we look at the annual plan, we focus on the next few months, and that's it'. These were not plans developed together. They were largely plans that the supplier proposes to the retailer at the start of each year. There appears to be a distinct absence of deeper and wider collaborative planning, including developing category plans together that will transform the category for a shopper.

As described earlier, we have seen a lot of merger discussion and activity in recent years. What all of them have in common is that the discussion on why they wanted to merge/buy isn't about the shopper, it's all about cost efficiencies. It often includes a focus on the suppliers and how an alternative approach can leverage even more value from suppliers. Virtually none of the discussion is about how the shopping experience will improve, making their lives simpler, better, quicker, and so on.

This is concerning. If the industry is being seen at the macro level as one with a cost-saving focus that is driven by a need for efficiencies, haven't we 'given up' on the consumer and shopper? The retailers involved will all point to price, and how these mergers will create bigger organisations that can leverage lower costs, and therefore deliver lower process to consumers. However, we know from extensive data sources that price is just one factor shoppers find important. They are looking for so much more from their shopping experience, quality inspiration, excitement, speed, and so on. If we carry on down this road, the consequences for the FMCG industry are severe.

However, the way the supplier is managing through these short-term demands may be changing. One senior manager explained to me that the balance of power could move back (even if slowly) towards the supplier. The reasons for this appear to be two-fold. The first is the introduction in the UK of the 'GSCOP' legislation, which has had the desired effect of thwarting the retailers' ability to make unreasonable demands of suppliers. Through this code of practice, suppliers now have a framework to use and a mechanism for complaint if they believe they are being treated unreasonably.

The second factor cited in these discussions was the supplier's gaining strength from both globalisation and the growth in the omni-channel. This means that firstly the suppliers' scale has not only grown, but their reliance on individual retailers in one country has declined. As one person said to me, 'if the supplier is investing for growth in the Far East markets, if we decline our business together in one retailer in the UK, it really doesn't make much difference to them'. This dynamic appears to have emboldened suppliers in this position to take a more assertive stance to retailers' demands. In the past, they may have given in to the demands, but not anymore.

In addition, the explosion in routes to market for the supplier (omni-channels) means they have many other options to sell to their consumers. This is a fast growing dynamic, with the number of options expanding all the time. In addition, as we have seen, the suppliers themselves can sell directly to their own consumers (DTC).

Underpinning these trends is the role of data and insights in enabling collaboration. Some retailers have a deep set of data and insights that they use (and sell) to their suppliers, other do not. Regardless, what no retailer has are the wider insights on what the consumer and shopper do when outside of their stores. This is the data and insight that suppliers hold. There appears to be a growing recognition that this is of great value to retailers, and they need access to it to develop winning propositions.

A final factor that was affecting collaboration was that of the availability of skilled people on each side to drive this work. As we have discussed, headcount reduction has been severe across the industry, with fewer people doing more work. In addition, those people are often being given sizeable areas of responsibility very early in their careers.

It's not too dramatic to say there is an emerging existential threat to the industry, where it's difficult to recruit into the industry, and there is less, and less money spent on training and developing those people. One opportunity for changing collaboration is helping each other develop skills and capabilities, so that retailers and suppliers can learn and develop together, resulting in better plans and results for both sides.

What all of this means for the future of collaboration is interesting. I propose we could see retailers now being more open to collaboration and reducing some of their focus on just the short term. If suppliers are now holding the resources and capabilities they value, and these are not 'guaranteed' anymore by the supplier, there is a genuine opportunity for better collaboration around the sharing of resources and capabilities.

One senior global retail leader told me that the opportunity is to move even further beyond the 'win-win' which is often cited as the goal of great collaboration. The idea they have pushed for in their collaborative work is 'give-give'. What they meant by this is that they want a position of freely sharing plans, data, and insights, even when the win isn't clear, so that they reach a different level of trust. That level is a trust that each side always has with the other's interests in mind and is looking for opportunities to help each other.

This is a very different end point for collaboration, and one that would require some incredible leaps in not only faith, but skills and capabilities for some retailers and suppliers! I would argue that is fine. Reaching that level of 'give-give', or maybe better described as 'share-share', would only be appropriate sometimes. The global retail leader I talked with showed that this was in place with maybe two suppliers out of the eight main global suppliers in their business.

In Summary: The Questions We Need to Address

I think based on all the challenges and opportunities we have discussed, there are a few important areas that need to change to transform the FMCG industry.

- First, is the work of collaboration particularly focussed on category management. This a process that was built in the late 1980s and the structure of the industry has been transformed significantly since then. What should be the work of collaboration now and into the future? What is the purpose of category management, and what work should it do? This isn't necessarily about a new process but rather about focussing on what is considered the important work, and how to do that work.
- How do we incorporate the new data and technologies that are now available? Where do we evaluate what's important and what isn't, and where in the collaborative process should they sit? There is a wealth of data and tools already available, and these are only going to increase. How do we manage through this?
- Can we address and overcome the retailers' short-term needs and focus, versus the opportunity for growth in the medium term, and the commitment this requires from both sides? All business has short-term needs, but when that becomes the only focus, then we are in danger of driving ourselves down in to a constant cost/price discussion and missing the opportunities to transform the shopper's experience.
- Finally, what are the skills and capabilities we will need to enable this fresh approach? The industry is seeing significant headcount losses, with fewer skilled people being asked to do enormous jobs. How can we address this in a way that gives those who need it the right skills and tools to do their jobs in a quick and efficient way?

It was against this background that I conducted my research with suppliers. I wanted to understand how they work now, and what this delivers in terms of value creation and capture. In the next chapter, we will review the important themes that provide the context for the research; look at what that 'theory' says about each area and then review the research findings, to compare what is happening now with the theory.

Chapter Summary

1. Suppliers are becoming larger and more powerful as they acquire competitors and globalise their ways of working.
2. Smaller local brands are emerging as significant players in driving innovation in categories.
3. The omni-channel challenge is providing growth opportunities alongside increased costs, complexity, and challenges to profitability for both retailers and suppliers.
4. Category management is being challenged as to effectiveness, with emerging areas such as RGM providing more obvious financial gains for suppliers.
5. Retailers are facing increased complexity driven by transformational changes in shopper behaviour.
6. Short-term demands and pressure are increasingly being used by retailers to the detriment of collaboration.
7. Both retailers and suppliers are recognising there is another way to growth, through improving their approach to collaboration.

References

Aastrup, J., Grant, D. and Bjerre, M. (2007) Value creation and category management through retailer-supplier relationships. *The International Review of Retail, Distribution and Consumer Research*, 17(5), pp.523-541.

Akçura, M.T. and Ozdemir, Z.D. (2019) Data-driven manufacturer-retailer collaboration under competition. *Enterprise Information Systems*, 13(3), pp.303-328.

Alan, Y., Dotson, J.P. and Kurtuluş, M. (2017) On the Competitive and Collaborative Implications of Category Captainship. *Journal of Marketing*, 81(4), pp.127-143.

ASDA Press Release (2021) Accessed at https://corporate.asda.com/newsroom/2020/10/14/asda-partners-with-toy-specialist-the-entertainer

Barclays Bank (2018) Scale, disruption and Brexit. A new dawn for the UK food supply chains? Accessed at https://www.barclayscorporate.com/content/dam/barclayscorporate-com/documents/insights/industry-expertise/grocery-sector-retail-report.pdf

Bazoche, S, Gaputis, D, Johnson, E, Turnbull, C. (2019). Magnifying Revenue Growth Management. Accessed at: https://www2.deloitte.com/content/dam/Deloitte/us/Documents/consumer-business/us-cb-c-and-m-magnifying-rgm-in-consumer-products.pdf

Bishop, E, Dias, S, Shankland, A, Volip, N. (2021). Revenue Management in the wake of economic recovery. Accessed at: https://www.kantar.com/inspiration/retail/revenue-growth-management-in-the-wake-of-economic-recovery

Brusset, X. and Agrell, P.J. (2017) Intrinsic impediments to category captainship. *Journal of Industrial and Management Optimization*, 13(1), pp.113-133.

Consultancy UK (2018). Globe's largest FMCG companies buying their way to faster growth. Accessed at https://www.thegrocer.co.uk/ranging-and-merchandising/asda-ready-to-slash-range-by-up-to-40-in-end2end-reset/655197.article

Conti, P, Jagusch, A, Zimmerman, K, McCroskey, B. 2021 Growth for Both: How US Brands and Retailers Grow the Profit Pool for All. Accessed at: https://www.bain.com/insights/growth-for-both-how-us-brands-and-retailers-grow-the-profit-pool-for-all/

Corsten, D. and Kumar, N. (2005) Do suppliers benefit from collaborative relationships with large retailers? An empirical investigation of efficient consumer response adoption. *Journal of Marketing*, 69(3), pp.80-94.

Dapiran, G.P. and Hogarth-Scott, S. (2003) Are co-operation and trust being confused with power? An analysis of food retailing in Australia and the UK. *International Journal of Retail and Distribution Management*, 31(5), pp.256-267.

Desrochers, D.M., Gundlach, G.T. and Foer, A.A. (2003) Analysis of antitrust challenges to category captain arrangements. *Journal of Public Policy and Marketing*, 22(2), pp.201-215.

ECR Europe (1994) *Category management best practice report.* Brussels: ECR Europe.

FMCG Magazine (2020). Morrisons to share more data with suppliers. Accessed at: https://fmcgmagazine.co.uk/morrisons-to-share-more-data-with-suppliers/

Gruen, T.W. and Hofstetter, J.S. (2010) The relationship marketing view of the customer and the service dominant logic perspective. *Journal of Business Market Management*, 4(4), pp.231-245.

HM Government Grocery Codes Adjudicator—GCA investigation into Tesco Plc—progress towards following GCA recommendations (2016) Accessed at: *https://www.gov.uk/government/news/gca-investigation-into-tesco-plc-progress-towards-following-gca-recommendations*

Hofstetter, J. (2006) Assessing the contribution of ECR. *ECR Journal: International Commerce Review*, 6(1), pp.20-29.

Hong, S., Misra, K. and Vilcassim, N.J. (2016) The perils of category management: the effect of product assortment on multicategory purchase incidence. *Journal of Marketing*, 80(5), pp.34-52.

Humby, C, Hunt, T, Phillips, T (2004). *Scoring Points: How Tesco is Winning Customer Loyalty.* Kogan Page, London

IDG, (2021). UK retail food and grocery market growth to slow sharply in the short term, according to latest IGD market forecasts. Accessed at: https://www.igd.com/articles/article-viewer/t/uk-retail-food-and-grocery-market-growth-to-slow-sharply-in-the-short-term-according-to-latest-igd-market-forecasts/i/28369

Kopka, U, Little, E, Moulton, J, Schmutler, R, Simon, P. (2020) What got us here won't get us there. A new model for the consumer good industry. Accessed at: https://www.mckinsey.com/industries/consumer-packaged-goods/our-insights/what-got-us-here-wont-get-us-there-a-new-model-for-the-consumer-goods-industry

Kotzab, H. and Teller, C. (2003). Value-adding partnerships and co-opetition models in the grocery industry. *International Journal of Physical Distribution and Logistics Management,* 33(3), pp.268-281.

Kuijpers, D, Simmons, V and van Wamelen, J, (2019). Mckinsey and Company. *Perspectives on retail and consumer goods, Number 7*

Leyland, A and Quinn, I. (2021) Sainsbury's asks suppliers for pricing talks after Aldi Price Match move. *The Grocer.* Accessed at: https://www.thegrocer.co.uk/sainsburys/sainsburys-asks-suppliers-for-pricing-talks-after-aldi-price-match-move/653687.article

Mantrala, M.K. and Kamran-Disfani, O. (2018) Category management and captains, in Gielens, K. and Gijsbrechts, E. (eds.), *Handbook of Research in Retailing*, Edward Elgar Publishing.

Neff, J. (2021). Wal Mart has some data they would like to sell you. *Ad Age.* Accessed at: https://adage.com/article/marketing-news-strategy/walmart-has-some-data-theyd-sell-you/2342911

Polman, P. (2006) Learning from long experience, *ECR Journal: International Commerce Review,* 6(1), pp.70-73.

Quinn, I (2021a). Groceries Code Adjudicator to probe Sainsbury's range reset. *The Grocer.* Accessed at: https://www.thegrocer.co.uk/sainsburys/groceries-code-adjudicator-to-probe-sainsburys-range-reset/656875.article

Quinn, I. (2016). Asda hands buying power to trading team in head office management cull. *The Grocer.* Accessed at: https://www.thegrocer.co.uk/supermarkets/asda-hq-job-cull-aims-to-simplify-trading-team-responsibility-/530413.article

Quinn, I. (2021b). Asda ready to slash SKUs by up to 40% in End2End reset ahead of Issa brothers arrival. *The Grocer.* Accessed at: https://www.thegrocer.co.uk/ranging-and-merchandising/asda-ready-to-slash-range-by-up-to-40-in-end2end-reset/655197.article

Rackham, N. and De Vincentis, J. (1999) *Rethinking the sales force: redefining selling to create and capture customer value.* New York: McGraw Hill Education.

Further Reading

Brandes, D., & Brandes, N. (2015). *Bare Essentials: The Aldi Success Story.* Wien, Linde.

3

The Theory, and How It Applies to the FMCG Industry

What we will cover in this chapter:

- Business-to-business exchange theory, and how relationship marketing and quality impact collaboration
- Relational quality and its link to conflict and equity (or inequity) in BTB relationships
- The impact of power in BTB relationships and collaboration
- BTB value creation and capture
- Key Account Management (KAM), how it works, the challenges, and how it applies to the grocery industry
- An introduction to the case study research aims and methodology

First, let me begin by addressing a question many practitioners tend to ask: why bother ourselves with the 'theory'! I know as a practitioner myself, there is often a reluctance to look at the theory around topics, with businesses often eager to just 'get to the solution'. In my view, this is a mistake. Delving into the previous research and gaining insights into what other industries have to teach us can help us not only improve the FMCG industry but begin the critical step of crafting and implementing a more collaborative working relationship.

It's worth noting that whilst there isn't a wealth of academic research into the FMCG industry, there are a number of relevant areas that can help inform our knowledge of how two businesses collaborate and look to create value in that exchange. There is also valuable insight into the area of power in BTB relations, and how this impacts the collaboration and its ability to create and capture value.

My aim in this chapter is to briefly discuss the research in those areas, and how I think it helps inform our interest in collaboration in the FMCG industry. It's a relatively high-level overview, but at the same time provides enough of a framework and context for my own research, which follows in the subsequent chapters, and the recommendations given later in the book.

Business-to-Business Exchange

Collaboration between two businesses is a method of business-to-business exchange (Kotler 1972), where all parties expect to be better off as a result of any exchange. In the nineteenth century, it was recognised that there is a need for a balanced approach to the business between a buyer and seller. Wanamaker was a retailer, whose thinking at the time ran counter to popular thinking on profit maximisation. He sought to focus on the need for the long term and to have a more balanced view that 'customers, retailers, and producers must have close contact for the benefit of all' (Hadjikhani and LaPlaca 2013).

This concept of 'benefits for all' is closely linked to the concept of value and is important in business-to-business exchange. Value is the 'primary force that drives market transactions and relationships alike' (Kotler 2000). Within this, as a supplier, it needs to be recognised that a key role is to create value for the customer (Keränen and Jalkala 2013; O'Cass and Ngo 2012) and also capture value for themselves (Dutta et al. 2003; Mizik and Jacobson 2003).

The foundation of business-to-business exchange theory was based upon the transaction itself as the unit of exchange and is known as Transactional Cost Economics (TCE) (Coase 1937; Williamson 1981). TCE considers the transaction as a unit of analysis, and, simply stated, looks to determine whether a firm will achieve a better business result (cost minimisation) from sourcing in the open market, or from developing its intra-firm solution (Mena et al. 2009). This is often characterised as 'make or buy decisions' (Ryals and Humphries 2010).

TCE has its limitations in helping to understand BTB exchanges more deeply. Firstly, it is a very narrow view of the exchange, when in reality most relationships are more complex and involve much more than an economic decision of any one exchange (Mena et al. 2009). Furthermore, it is recognised that the transactions between firms are more than independent one-off transactions and contain social interaction and relationships between the two businesses that impact on the exchange (Granovetter 1985).

In summary, it has been argued that the management practice based on TCE could even be damaging (Ryals and Humphries 2010). It is these limitations in TCE which led to the development of theories that looked at the broader relationship in the business-to-business exchange.

BTB Relationship Marketing

Given TCE's limitations as a theory to understand the business-to-business exchange, it was recognised that the exchange between businesses exists in a social context. This means that factors other than the cost minimisation can influence and create an impact on the relationship between the two firms in a transaction (Ryals and Humphries 2010).

The concept of Relationship Marketing (RM) explains a wider context in which a business-to-business relationship takes place. The key features of RM are collaboration with profitable customers and the generation of customer value (Sheth and Parvatiyar 1995). There are two important concepts to explore in these features. Firstly, the concept of 'profitable customers', indicating it is important to be able to identify who the customers are, often achieved through some form of segmentation of the supplier's customer base (Sullivan et al. 2012).

Secondly, with reference to customer value, it has been recognised that the creation of customer value is the foundation of business performance for a supplier (Woodruff 1997) and that there are dimensions of value creation on which a supplier can focus to create the value (Ulaga and Eggert 2006). These dimensions can include both the transactional elements of the relationship and the interpersonal and relational elements (Möller and Törrönen 2003).

Therefore, RM is a complex blend of personal, non-economic, and economic benefits (Dwyer et al. 1987). Hence, it indicates that the management of the interface between supplier and customer is not only important, but potentially complex as well. This complexity suggests that the sales function in a manufacturer organisation is an increasingly important manager and facilitator of the BTB relationship between themselves and their customers (Anderson et al. 2007).

It is the function of the Key Account Management or KAM team to build this mix of both economic and personal benefits with the intention of building long-term sustainable relationships (Storbacka et al. 2009). If RM is significant in understanding the BTB exchange, it is also important to understand the factors that drive the quality of the relationship or Relational Quality (RQ).

BTB Relational Quality

Relational Quality reflects the overall depth, closeness, and climate in the inter-organisational relationships (Jiang et al. 2016). The benefits of improving RQ to a business are found not only in improved financial results (Ford 1980) but also in the fact that RQ is an indicator of long-term KAM success (Ivens and Pardo 2007).

There have been multiple variations of defining the dimensions of relational quality. Jiang et al. (2016) researched more than 30 papers based on the dimensions of RQ. Their review proposes that there are four key constructs for measuring relational quality: Communication, Long-Term Orientation, Social Satisfaction, and Economic Satisfaction (Fig. 3.1).

According to Jiang et al. (2016), the factors driving relationship quality are summarised in Table 3.1.

These RQ factors all interplay in how the quality of a relationship is perceived and can be measured. The challenge for a supplier in developing the relationship over time is how to manage and balance each of the factors with the objective to move from the transactional relationships to longer-term partnership relationships (Pinnington and Scanlon 2009). It is also important to reflect that if a supplier can improve trust, satisfaction, and commitment, then their performance with their customer has been shown to improve

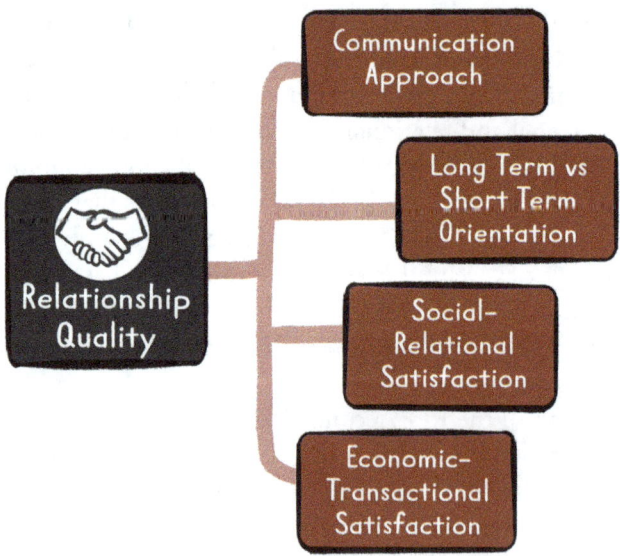

Fig. 3.1 Relationship quality factors. (Source: Adapted from Jiang et al. 2016)

Table 3.1 Description of factors driving relationship quality

Factor	Description
Communication approach	The formal and informal sharing of the meaningful and timely information between the buyer and the supplier, as perceived by the buyer
Long-term versus short-term orientation	The perception of the interdependence of outcomes in which both a supplier's outcomes and joint outcomes are expected to benefit the buyer in the long run
Social-relational satisfaction	The buyer's satisfaction with the social outcomes of the relationship with the supplier
Economic-transactional satisfaction	The measure of economic satisfaction indicates the extent to which the buyer is satisfied with the economic rewards based on his/her relationship with the supplier

Source: Adapted from Jiang et al. (2016)

(Vieira et al. 2014). Within these factors, it is recognised that there is the potential for conflict and challenge, as suppliers look to develop their relationships with customers.

BTB Relationship Conflict and Asymmetry

In any business-to-business relationship, there will be conflict and asymmetry in the relationship, often changing over time, and it could be argued that symmetry in the relationship may be the unusual state (Stanko et al. 2007). Furthermore, the desire to develop a long-term relationship as an objective from a supplier can cause conflict in the relationship with their customers. While a supplier may strive for longer-term relationships, it may not be a desire on the part of the customer and could negatively impact the customer's commitment to the supplier (Stanko et al. 2007).

The second area of potential conflict between supplier and customer is that of equity. Not all relationships realise mutually beneficial outcomes (Narayandas and Rangan 2004) and hence, many relationships may result in inequity (Blois 2009). Striving for equity may be both unrealistic and potentially unachievable from the outset. In evaluating the equity of the relationship, the supplier's perception is an important factor, with their perception being influenced by the transparency of the relationship, that is, how each party is informed and is informing each other of its actions with regards to the relationship (Eggert and Helm 2003).

The concept of equity in the relationship is an important consideration in the UK Grocery Industry, where the suppliers can be described as dominated by their customers (Blois 2009). In this market context, the supplier could tolerate inequity, either because the supplier may not perceive their relationship as inequitable (based upon comparison to others) and they may believe there is no realistic alternative (Blois 2009). It could be argued that the partnership may be more successful if the supplier partner accepts that the retailer is dominant in the relationship (Hingley 2005).

The management of all these challenges between the supplier and the customer is the responsibility of the Key Account team (Anderson et al. 2007). The KAM structure is the approach used by most suppliers in the UK Grocery Industry, and the KAM approach will be reviewed in detail later in this chapter.

In summary

- BTB exchange is a mechanism where both parties need to benefit.
- There is a relational element to the BTB exchange, a complex blend of personal, economic, and non-economic benefits.
- Relational Quality (RQ) reflects the depth, closeness, and climate in the BTB relationship.
- There will be conflict in any BTB relationship, and the benefits may not be equal for each side or equitable comparing one supplier to another.

Power in BTB Relationships

Power as a phenomenon in business-to-business relationships could be argued as the major influencing factor in collaboration, in that it contains the idea of 'the control, influence or direction of one party's behaviour by another' (Dapiran and Hogarth-Scott 2003, p. 258). It has also been recognised that even though power may not always be evident in the relationship, its potential influence always exists and 'that power is the base atomic particle of relationships' (Dapiran and Hogarth-Scott 2003, p. 258).

The concept of power in a business-to-business relationship is therefore important to understand, although this has not always been the case in the BTB literature (Hingley 2005). It has been argued that both the TCE literature (discussed earlier) and the IMP Group have each 'marginalised the role of power in BTB exchanges' (Chicksand 2015, p. 123). The IMP group work focuses on the BTB relationship as a complex set of interactions and this has led to the development of their 'interaction model' (Håkansson 1982). However, it has been argued that this work places too great an emphasis on social interactions versus the role of power (Chicksand 2015).

The areas of interest to this research cover the definition of power, how it exists in different levels of the organisation, and the concept of power balance between the retailer and the supplier as it relates to the UK Grocery Industry. Each of these areas will be discussed in turn.

Looking firstly at the definition of power, French and Raven (1959) identified the types of power that can exist in relationships. These are:

- **Expert power** is the power that a customer has, based on knowledge, expertise, or skills that are desired by a supplier.
- **Referent power** exists when a supplier values identification with the customer.
- **Legitimate power** is natural power: the supplier believes that certain customers have a natural right to influence its actions.
- **Reward power** exists when the customer provides rewards that are attractive to the supplier. When the customer is pleased with a supplier, it may increase the frequency or quantity of its purchases.
- **Coercive power** exists when the customer can provide punishments that are detrimental to the supplier. (Adapted from Lacoste and Blois 2015)

Power can exist at three levels in the collaborative relationship. It can be at an organisational level, based on one organisation's ability to control the economic or operational basis of the relationship (Pinnington and Scanlon 2009; Dapiran and Hogarth-Scott 2003), as well as at a personal level, or at the social level (i.e., involving teams of people). In this research, the focus is on the social and organisational level, not the personal level, with the focus of our interest on the KAM team within the supplier organisation, and its relationship with retail customers.

Turning to the management of power between the two firms, it has been proposed that an understanding of each partners' resources can help identify their potential behaviours, in order to facilitate better management outcomes on collaboration (Cowan et al. 2015). Furthermore, this research argues that understanding the benefits of the collaboration before entering into it is an important prerequisite for success (Cowan et al. 2015). The summary of their research is highlighted in the model provided in Fig. 3.2.

The model proposes reviewing the relative power position of each party, in order to place the relationship in one of four boxes. Exploitative relationships are often evident in very competitive markets, and a dependent partner may just be looking for self-preservation as a goal, or a move across to the 'tolerable relationship' quadrant (Cowan et al. 2015). This could be argued to be a significant relationship style that exists in the UK Grocery Industry (Hingley

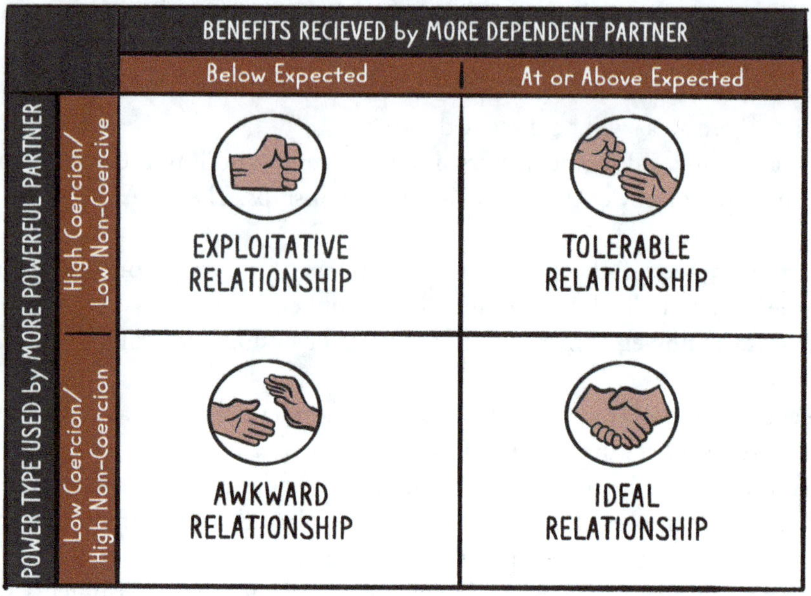

Fig. 3.2 Power benefit matrix in an inter-firm relationship. (Source: Adapted from Cowan et al. 2015)

2005). Tolerable relationships are where benefits are increased versus the exploitative relationship, but still the dominant partner exerts power and control over the less dominant party (Cowan et al. 2015).

Reviewing the quadrant 'awkward relationship', relationships in this area are characterised by benevolence and potential future benefits (Cowan et al. 2015). The final quadrant, 'ideal relationship', would see the closest characterisation of an inter-firm partnership (Cowan et al. 2015). From this brief review, it is firstly evident that, as discussed, suppliers in the UK Grocery Industry could be characterised as having exploitative or tolerable relationships in this model. Secondly, the KAM team will play the lead role in the supplier in managing the relationships (Baumann et al. 2017).

The KAM team has the purpose of developing the relationship between the retailer and their own business. It is acknowledged that a difference in power between the two parties can influence the success of the partnership, more so than other factors such as trust or commitment (Chicksand 2015). Further, it has been argued that if power is imbalanced then actions should be considered to try and reduce the imbalance as far as is possible (Chicksand 2015).

The balance of power is therefore an important factor that can influence the BTB relationship. This concept looks to identify if each party is equally

3 The Theory, and How It Applies to the FMCG Industry

powerful in the relationship (symmetry) or is one party dominant over the other (asymmetry) (Hingley 2005). Factors that can impact this balance include a supplier's drive for longer-term relationships with their customers, which can conflict with the customer's desire (Stanko et al. 2007) and striving for equity, that is, the supplier recognising that not all relationships realise mutually beneficial outcomes (Narayandas and Rangan 2004).

It may appear at first glance that the concept of one party exerting power over another runs counter to the central premise of collaboration between two businesses. Indeed, much of the discussion in the relationship marketing literature appears to claim that power is a negative (Hingley 2005). However, Hingley goes on to assert that this is clearly false, as power is always ever-present in any business-to-business relationship, and that 'power play and relationship development co-exist alongside one another' (Hingley 2005, p. 855).

How widespread is the issue of imbalance? It has been said that many BTB relationships can result in inequity (Blois 2009) because of imbalance and, furthermore, others have viewed a balanced or symmetrical relationship (i.e., equal power on each side) as being the unusual state (Hingley 2005). Moreover, the acceptance of asymmetry (imbalance of power) by a supplier may still lead to a collaborative relationship with a customer (Hingley 2005). This is linked to the KAM role, where managing this imbalance in the relationship is a key; 'conflict is seen as an inherent condition of the key account management selling role' (Speakman and Ryals 2012, p. 367).

How can a rebalance of power be achieved, especially in a market context such as the UK Grocery Industry, where retailers are the dominant partner? (Maglaras et al. 2015). One argument is that the imbalance in power is best mitigated through aiming to develop goal congruence (Maglaras et al. 2015), and particularly financial goal congruence (Marcos-Cuevas et al. 2014). Through this balancing of financial goals, power can be better balanced and trust issues can be mitigated (Maglaras et al. 2015). However, how this works in practice is through an acknowledged gap in the power literature as it relates to the UK Grocery Industry (Hingley et al. 2015a), and one this research intends to explore.

As discussed earlier, this concept of balance is an important consideration in the UK Grocery Industry where it has been argued that suppliers are dominated by their customers (Blois 2009; Maglaras et al. 2015). There has also been a marked shift in power to the retailers in recent years (Fernie 2014). It is recognised that suppliers are under increased short-term pressure for better margins and increased funding from retailers (Perrett 2010), and the consequence of all these factors is that as the retailer exerts their dominant power, the relationship between the retailer and supplier becomes damaged (Maglaras et al. 2015).

As further evidence of this damage, a UK government enquiry into the industry in 2000 concluded that 'the major retailers could exercise power in the marketplace that adversely affects the competitiveness of some of their (dependent) suppliers and distorts competition in the market' (Dapiran and Hogarth-Scott 2003, p. 257). The situation since 2000 may even have worsened, with the government setting up a Groceries Supply Code of Practice and an Adjudicator, to manage the issues and challenges suppliers are facing with their customers (HM Government Competition and Markets Authority 2008).

In this market context, the supplier could potentially tolerate an inequitable role, either because the supplier may not perceive their relationship as inequitable (based upon comparison to others) and they may believe there is no realistic alternative (Blois 2009; Towill 2005).

It has been argued that the supplier could have a more successful partnership if the supplier accepts that the retailer is dominant in the relationship (Hingley 2005). This power asymmetry has been argued to be even more pronounced for private label suppliers, arguing that 'in such conditions, the retailer has brand control over the supplier, and private rules enforce dependency in private label supply' (Hingley et al. 2015b).

As stated earlier, the suppliers will often accept the power imbalance as long as they perceive that they are being dealt with in a 'fair' way. This fairness is underpinned by the concepts of justice in the relationship along with the suppliers evaluating their position relative to the competition in the areas of 'procedural justice' and 'distributive justice' (Duffy et al. 2003). In other words, a supplier may be accepting a weaker power position in a relationship with its customer, if it is perceived that the supplier is being dealt with similarly to the other competition suppliers (procedural justice) and is receiving the same benefits and rewards as other suppliers (distributive justice).

Concerning the grocery industry, the collaborative industry process such as ECR and category management has been cited as examples of 'expert power' (French and Raven 1959), in that they attempt to use superior knowledge and insights to drive better business plans through collaboration.

This raises a question as to where this power lies. Is category management used as a power mechanism by the retailers to exert power over the suppliers? Dapiran (2003) and other scholars have argued that category management enables the suppliers to exert power, as most category information and insights are sourced from the category partners or captains who are, in fact, suppliers (Lindblom and Olkkonen 2008). This research looks to bring insight into this area of collaboration and understand more deeply how category management activities are used by the supplier to create and capture value with their customers.

In summary:

- Power is a major factor in BTB relationships—the atomic particle ever presents even if unseen.
- There are different types of power that can be exerted, each with unique characteristics and implications.
- Power clearly impacts collaboration, and its success, so it's important to understand where the power lies before entering into collaboration.
- There is an imbalance of power in the UK Grocery Industry, in favour of the retailer, which has been seen to cause competitive issues.
- Collaboration processes such as ECR and category management are unclear in who they benefit most in terms of power and balance in the collaboration between retailer and supplier.

Value Creation and Capture: What Is It and What Is Happening?

Business-to-Business Value Creation

When reviewing the literature on value in business-to-business (BTB) relationships, the first challenge is to define what value is and what it involves. There are typically three areas of value definition and concepts used in the literature. Firstly, the concept of value creation from a customer's perspective, that is, how a customer perceives the value they receive in the business-to-business exchange. The second area is the types of value created in the exchange, typically a combination of relational and transactional value elements. The final area is value capture, that is understanding what value is captured and how is it captured by the actors in the BTB relationship.

At first, the researcher looked at the value and its creation in the exchange from the perspective of the customer. This concept is closely related to the exchange theory of marketing (Georges and Eggert 2003) and is defined as 'the tradeoff between multiple benefits (what you get) and sacrifices (what you give) in a market exchange' (Eggert and Ulaga 2002, p. 678).

The focus of this research is the supplier for which the definition of value creation does not translate directly to the supplier's value creation. However, the definition offered by Georges and Eggert does offer some useful guidance on a supplier's value creation approach. The reference to 'multiple benefits and sacrifices of a suppliers offering' (Eggert and Ulaga 2002, p. 678) indicates that the supplier has to create an 'offer' for customers to create value and this 'offer' needs to aim the key decision makers in the customer organisation to create and capture a value of their own.

Exploring more deeply the concept of a supplier 'offer', in their literature review, Georges and Eggert (2003) highlighted four recurring themes in identifying customer perceived value: (1) value is a subjective concept, (2) it is conceptualised as a tradeoff between benefits and sacrifices, (3) benefits and sacrifices can be multi-faceted, and (4) value perception is relative to competition. This further informs how a supplier can approach value creation for their customer.

Firstly, a recognition that suppliers are offering 'multiple benefits and sacrifices' to their customers has been considered. The benefits can be gathered from the products they sell, and the services they also provide (such as category management). The sacrifices are potentially the 'costs' involved in the relationships with the supplier, be it the direct product and distribution costs, or hidden costs such as complexity, and relational elements involved in the transaction.

The second proposal from Georges and Eggert's review is the concept of 'perceived' value by the decision makers. This recognition of perception of value is highlighting the fact that identifying and meeting the needs of decision makers for suppliers is crucial if they are to be perceived as adding value to the retailer. In short, this recognises the need for developing a personal relationship with the decision makers to create value.

The final area of Georges and Eggert's review is that of available alternative suppliers. This is a vital context to the UK grocery market, where there are often many branded (and own-brand) supplier alternatives for a retailer to choose from. As will be discussed later in the research, this market context and how it influences the retailer-supplier relationship is potentially a major factor in how a supplier creates and captures value.

Whether the value concept is examined from the perspective of the customer or the supplier, it is impacted by differing perceptions of their definitions of value, with the two actors often not agreeing on what value is (Möller 2006). As discussed earlier, at the core of customer perceived value is the suppliers' 'offer'. The challenge is to verify how the customers perceive the value created by the suppliers for them (Möller 2006).

Value Creation Types

In exploring the levels of value created from the business-to-business exchange, Pardo et al. (2006) proposed that there are three types of value creation (Fig. 3.3):

1. *Proprietary Value*—value developed by either supplier or customer entirely for its benefit
2. *Exchange Value*—a value which suppliers deliver, and the customer receives the benefits
3. *Relational Value*—the value created through interrelated activities between the supplier and buyer

When reviewing this model in the context of the research question, the proprietary value and exchange value could be argued to be the major focus of the transaction between the supplier and the retailer. This focal point is the selling of products (brand and own-brand) to the retailer, with a negotiation around the cost price and other investments that the supplier will make for the retailer to 'list' (stock) the product. This activity for the supplier is a balance between how much value they can keep in the negotiation (proprietary value) and how much they transfer across to the retailer (exchange value).

When looking at relational value, the challenge is not just to identify the activities it involves, but also to understand whether the customer places a value on them. This area is difficult to assess, as it is created jointly between the two actors, with each bringing their resources and competencies to the

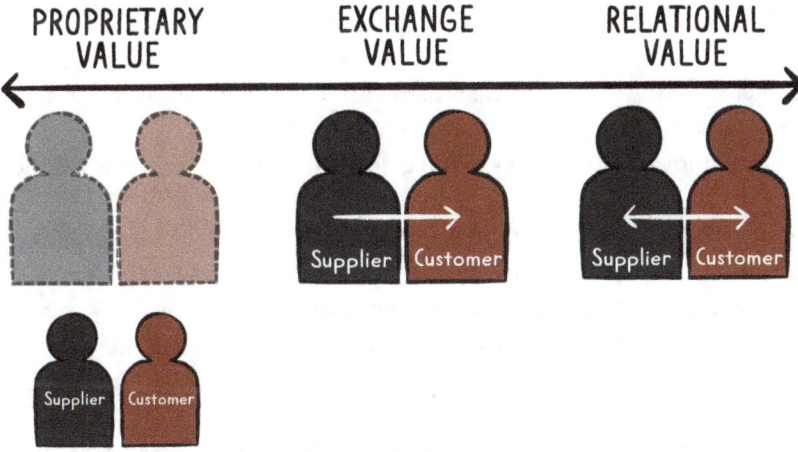

Fig. 3.3 Types of value in BTB exchange. (Source: Adapted from Pardo et al. 2006)

collaboration. Moreover, it can bring a managerial complexity not only between the two businesses but within the supplier's business (Möller 2006) since the supplier may have to align and organise different resources across different functional teams (Grant 2005).

Another area of potential complexity with relational value production is to find out how much of the relational value is created for the short or long term. It is argued that short-term value creation is often characterised by known and trusted activities, with a future orientation being more characterised by the new and radical changes to the norm (Möller and Törrönen 2003). This difference presents managerial challenges to the supplier due to the tradeoff between cost and complexity, versus the period to realise a financial return.

For a supplier to effectively create and capture value, they need to understand the customers' competencies. It can be difficult for the suppliers to align the competencies that are important in the creation of value (Möller 2006). This latter point is important, as it is in the transformation of these competencies and resources that a supplier creates the value. For a supplier to create value for themselves and their customers in a BTB collaboration, it is important that they understand which of their competencies can create value, and crucially what customer benefits they can deliver (Golfetto et al. 2007).

From a supplier perspective, understanding a customer's needs may not be as simple as just asking them; rather, that understanding needs to be related to the customer's business model (Beverland 2012).

This understanding then enables the suppliers to translate their competencies to value creation and capture the activities with their customers. These decisions can be characterised as value creation strategies. These strategies can vary in their future orientation and complexity and are described by Möller (2006) as:

- Market Offering—the strategies offering similar activities to others.
- Value-added strategies more tailored to the actor.
- Radical innovation strategies tailored and differentiated to the actor's needs.

Figure 3.4 highlights the model that proposes that there are implications for choosing strategic options that do not match the buyer (customer) and supplier needs. Each approach comes with implications on how much the current value system needs to change, the complexity that the choice will place on the relationship, and the impact on the timescale to create and capture the value.

The key point is understanding each actor's strategy (current or desired) and ensuring the value creation strategy proposed is matched to each actor's

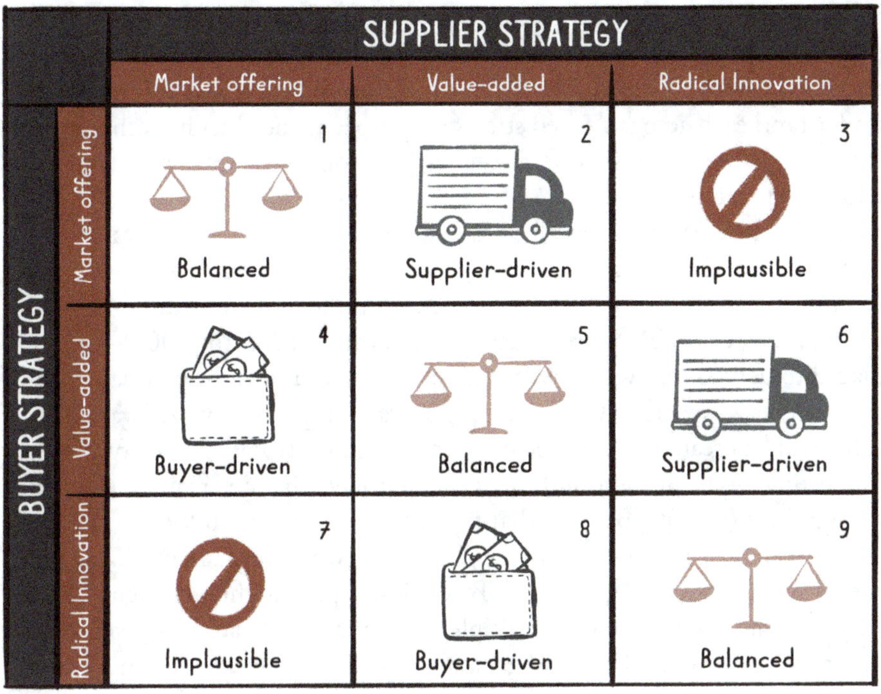

		SUPPLIER STRATEGY		
		Market offering	Value-added	Radical Innovation
BUYER STRATEGY	Market offering	1 Balanced	2 Supplier-driven	3 Implausible
	Value-added	4 Buyer-driven	5 Balanced	6 Supplier-driven
	Radical Innovation	7 Implausible	8 Buyer-driven	9 Balanced

Fig. 3.4 Basic value strategies in business-to-business marketing. (Source: Adapted from Möller 2006)

needs. If the strategy mismatches, then it leads to no value creation as each side struggles to understand and implement the strategy (Möller 2006).

In relating this to the UK Grocery Industry, it could help to highlight how some of the shorter term demands and tensions discussed earlier in this literature review are creating challenges for the suppliers. The retailers are demanding short-term funding and other mechanisms for a limited value gain in a very competitive environment versus discounters, and so on.

In contrast, the suppliers are reluctant to collaborate on this basis, looking for a longer-term solution. This mismatch in strategy could either indicate a lack of understanding of each other's strategic intent and the wrong choice of strategy that both can collaborate around to create joint value.

This underlines the importance of understanding the value creation strategies from both sides of the relationship; the result of a mismatch in value creation strategy at this stage will be at best ineffective value creation and capture, at worst customer dissatisfaction at potentially being asked to deploy resources and investments for what they perceive as a 'cost' to their business.

The real danger for a supplier is that they add 'value' to the collaboration that the customer does not recognise, or want, which carries both cost and risk. In developing the appropriate value creation strategy, it is important to understand each actor's desired strategic approach, and then have the capability to align the organisation's resources and competencies against the most appropriate strategy.

As it is the customer that will provide the ultimate measure of value in the collaboration (Möller 2006), it may be that actors who can provide more resources that are 'valuable, rare, inimitable, and non-substitutable'—what are referred to as VRIN attributes (Eisenhardt and Martin 2000)—are best placed to deliver that value. What is also clear is that it is the competencies of the firms involved that will have a significant impact on which variables of value will be created. It is in the gap between the customer's own competency in creating a type of value and that of its suppliers that determines its reliance on suppliers (or not) to create that type of value (Möller 2006).

As a result, this presents the supplier with two management challenges if they are to create value in the BTB relationships. The first challenge is that they typically operate across multiple customers, and each may well have a different strategic need regarding value creation. This means the supplier will need to make choices about whom to collaborate with, and how to collaborate to create value and optimise the resources of the firm (Möller 2006).

The role of the salesperson in the creation of value between the two businesses is important to understand in the value creation process (Baumann et al. 2017). The salesperson does take on a distinct role in the value creation process, versus the role taken by the customer, acting as the lead for their own organisation as well as translating the customer needs back into their own business (Blonska et al. 2013).

It could be argued that the salesperson is the key actor in the value creation process, with their ability to develop 'sustained, purposeful engagement' with the customer a key factor in successfully creating value with that customer (Marcos-Cuevas et al. 2014). This importance is perhaps stressed further when looking at what can happen if the salesperson is not behaving as intended. Research has shown that in value co-creation relationships between the supplier and customer, if the salesperson does not deliver the promised co-creative behaviour, this can lead to a breakdown in the collaborative relationship (Baumann et al. 2017).

All of this focus on the importance of the salesperson in the value creation between the two parties means that the relationship between the salesperson and customer could be described as the nucleus of the value creation process

(Baumann et al. 2017). The question for the supplier is then, after understanding this importance, and generating value through collaboration, how do they capture value for themselves?

Value Capture

Value capture is concerned with how much of the value in a transaction is retained by the supplier (Leischnig et al. 2018). The research on supplier value capture in BTB relationships is limited, with the studies undertaken mostly by looking at the customer and the value they desire and realise (Flint et al. 2002). This process focus versus an outcome focus is a potential gap in the research and is made all the more challenging when looking to assess the value of complex relationships that include intangible as well as tangible value elements (Keränen and Jalkala 2013).

The capture of value requires the supplier firm to have the process and skill to measure the value created for each party, and this is acknowledged as a challenge for suppliers (Keränen and Jalkala 2013; Storbacka 2012). Within this, it is perhaps even more complex as the measurement needs to be able to evaluate both financial and non-financial benefits (Biggemann and Buttle 2012); this evaluation could be characterised as supplier-perceived value (Songailiene et al. 2011).

Supplier-perceived value can be argued to have three dimensions of financial, strategic, and co-created value (Songailiene et al. 2011). Examining these areas more closely, they can be characterised as:

- Financial Value—based on a customer's ability to generate volume and profit
- Strategic Value—the customer's ability to generate growth and referral
- Co-Created Value—value derived … through customer co-operation. (Songailiene et al. 2011)

Although these dimensions are informative in showing how suppliers perceive the value they capture, they do not explain how suppliers measure these types of value in their collaboration with customers. Research by Keränen and Jalkala (2013) proposed a process for customer value assessment, but this approach was looking only at supplier value created FOR the customer, not the value captured BY the supplier.

This gap in the literature is intended to be addressed in some part by my research. The gap in knowledge on value capture for the supplier is interesting, in that one major factor impacting on a supplier's ability to capture value could be the influence of power, which will be discussed next.

In summary:

- There is a need to define value for both the customer and supplier before being able to decide on how to create value.
- Value is often subjective, is a trade-off between multiple benefits and sacrifices, can be multi-faceted and its perception is relative to competition.
- There are number of joint value creation strategies available, each with characteristics that need to be mapped to the retailer and suppliers' own strategy.
- The KAM team are a very important facilitator of the identification and creation of value between the retailer and supplier.
- Value capture literature is limited, but appears to involve financial value, strategic value, and co-created value elements.

Key Account Management

In developing an understanding of the Key Account Management (KAM) approach, it is important to understand the wider context in which the management of the customers operates for a supplier. The traditional view of the firm would see the goods being sold by a supplier and supplied to a retail customer, along with a value chain. It would then be the role of the sales department in the organisation to manage that process and supply of the goods in a timely and profitable way.

As discussed earlier, KAM is a relationship management mechanism and is defined as 'a relational capability, involving task dedicated actors, who allocate the resources of the firm and its strategically important customers, through the management practices that aim at inter and intra organisational alignment' (Storbacka 2012, p. 261). KAM brings benefits to both the suppliers and the customers (Davies and Ryals 2014), but it also brings challenges, as will be discussed later.

KAM as a management mechanism can also be argued to be rooted in the 'Service-Dominant Logic' (SDL). SDL looks at the whole value chain and the roles of the actors within the chain. It creates a link between the supply chain and marketing theories of exchange and value creation. SDL argues that the firm is now shifting from the logic of the exchange of goods to the logic of the exchange of services, and the customers are seeking to 'buy offerings that render service and create value' (Vargo and Lusch 2004).

If the focus of SDL is on the co-creation of value through service, then the role of the KAM team can be argued to be vitally important in a supplier organisation. The KAM team's responsibility is to understand their customers' needs and collaborate with them, to build their mutual business. To achieve this, the KAM team will need the required resources, and importantly the personal and organisational capability to execute their goals (Vargo and Lusch 2004).

More recent thinking in this area has directly linked the concept of SDL to selling as a concept and how it relates to KAM as an organisational structure (Storbacka et al. 2009; Hartmann et al. 2017). This new thinking proposes that there are a broad set of actors engaged in the organisational sales process, and their roles and participation are changing from 'selling' to 'the interaction between actors aimed at creating and maintaining thin crossing points (the locations at which service can be efficiently exchanged for service) through the ongoing alignment of institutional arrangements' (Hartmann et al. 2017, p. 2).

This emergent thinking further appears to support the concept of KAM as a multi-faceted, multi-functional team across an organisation. KAM's role is recognised as an opportunity for business to deliver 'collaborative innovation' through partnerships with their selected customers (Hartmann et al. 2017).

This new sales context for SDL conceptually fits with the move from a traditional sales management approach to a KAM approach. Sales management was traditionally founded on the idea of translating the 'features' of a product that has been sold into 'benefits' for the customers. This is often explained as the 'seven steps process' and has been recognised as being in place for many years as the foundation process for sales (Moncrief and Marshall 2005).

However, this approach has been refined and replaced as the customer needs and sophistication levels have increased. Specifically, 'rising customer expectations, consumer avoidance of the buyer-seller negotiations, expanding the power of giant retailers, globalisation and de-basification of domestic markets are radically changing the way sales-people perform their jobs' (Anderson 1996).

The foundation of the KAM approach is for the selling organisation to recognise the need for closer and longer-term relationships with selected customers or accounts (Millman and Wilson 1995). It also has to have a focus on the creation and capture of value (Rackham and De Vincentis 1999). To achieve this, the skill and competency of the KAM team are vital in delivering a collaborative approach between a supplier and its customers (Arnett et al. 2005).

Considering the concepts of RM previously discussed, it could be argued that the overall purpose of the KAM team is to create a relationship marketing benefit between the buying and selling organisation that brings benefits in two areas. One area is collaborative relationships with the buyers to increase the buyer's relationship commitment, and the other refers to the increased sell-through of the supplier's products, thereby enhancing a buyer's competitive advantage (Arnett et al. 2005).

Successful implementation of a KAM approach to managing the customers requires some elements to be present. These elements include (1) account planning and selection, (2) top management involvement, (3) KAM 'esprit de corps', (4) use of teams, (5) KAM activities, and (6) KAM evaluation (Homburg et al. 2002).

A detailed account plan to direct and manage the collaborative relationship is also a key factor for the success of KAM (Ryals and Rogers 2007). The account plan is not only a tool for developing strategies and tactics but also a mechanism to inform decision makers of the presence of defined strategies for Key Account Management that can contribute to resource efficiency of the firm (Ryals and Rogers 2007).

The second feature of a successful KAM approach is the development of the KAM 'team'. This is where the supplier develops a Customer Business Team structure to match 'expert to expert' in the customer organisation. This team 'jointly develops plans that deliver improved offerings to their common customer and the shoppers/consumers in store' (Gruen and Hofstetter 2010, p. 239). This organisational structure has been often characterised as the 'reverse bow tie' (Fig. 3.5):

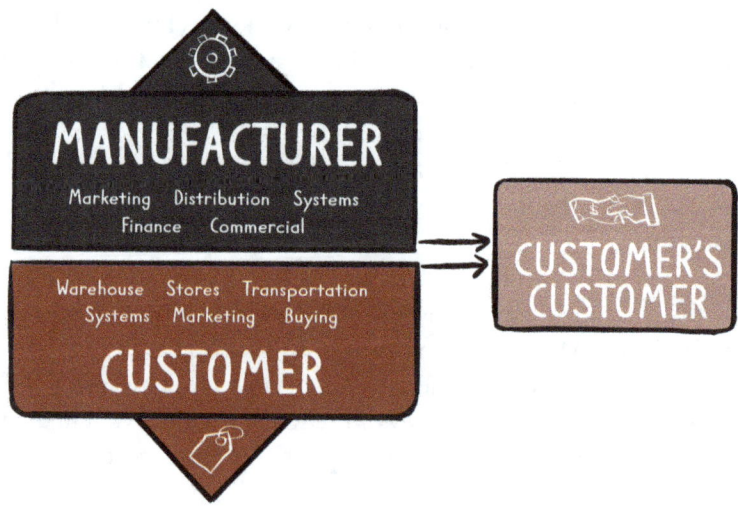

Fig. 3.5 Customer business development team model. (Source: Adapted from Gruen and Hofstetter 2010)

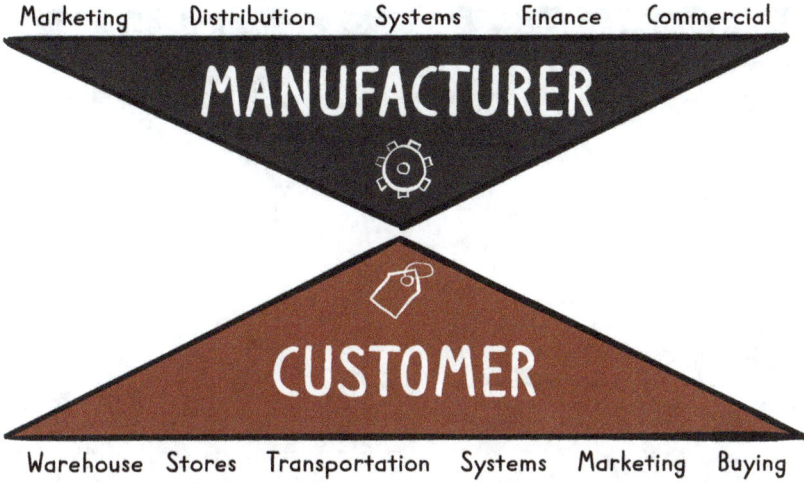

Fig. 3.6 Tradition supplier-customer relationship model. (Source: Adapted from Gruen and Hofstetter 2010)

As indicated, the roles in the KAM team are often cross-functional and cover areas such as marketing, distribution, systems, and finance from a supplier's perspective. The concept is that these multi-functional contacts develop relationships with their counterparts in the customer in order to deliver initiatives and plans for a mutual benefit. This approach is consistent in looking at the whole value chain to manage the business-to-business relationship (Vargo and Lusch 2004).

The customer business team development model is a move away from the 'old' model of sales management that considers an account manager from a supplier and a 'buyer' from a customer as the only points of contact between each business (as illustrated by Fig. 3.6).

What resources and capabilities need to be in place when building a KAM organisation? A systematic review by Guesalaga et al. (2018) proposed both tangible and intangible resources and capabilities that together identify a resource-based KAM framework, as shown in Fig. 3.7.

Looking firstly at the KAM resources, as discussed, the review proposes that the tangible resources of a KAM team and organisation need to be in place, along with the intangible resources of top management support, culture, and team spirit (Homburg et al. 2002). The model proposes that this is further supported by customer knowledge and relational quality. This again fits in with the earlier discussion on the importance and role of relational quality, as well as how this can be built and developed.

Fig. 3.7 Resource-based KAM framework. (Source: Adapted from Guesalaga et al. 2018)

Turning to KAM capabilities, the model highlights how in identifying and developing relationships, the importance of account selection (segmentation) and building relationships and trust (previously discussed in RM) becomes evident. Value creation is proposed as a core capability for KAM, as was discussed earlier in this chapter. The final areas identified in the model are the dynamic capabilities of KAM planning support and KAM implementation. The inclusion here of continuous improvement is consistent with the new perspective on selling, adopted by Hartmann et al. (2017).

KAM Challenges

The KAM approach brings challenges and risks to the supplier companies. Early in its adoption by suppliers, a KAM approach was seen as a competitive advantage, as the business adopted the latest thinking. As KAM adoption by suppliers has developed, it is now seen as a hygiene factor that does not bring any competitive advantage (Piercy and Lane 2006).

Adopting a KAM approach does require the development of multi-functional teams (Gruen and Hofstetter 2010). The intent behind this is to enable value development and delivery for the customer, through the KAM team (Piercy 2006). However, these teams are complex to manage, and this inter-company complexity has been found to bring challenges to the supplier company (Mena et al. 2009).

Moving to a KAM approach also brings additional complexity in the management of the customer base for a supplier. An important feature of a KAM approach is the segmentation of customers (Tzempelikos and Gounaris 2015). The purpose of this segmentation is to enable the suppliers to prioritise their customers, based on the size, growth potential, and other metrics to indicate scale and an assessment of strategic fit.

This prioritisation enables the suppliers to tailor their approach and levels of the resources invested for the customers, based on the segmentation. This brings complexity to a supplier both in making those choices and in delivering the different approaches to the varied customer portfolio (Piercy 2006). Is this complexity necessary? Research has shown that making 'indiscriminate investments' into customers, rather than those who have made a commitment to the supplier, is inefficient and leads to lower sales (Vieira et al. 2014).

These organisational challenges are recognised and can occur at almost every step of KAM implementation, from leadership through planning to targets and execution (Pressey et al. 2014). Furthermore, as a supplier looks to continuously improve their KAM capability, this improvement activity can also provide a challenge to the organisation (Guesalaga et al. 2018) as the new activities drive changes such as the supplier re-evaluating their value proposition, reassigning the importance of certain accounts, or changing the skills needed in the organisation (Guesalaga et al. 2018).

Looking more deeply at the KAM approach, the KAM plan, a central focus of the approach, can be a particular area of weakness. The findings of Pressey et al. indicated that plans could be resisted or fail due to 'a belief that following a certain course of action is redundant due to externalities' (Pressey et al. 2014, p. 1167). This is of particular interest to this research, where the fast-moving nature of the UK Grocery Industry can impact a supplier's business with a retailer with short-term demands and changes, that can challenge the KAM plan that has been developed.

Overall, the financial benefits of adopting a KAM approach can be unclear for the suppliers. As discussed, KAM requires increased resources and investments for suppliers to implement a KAM organisation (Homburg et al. 2002). It could be argued that this has led to profit challenges, as suppliers have formed closer collaborations with their important customers, which could have led them demanding ever lower prices (Davies and Ryals 2013).

In contrast, some suppliers have found that they can bring higher profitability by implementing a KAM approach to manage the customers (Kalwani and Narayandas 1995). It is perhaps as a result of these mixed findings that KAM implementation can not only be challenged but sometimes actively resisted in the supplier organisation.

KAM Grocery Market Context and Practice

Specifically, in the grocery industry, the emergence of collaborative KAM approaches has been supported by 'formalised' approaches such as 'Efficient Consumer Response' by the various industry bodies across Europe and the world. The effectiveness of ECR approaches is under debate, as ECR is said to have developed a new approach to collaboration and co-operation in the grocery industry (Kahn and McAlister 1997), whereas others have argued that ECR is more focused on aligning around a common process between retailer and supplier than on the creation of value (Hofstetter 2006).

The reason for the development of ECR was to enhance the collaborative nature of relationships and the value developed in the industry to avoid the industry declining into stagnation (Kotzab and Teller 2003). Within ECR, the category management (CM) is a process that looks to build demand growth plans in a product category, typically as a collaborative approach between a retailer and key supplier(s). It intends to formalise a collaborative process to co-create value through the use of expert information and capability (Aastrup et al. 2007).

Although a limited amount of research has been undertaken in the ECR/category management field, there are conflicting views on its effectiveness. Some researchers have viewed it as a positive process to enable collaboration and create joint value (Lindblom and Olkkonen 2008). However, others have argued that category management is a collaborative process and a mechanism for the retailers to exert power over the suppliers (Dapiran and Hogarth-Scott 2003). Part of the challenge in the ECR approach could be its attempt to be both collaborative, yet at the same time involve partners who are competitive and part of the so-called competition models (Kotzab and Teller 2003).

This change to supplier relationships, with a few strategic customers becoming increasingly important to their business, is a known phenomenon for companies engaged in a KAM-way of working, 'Strategic customers have become more difficult to acquire and retain, as markets mature, and customers demand even better service at ever lower prices' (Ryals and Holt 2007, p. 403).

3 The Theory, and How It Applies to the FMCG Industry

A government enquiry has recognised these challenging dynamics. As far back as 2008, the Competition Commission looked at the grocery market (HM Government Competition and Markets Authority 2008), its dynamics, and potential abuses of power. In its research, the Commission found evidence of retailers using their power to try and stop suppliers supplying other (competitor) retailers, demanding large lump-sum payments to continue trading, retrospective pricing demands, and transfer of risk in deals to the supplier. Figure 3.8 highlights the complaints from the suppliers which were analysed by the Competition Commission.

The buyer-seller relationship in the grocery market is arguably also made more complex by the fact that the suppliers are largely selling branded products, and so are aiming to reach an end consumer, to whom they advertise directly, via shoppers in their retail customer's stores. This can give rise to tension within a supplier's business, as they try to balance the marketing team's needs that are driven by brand strategy and are largely focused on the end consumer, the sales team, and their customer management strategies related to the retailer. It can be argued that the emergence of fewer, larger, and more powerful retail customers has affected the balance of power between the supplier companies (Pressey et al. 2014).

Further to this, for both suppliers and retailers, it used to be the case that powerful brands were at the centre of the relationship, but with the emergence and growth of own label supermarket brands, this is no longer the case. As of 2021, own label accounts for over 50% share of grocery sales. This dynamic is having two effects for suppliers. Firstly, they are potentially

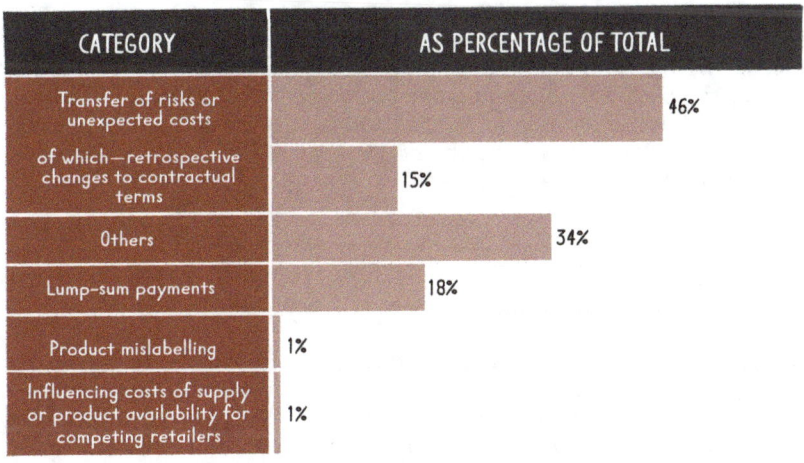

Fig. 3.8 Competition Commission retailer power abuses instances reported. (Source: Adapted from HMRC Competition Commission Report—Appendix 9.8 2008)

competing for sales with their own customers (unless they choose to manufacture the own-brand themselves), and, secondly, increasingly suppliers need to find the other ways to grow their business with their customers and gain a competitive advantage over their (supplier) competitors (Pressey et al. 2014).

Building from these challenges, the current reality for large suppliers in the industry is that, although collaborative approaches are well understood, and ECR as a theoretical ideal is broadly embraced, the day-to-day realities of the relationship with their customers are challenging these beliefs in taking a collaborative approach.

An annual industry survey by the 'Advantage Group' regularly places 'having a collaborative approach', and 'building joint category business plans' as key factors retailers wish to see from their suppliers (Advantage Group International 2015). In their day-to-day dealings, many suppliers are under increased short-term pressure for better margins and increased funding from retailers (Perrett 2010) that seem a long way from their desire to collaborate and work within an 'ECR' framework.

A 2016 report by the Grocery Code Adjudicator, Christine Tacon, found evidence in Tesco of this behaviour. Specifically, she highlighted issues around delays in payments and invoicing, and detailed issues in delaying supplier payments to manipulate joint business plan targets (HM Government Grocery Codes Adjudicator 2016).

> It was clear from the evidence that a major focus of the Tesco commercial team during the investigation period was on hitting budgeted margin targets. A percentage margin target was a key element of many of the Joint Business Plans ("JBP") which Tesco negotiated with suppliers on a periodic basis. Payments to maintain the margin target were requested from suppliers by Tesco regardless of whether the planned growth had been achieved and regardless of whether Tesco had delivered on its own JBP commitments. I found that the direction being given to Tesco's buying team as to the status and enforceability of JBP targets was contradictory and unclear.

And further:

> I received internal Tesco emails which encouraged Tesco staff to seek agreement from suppliers to the deferral of payments due to them in order temporarily to help Tesco margin. I also saw internal Tesco emails suggesting that payments should not be made to suppliers before a certain date in order to avoid underperformance against a forecasted margin. I found that Tesco knowingly delayed paying money to suppliers in order to improve its own financial position.

In its defence, Dave Lewis, then the Tesco CEO (appointed after that GCA investigation) indicated that this behaviour was no longer in place. 'We have made a lot of progress, but there is still more we can do … today our colleagues are empowered to do the right thing for our customers and our suppliers, and I am extremely proud of the way they have responded over the past year' (McShane 2017).

Lewis, after his appointment, has publicly recognised the behaviours of the past and how these had impacted their business. 'We lost the virtuous circle. We focused on margin, not customers. We made some bad choices' (Anderson 2015). To improve the situation, Tesco both changed its approach to funding by simplifying its terms structure, and it also launched a 'Tesco Supplier Network', a portal for suppliers to communicate directly with Tesco (Tesco Plc Press Office 2015).

The Tesco example of demands for increased funds is indicative of a known challenge in moving towards a collaborative way of working. 'The benefits to the customer of being treated as a strategic account are clear; what is less clear is what the benefits are to the supplier of entering into such relationships' (Ryals 2005, p. 404).

At the heart of this debate appears to be the concept of value creation and its creation in a KAM relationship, and then, the subsequent sharing of that value. What is clear is that there is a tension between the creation of value and the sharing of value, with the creation of value being a cooperative activity, and the sharing of value being a competitive activity between the two parties (Nalebuff and Brandenburger 1997).

In light of this tension, it is perhaps not unsurprising that some suppliers are now looking at their current approaches towards strategic key accounts. This shift in the thinking of suppliers is supported by recent findings from the Grocery Codes Adjudicator. Although improvements were noted in their findings, problems were still persisting in the way suppliers were treated (Mclean 2016). In that connect, Ben Baruch of the Federation of Small Business commented on the GCA report findings, stating 'Pay to stay [cash to secure shelf space] is front and centre of the complaints we receive—it's supply chain bullying and anti-competitive'.

More recently the proposed merger by ASDA and Sainsbury's in 2019 was highlighted to increase pressure on suppliers for better costs, not just by the combined group, but by the reaction of their competition as well.

> *The upshot for suppliers is when input cost pressures are increasing, and (increased) pricing is not an option in this hostile retail environment, margins will inevitably get squeezed, requiring more cost savings to plug the gap—and so the vicious cycle accelerates. The weakest could go to the wall. It could get ugly very quickly and may even prompt more retail consolidation across Europe. (Ackerman, The Grocer, 2018)*

In summary

- KAM operates as a method for the suppliers to organise their resources and competencies in a way to focus on co-creating value with chosen key customers.
- KAM has been shown to bring benefits for the supplier and customer, through the delivery of elements such as the KAM plan and KAM team (Davies and Ryals 2014).
- However, KAM also leads to challenges regarding developing and delivering plans and value for the supplier, as it requires the coordination and management of cross-functional teams within the supplier, and then with the customer.
- KAM in the grocery market has been established for many years, founded in the collaborative approach of ECR and category management.
- Category management is a core capability of KAM, but its effectiveness is open to question based on research.
- Collaborative efforts have been challenged by short-term retailer behaviours and demands resulting in a code of practice being introduced by the government.

In summary

- Business-to-business collaboration
  - BTB exchange is a mechanism where both parties need to benefit.
  - There is a relational element to the BTB exchange, a complex blend of personal, economic, and non-economic benefits.
  - Relational Quality (RQ) reflects the depth, closeness, and climate in the BTB relationship.
  - There will be conflict in any BTB relationship, and the benefits may not be equal for each side or equitable comparing one supplier to another.
- Power in BTB relationships
  - Power is a major factor in BTB relationships; the atomic particle ever presents even if unseen.
  - There are different types of power that can be exerted, each with unique characteristics and implications.
  - Power clearly impacts collaboration, and its success, so it's important to understand where the power lies before entering into collaboration.

- There is an imbalance of power in the UK Grocery Industry, in favour of the retailer, which has been seen to cause competitive issues.
- Collaboration processes such as ECR, and category management, are unclear when it comes to who they benefit mostly in terms of power and balance in the collaboration between retailer and supplier.

- BTB value creation and capture

  - There is a need to define value for both the customer and supplier before being able to decide on how to create value.
  - Value is often subjective, is a trade-off between multiple benefits and sacrifices, can be multi-faceted, and its perception is relative to competition.
  - There are number of joint value creation strategies available, each with characteristics that need to be mapped to the retailer and suppliers' own strategy.
  - The KAM team are a very important facilitator of the identification and creation of value between the retailer and supplier.
  - Value capture literature is limited, but appears to involve financial value, strategic value, and co-created value elements.

- Key Account Management

  - KAM operates as a method for the suppliers to organise their resources and competencies in a way to focus on co-creating value with chosen key customers.
  - KAM has been shown to bring benefits for the supplier and customer, through the delivery of elements such as the KAM plan and KAM team.
  - However, KAM also leads to challenges regarding developing and delivering plans and value for the supplier, as it requires the coordination and management of cross-functional teams within the supplier, and then with the customer.
  - KAM in the grocery market has been established for many years, founded in the collaborative approach of ECR and category management.
  - Category management is a core capability of KAM, but its effectiveness is open to question based on research.
  - Collaborative efforts have been challenged by short-term retailer behaviours and demands resulting in a code of practice being introduced by the government.

Introduction into Research Aims and Methodology

The discussion of the theory highlighted some interesting questions and challenges for the FMCG industry. These questions were then used to inform my research into the current state of collaboration, and to do that I decided on a case study approach to the research. Case studies allow for deep understanding of a situation and are particularly useful for developing answers to why and how things work.

The case studies were developed through qualitative one-to-one interviews, a detailed document review of relevant strategies and plans, and attendance at a Customer Team meeting. The research questions I looked to answer were:

- How do grocery suppliers generate and capture value through key account relationships?

The following sub questions were explored:

(a) What are the benefits of collaborative supplier/customer relationships in the UK Grocery Industry, to the supplier?
(b) How is value created and captured by suppliers in the UK Grocery Industry?
(c) What is the influence of power on the supplier's collaboration with the retailer?
(d) How are collaborative models such as ECR, category management, and KAM used in the UK Grocery Industry?
(e) How do these models influence collaborative practices of the supplier when working with their customers?

Identifying the Research Population

When identifying the research population, a number of factors were used to identify the appropriate companies. These were company scale, product type, company ownership structure, and the supply of brands versus own-brand.

Firstly, the scale of the company is important. For this research, each case company needed to be large enough to have a KAM organisation structure in place, which would appear to preclude small business from being part of the research population as they lack the resources (or need) to have a KAM organisation in place to manage their business with the retailer.

The second factor under consideration is type of product sold, and the associated supply chain. It could be instructive to understand if the supplier for fresh or shorter life products (e.g., dairy) is operating in a different way towards longer life products (grocery and non-food items).

3   The Theory, and How It Applies to the FMCG Industry

A third factor was company ownership structure. There are public and privately owned companies in operation in the UK Grocery Industry. The final factor reviewed was that of the supply of brand and own-brand product, or both. This dynamic is potentially interesting as to what level of access and collaboration a customer may exhibit with these different types of suppliers.

Own-brand suppliers have a relationship where the individual retailer is the only customer for that product range, whereas branded suppliers sell the same brands across multiple retailers. This difference could be a factor in how the supplier collaborates with the retailer, and how the retailer responds to their collaborative efforts.

In selecting the cases, the criteria for inclusion are that they are a UK grocery supplier to one of the top-five UK grocery retailers and operate under a 'KAM' organisational structure.

The businesses selected were:

- **Alpha**, a multi-product category multinational manufacturer
- **Beta**, the brand leader in a fresh product market
- **Gamma**, a privately owned brand and own-brand manufacturer
- **Delta**, a public company which supplies only own-brand products to UK grocery retailers

Data Gathering

It was decided to utilise three research instruments to provide the triangulation of data required: one-to-one interviews, key document review, and attendance at an internal KAM team meeting for observation.

Table 3.2 highlights the overview of the three approaches with their respective characteristics, as related to the variables being captured, the timeframe under consideration, and the thematic framework for each data type.

The one-to-one interviews were carried out with members of the extended KAM teams. This means it included both the people formally managing the customer and wider team members, such as category managers.

The second instrument selected was that of meeting attendance. This was an internal supplier meeting of the KAM team, usually monthly in frequency. This meeting was observed and recorded, so no interview guide or questions were used. This instrument looked to understand how direction or strategy was executed as a team, and how issues and opportunities were understood and managed.

Table 3.2 Research framework for case studies

Unit of analysis/ unit of observation	Variables	Time frame	Data type	Thematic framework
Companies	Ownership type Brand/own-brand supply	Snapshot	One-to-one interviews Document review	Structured questions interview Structured questions—document analysis
People	Roles Time in role		Meeting observation	Emerging themes from meeting observation

The third instrument used was a document review. As noted in Table 3.3 various documents were selected against their ability to answer questions around the types and levels of plans used in the company, and how these directed the type and amount of collaboration with customers.

Research Anonymity

When deciding to be involved in this research, the key factor for all companies was the anonymity for the company and interviewees. The relationships between the companies and their major customers are often challenging and sometimes confrontational. For that reason, anonymity at both the company and individual level was paramount. This has been respected in the research, and subsequently in this book.

Chapter Summary

- The review of the theory identified three major areas of interest that are relevant to collaboration in the FMCG industry
    - BTB collaboration identified how businesses work together, and work towards developing value, but within that the quality of the relationship, and conflict, can be important factors.
    - Power is an always present factor in BTB relationships and is often unbalanced towards one side. In the FMCG industry this provides a constant challenge and impact on the relationship between retailer and supplier.
    - Value creation and capture is at the heart of the BTB relationship, and it is the sharing of that value that is the cause of conflict.

Table 3.3 Research instruments objectives

Data area	Data collection plan	Objectives
1. Document review	Review of key documents: • Company strategy • Sales strategy • Customer business plan (CBP)/joint business plan (JBP) • Customer account profitability • Commercial organisation structure and roles—skills	• To understand the company direction and the role and importance of customers • To understand the importance of collaboration • To identify the types of collaboration in customer plans • To understand the level of account profitability and the impact on collaboration • To understand the amount, type, and skills of resources in the team
2. One-to-one semi-structured interviews	• Commercial/sales director • National Account Controller x 2 • National Account Manager x 3 • Category manager x 2 • Other customer resources x 1	• To understand the direction given to the KAM regarding collaboration and value creation and capture • To identify how customers are selected for collaboration and the implications • To identify evidence of collaboration with customers • To understand the role the individual plays in collaboration with the customer • To understand how the individual values collaboration with the customers
3. Meeting participation	• Internal account planning meeting	• To understand how Customer Teams plan and deliver their collaborate with customers • To understand the processes used in collaboration • To review the different approaches used with different customers • To understand how the Customer Team manages issues and conflict with the customer • To understand how value creation and capture is described by the Customer Team

- KAM is an important approach in the FMCG industry to manage the relationship. It is often complex, involves multiple teams of people, with category management being an important facilitator of collaboration work.

- Four cases of differing company types were identified to answer the research questions and gain an in-depth knowledge of how suppliers create and capture value through collaboration with retailers.

References

Aastrup, J., Grant, D. and Bjerre, M. (2007) Value creation and category management through retailer-supplier relationships. *The International Review of Retail, Distribution and Consumer Research*, 17(5), pp. 523–541.

Ackerman, W. (2018) The sky's not sunny: how Asda and Sainsbury's merger will end up hurting suppliers. *The Grocer* Website, 02 May 2018.

Advantage Group International—Retailer Benchmarking Study UK (2015) Available at: https://www.advantagegroup.com/solutions/supplier-report (Accessed August 2015).

Anderson, J., Kumar, N. and Narus, J. (2007) *Value Merchants: Demonstrating and Documenting Superior Value in Business Markets*. Boston, MA: Harvard Business School Press.

Anderson, M. (2015) Dave Lewis is steering Tesco through a 'fundamental reset' of how it does business. *Campaign Magazine*, 07 October 2015. Available at: https://www.campaignlive.co.uk/article/dave-lewis-steering-tesco-fundamental-reset-does-business/1367466

Anderson, R.E. (1996) Personal selling and sales management in the new millennium. *Journal of Personal Selling and Sales Management*, 16(4), pp. 17–32.

Arnett, D.B., Macy, B.A. and Wilcox, J.B. (2005) The role of core selling teams in supplier-buyer relationships. *Journal of Personal Selling & Sales Management*, XXV(1), pp. 27–42.

Baumann, J., Le Meunier-FitzHugh, K. and Wilson, H.N. (2017) The challenge of communicating reciprocal value promises: buyer-seller value proposition disparity in professional services. *Industrial Marketing Management*, 64, pp. 107–121.

Beverland, M.B. (2012) Unpacking value creation and delivery: orientation, capabilities, practices, and outcomes. *Industrial Marketing Management*, 41(1), pp. 8–10.

Biggemann, S. and Buttle, F. (2012) Intrinsic value of business-to-business relationships: an empirical taxonomy. *Journal of Business Research*, 65(8), pp. 1132–1138.

Blois, K. (2009) Equity within business-to-business relationships. *Journal of Marketing Management*, 25(5–6), pp. 451–459.

Blonska, A., Storey, C., Rozemeijer, F., Wetzels, M., and de Ruyter, K. (2013) Decomposing the effect of supplier development on relationship benefits: the role of relational capital. *Industrial Marketing Management*, 42(8), pp. 1295–1306.

Chicksand, D., 2015. Partnerships: The role that power plays in shaping collaborative buyer-supplier exchanges. *Industrial Marketing Management*, 48, pp. 121–139.

Coase, R.H. (1937) The nature of the firm. *Economica*, 4(16), pp. 386–405.

Cowan, K., Paswan, A.K. and Van Steenburg, E. (2015) When inter-firm relationship benefits mitigate power asymmetry. *Industrial Marketing Management*, 48, pp. 140–148.

Dapiran, G.P. and Hogarth-Scott, S. (2003) Are co-operation and trust being confused with power? An analysis of food retailing in Australia and the UK. *International Journal of Retail and Distribution Management*, 31(5), pp. 256–267.

Davies, I.A. and Ryals, L.J. (2013). Attitudes and behaviours of key account managers: are they really any different to senior sales professionals? *Industrial Marketing Management*, 42(6), pp. 919–931.

Davies, I.A. and Ryals, L.J. (2014) The effectiveness of Key Account Management practices. *Industrial Marketing Management*, 43(7), pp. 1182–1194.

Duffy, R., Fearne, A. and Hornibrook, S. (2003) Measuring distributive and procedural justice: an exploratory investigation of the fairness of retailer-supplier relationships in the UK food industry. *British Food Journal*, 105(10), pp. 682–694.

Dutta, S., Zbaracki, M.J. and Bergen, M. (2003) Pricing process as a capability: A resource-based perspective. *Strategic Management Journal*, 24(7), pp. 615–630.

Dwyer, F.R., Schurr, P.H. and Oh, S. (1987) Developing buyer-seller relationships. *Journal of Marketing*, 51(2), pp. 11–27.

Eggert, A. and Helm, S. (2003) Exploring the impact of relationship transparency on business relationships a cross-sectional study among purchasing managers in Germany. *Industrial Marketing Management*, 32(2), pp. 101–108.

Eggert, A. and Ulaga, W. (2002) Customer perceived value: a substitute for satisfaction in business markets? *Journal of Business and Industrial Marketing*, 17(2/3), pp. 107–118.

Eisenhardt, K.M. and Martin, J.A. (2000) Dynamic capabilities: What are they? *Strategic Management Journal*, 21(10/11), pp. 1105–1121.

Fernie, J. (2014) Relationships in the supply chain, in Fernie, J. and Sparks, L. (eds.), *Logistics and Retail Management: Emerging Issues and New Challenges in the Retail Supply Chain*, London: Kogan Page.

Flint, D.J., Woodruff, R.B. and Gardial, S.F. (2002) Exploring the phenomenon of customers' desired value change in a business-to-business context. *Journal of Marketing*, 66(4), pp. 102–117.

Ford, D. (1980). The development of buyer-seller relationships in industrial markets. *European Journal of Marketing*, 14(5/6), pp. 339–353.

French, J.R.P. and Raven, B. (1959) The bases of social power, in Cartwright, D. (ed.) *Studies in Social Power*, Ann Arbor, MI: Institute for Social Research, The University of Michigan, pp. 150–167.

Georges, L. and Eggert, A. (2003) Key account managers' role within the value creation process of collaborative relationships. *Journal of Business-to-Business Marketing*, 10(4) pp. 1–22.

Golfetto, F., Salle, R., Borghini, S. and Rinallo, D. (2007) Opening the network: bridging the IMP tradition and other research perspectives. *Industrial Marketing Management*, 36(7), pp. 844–848.

Granovetter, M. (1985) Economic action and social structure: the problem of embeddedness. *American Journal of Sociology*, 91(3), pp. 481–510.

Grant, D.B. (2005) The transaction-relationship dichotomy in logistics and supply chain management. *Supply Chain Forum: An International Journal*, 6(2), pp. 38–48.

Gruen, T.W. and Hofstetter, J.S. (2010) The relationship marketing view of the customer and the service dominant logic perspective. *Journal of Business Market Management*, 4(4), pp. 231–245.

Guesalaga, R., Gabrielssona, M., Rogers, B., Ryals, L.J. and Marcos-Cuevas, J. (2018) Which resources and capabilities underpin strategic key account management? *Industrial Marketing Management*, 75(May 2018), pp. 160–172.

Hadjikhani, A. and LaPlaca, P. (2013) Development of B2B marketing theory. *Industrial Marketing Management*, 42(3), pp. 294–305.

Håkansson, H (1982) An interaction approach, in H. Håkansson (ed.), *International Marketing and Purchasing of Industrial Goods*, Chichester: Wiley.

Hartmann, N.N., Wieland, H. and Vargo, S.L. (2017) Converging on a new theoretical foundation for selling. *Journal of Marketing*, 82(2), pp. 1–18.

Hingley, M. K. (2005) Power to all our friends? Living with imbalance in supplier-retailer relationships. *Industrial Marketing Management*, 34(8), pp. 848–858.

Hingley, M., Angell, R. and Lindgreen, A. (2015a) The current situation and future conceptualization of power in industrial markets. *Industrial Marketing Management*, 48, pp. 226–230.

Hingley, M., Lindgreen, A. and Grant, D.B. (2015b) Intermediaries in power-laden retail supply chains: an opportunity to improve buyer-supplier relationships and collaboration. *Industrial Marketing Management*, 50, pp. 78–84.

HM Government Competition and Markets Authority—Grocery Market Investigation (CC) (2008) Available at: https://www.gov.uk/cma-cases/groceries-market-investigation-cc

HM Government Grocery Codes Adjudicator—GCA investigation into Tesco Plc—progress towards following GCA recommendations (2016) Available at: https://www.gov.uk/government/news/gca-investigation-into-tesco-plc-progress-towards-following-gca-recommendations

Hofstetter, J. (2006) Assessing the contribution of ECR. *ECR Journal: International Commerce Review*, 6(1), pp. 20–29.

Homburg, C., Workman, J.P. and Jensen, O. (2002) A configurational perspective on key account management. *Journal of Marketing*, 66(2), pp. 38–60.

Ivens, B. and Pardo, C. (2007) Are key account relationships different? Empirical results on supplier strategies and customer reactions. *Industrial Marketing Management*, 36(4), pp. 470–482.

Jiang, Z., Shiu, E., Henneberg, S. and Naudè, P. (2016) Relationship quality in business-to-business relationships—Reviewing the current literatures and proposing a new measurement model. *Psychology & Marketing*, 33(4), pp. 297–313.

Kahn, B.E. and McAlister, L. (1997) *Grocery Revolution—The New Focus on the Consumer*. Reading, MA: Addison Wesley Educational Publishers Inc.

Kalwani, M.U. and Narayandas, N. (1995) Long-term manufacturer-supplier relationships: do they pay off for supplier firms? *Journal of Marketing*, 59(1), pp. 1–16.

Keränen, J. and Jalkala, A. (2013) Towards a framework of customer value assessment in B2B markets: An exploratory study. *Industrial Marketing Management*, 42(8), pp. 1307–1317.

Kotler, P. (1972) A Generic concept of marketing. *Journal of Marketing*, 36(2), pp. 46–54.

Kotler, P. (2000). *Marketing Management, Millennium Edition*, 10th edn. Upper Saddle River, NJ: Prentice Hall Inc.

Kotzab, H. and Teller, C. (2003). Value-adding partnerships and co-opetition models in the grocery industry. *International Journal of Physical Distribution and Logistics Management*, 33(3), pp. 268–281.

Lacoste, S. and Blois, K. (2015) Suppliers' power relationships with industrial key customers. *Journal of Business and Industrial Marketing*, 30(5), pp. 562–571.

Leischnig, A., Ivens, B., Niersbach, B. and Pardo, C. (2018) Mind the gap: a process model for diagnosing barriers to key account management implementation. *Industrial Marketing Management*, 70, pp. 58–67.

Lindblom, A. and Olkkonen, R. (2008) An analysis of suppliers' roles in category management collaboration. *Journal of Retailing and Consumer Services*, 15(1), pp. 1–8.

Maglaras, G., Bourlakis, M. and Fotopoulos, C. (2015) Power-imbalanced relationships in the dyadic food chain: An empirical investigation of retailers' commercial practices with suppliers. *Industrial Marketing Management*, 48, pp. 187–201.

Marcos-Cuevas, J., Nätti, S., Palo, T. and Ryals, L.J. (2014) Implementing key account management: Intraorganizational practices and associated dilemmas. *Industrial Marketing Management*, 43(7), pp. 1216–1224.

Mclean, P. (2016) Supermarkets and suppliers take stock of relationships. *The Financial Times*, 21 August 2016. Available at: https://www.ft.com/content/b1705e06-53de-11e6-befd-2fc0c26b3c60

McShane, G. (2017) Tesco pledges to improve supplier relationships after GCA finds it breached code of practice. *Produce Business UK*, 26 January 2017. Available at: http://www.producebusinessuk.com/purchasing/stories/2016/01/26/tesco-pledges-to-improve-supplier-relationships-after-gca-finds-it-breached-code-of-practice (Accessed 26 January 2017).

Mena, C., Humphries, A. and Wilding, R. (2009) A comparison of inter- and intra-organizational relationships: two case studies from UK food and drink industry. *International Journal of Physical Distribution & Logistics Management*, 39(9), pp. 762–784.

Millman, T. and Wilson, K. (1995) From key account selling to key account management. *Journal of Marketing Practice: Applied Marketing Science*, 1(1), pp. 9–21.

Mizik, N. and Jacobson, R. (2003) Trading off between value creation and value appropriation: the financial implications of shifts in strategic emphasis. *Journal of Marketing*, 67(1), 63–76.

Möller, K.E.K. (2006) Role of competences in creating customer value: a value-creation logic approach. *Industrial Marketing Management*, 35(8), pp. 913–924.

Möller, K.E.K. and Törrönen, P. (2003) Business suppliers' value creation potential a capability-based analysis. *Industrial Marketing Management*, 32(2), pp. 109–118.

Moncrief, W.C., and Marshall, G.W. (2005) The evolution of the seven steps of selling. *Industrial Marketing Management*, 34(1), pp. 13–22.

Nalebuff, B.J. and Brandenburger, A.M. (1997) Co-opetition: competitive and cooperative business strategies for the digital economy. *Strategy and Leadership*, 25(6), pp. 28–33.

Narayandas, D. and Rangan, V.K. (2004) Building and sustaining buyer-seller relationships in mature industrial markets. *Journal of Marketing*, 68(3), pp. 63–77.

O'Cass, A. and Ngo, L.V. (2012) Creating superior customer value for B2B firms through supplier firm capabilities. *Industrial Marketing Management*, 41(1), pp. 125–135.

Pardo, C., Henneberg, S.C., Mouzas, S. and Naudè, P. (2006) Unpicking the meaning of value in key account management. *European Journal of Marketing*, 40(11), pp. 1360–1374.

Perrett, M. (2010) Tesco delivers £8.8m duty blow on promos. *The Grocer* Website, 05 June 2010.

Piercy, N.F. and Lane, N. (2006) The underlying vulnerabilities in key account management strategies. *European Management Journal*, 24(2-3), pp. 151–162.

Piercy, N.F. (2006) The strategic sales organization. *The Marketing Review*, 6(1), pp. 3–28.

Pinnington, B.D. and Scanlon, T.J. (2009). Antecedents of collective-value within business-to-business relationships. *European Journal of Marketing*, 43(1/2), pp. 31–45.

Pressey, A.D., Gilchrist, A.J.P. and Lenney, P. (2014) Sales and marketing resistance to Key Account Management implementation: an ethnographic investigation. *Industrial Marketing Management*, 43(7), pp. 1157–1171.

Rackham, N. and De Vincentis, J. (1999) *Rethinking the sales force: redefining selling to create and capture customer value*. New York: McGraw Hill Education.

Ryals, L.J. (2005) Management work: the measurement and profitable management of customer relationships. *Journal of Marketing*, 69(4), pp. 252–261.

Ryals, L.J. and Holt, S. (2007) Creating and capturing value in KAM relationships. *Journal of Strategic Marketing*, 15(5), pp. 403–420.

Ryals, L.J. and Rogers, B. (2007) Key account planning: benefits, barriers, and best practice. *Journal of Strategic Marketing*, 15(2), pp. 209–222.

Ryals, L.J. and Humphries, A.S. (2010) Efficiency versus value maximisation in co-manufacturing relationships. *The International Journal of Logistics Management*, 21(2), pp. 309–330.

Sheth, J.N. and Parvatiyar, A. (1995) The evolution of relationship marketing. *International Business Review*, 4(4), pp. 397–418.

Songailiene, E., Winklhofer, H. and McKechnie, S. (2011) A conceptualisation of supplier perceived value. *European Journal of Marketing*, 45(3), pp. 383–418.

Speakman, J.I.F. and Ryals, L.J. (2012) Key account management: the inside selling job. *Journal of Business and Industrial Marketing*, 27(5), pp. 360–369.

Stanko, M.A., Bonner, J.M. and Calantone, R.J. (2007) Building commitment in buyer-seller relationships: a tie strength perspective. *Industrial Marketing Management*, 36(8), pp. 1094–1103.

Storbacka, K. (2012) Strategic account management programs: alignment of design elements and management practices. *Journal of Business and Industrial Marketing*, 27(4), pp. 259–274.

Storbacka, K., Ryals, L.J., Davies, I.A. and Nenonen, S. (2009) The changing role of sales: viewing sales as a strategic, cross-functional process. *European Journal of Marketing*, 43(7/8), pp. 890–906.

Sullivan, U.Y., Peterson, R.M. and Krishnan, V. (2012) Value creation and firm sales performance: the mediating roles of strategic account management and relationship perception. *Industrial Marketing Management*, 41(1), pp. 166–173.

Tesco Plc Press Office—Tesco launches new online supplier community, 22 January 2015. Available at: https://www.tescoplc.com/news/news-releases/2015/tesco-launches-new-online-supplier-community/

Towill, D.R. (2005) A perspective on UK supermarket pressures on the supply chain. *European Management Journal*, 23(4), pp. 426–438.

Tzempelikos, N. and Gounaris, S. (2015) Linking key account management practices to performance outcomes. *Industrial Marketing Management*, 45(1), pp. 22–34.

Ulaga, W. and Eggert, A. (2006) Value-based differentiation in business relationships: gaining and sustaining key supplier status. *Journal of Marketing*, 70(1), pp. 119–136.

Vargo, S.L. and Lusch, R.F. (2004) Evolving to a New Dominant Logic. *Journal of Marketing*, 68(1), pp. 1–17.

Vieira, A.L., Winklhofer, H. and Ennew, C.T. (2014) The effects of relationship marketing on share of business: a synthesis and comparison of models. *Journal of Business-to-Business Marketing*, 21(2), pp. 85–110.

Williamson, O. (1981) The economics of organization: the transaction cost approach. *The American Journal of Sociology*, 87(3), pp. 548–577.

Woodruff, R. (1997) Customer value: the next source for competitive advantage. *Journal of the Academy of Marketing Science*, 25(2): pp. 139–153.

4

Collaboration in Action: Four Case Studies

In this chapter we will be turning our attention to what is happening in reality when suppliers look to collaborate with their retail customers. Each of the cases represents companies of different types and ownership, as highlighted in the previous chapter. However, in all four there are questions that arise that the cases look to answer. These are

- How do the companies choose who to collaborate with?
- What does the work of collaboration contain?
- What are the barriers to collaboration?
- What influence does power have in the collaboration?
- How do the companies create and capture value?

The cases will provide answers to these questions and show examples and insights to bring into light this often 'secretive' area of business between the retailer and supplier. As already discussed, for this reason these cases are anonymised, but I do describe characteristics of each company so you can get a sense of the type of company involved.

These cases are intended to bring depth of insights to what is happening and why. Case study research of this type does not provide answers to 'how many' companies behave in this way. That would need new, quantitative research. However, I wanted to get deep understanding of the issues and challenges that are at play in suppliers when they are collaborating with their customers. The findings you will see here provide the basis of the recommended ideas and actions we will discuss in Chap. 6.

The Alpha Case Study: A Multinational Multi-category Supplier Demonstrating a Global to Local Approach

After reading this case you will discover:

1. How Alpha has a clear focus, process, and approach to collaborating with their major customers.
2. The way Alpha uses guidance and help from a global team to help the local team use standard tools and approaches to facilitate the choice of collaborative customers, and the plans and approaches that can be used.
3. The ways Alpha creates and captures value from its collaboration with customers, using joint scorecards and the setting of ROI targets to understand what value has been created and captured.
4. How Alpha experiences and manages the influence of power is present in relationships with its customers.
5. Alpha's approach to creating and capturing value from its collaborative relationships.

Introduction

Alpha is a publicly company, operating globally across a number of product categories. It has a portfolio of large brands in each of its main product categories, with brand leadership in some of their product categories. It sells to customers across all channels of trade, but it is its relationship with its major retailer customers in the UK that is the focus of this case study.

The key accounts team at Alpha is responsible for managing the business-to-business relationship and is organised into four customer teams. Each major customer has a dedicated team allocated to it for the management of the joint business.

Team Structure

These teams comprise an Account Director, managing a team of Account Managers and Executives, and in some instances a dedicated Supply Chain Executive. There is also a dedicated resource in the 'virtual' team, covering the areas of Category and Shopper Marketing, specifically for those customers.

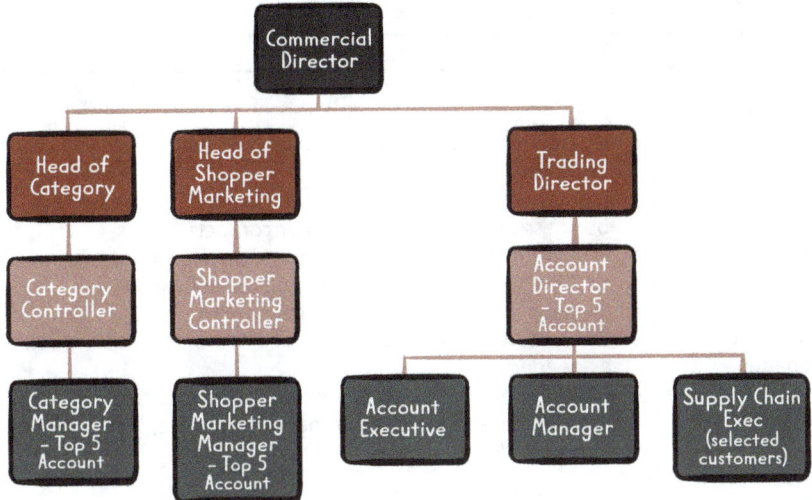

Fig. 4.1 Alpha commercial team structure

The structure of the team is illustrated in Fig. 4.1, and the individual work roles and responsibilities in the Customer Team are highlighted in Table 4.1.

Alpha Case Themes

In analysing the research findings, three main categories emerged as significant in answering the overall research question. These categories and their subcategories are characterised in Table 4.2.

The three high-level themes that have emerged are 'Collaboration', 'Power', and 'Value'.

Collaboration is the area of work that exists so that Alpha works more closely with its customers. This may be work with the customer (e.g., joint product development) or work developed for the customer alone by Alpha (e.g., market data analysis and reporting).

Power is evidence of the impact of retailer power specifically on Alpha's ability to collaborate with the customer in question and/or its ability to generate and capture value. This is evidenced with specific instances of the retailer withdrawing from collaborative activities and asking for funding over, above, and outside the formal business plans and agreed activities.

Value is evidence of work aimed at directly creating value for Alpha. Value creation, for example, could cover work such as joint business planning, and work areas showing evidence of value capture for Alpha could include

Table 4.1 Alpha Customer Team roles and responsibilities

Role	Responsibility in Customer Team
Full-time team member	
Account Director	• Overall management responsibility of the customer P&L and team management
Account Manager	• Day-to-day responsibility for relationship and delivery of business plan with key customer contacts
Category Manager	• Provide total category insights and advice to the customer on how to grow the (customers) overall business
Shopper Marketing Manager	• Develop tailored marketing programmes for Alpha brands in the customer, working with the customers marketing team as needed
Customer Implant	• Undertakes analysis and reporting for the customer for their business, based in the customers head office, but paid for and provided by Alpha
Part-time team member	
Supply Chain Manager	• Ensures the on time in full delivery of Alpha products to the customer, working with customer supply chain operations
Retailer Operations Manager	• Delivers the in-store activation and display of Alpha products in the retailers' stores, working with the retailer's store operations and retail management

evidence of initiatives undertaken with their ROI for the Alpha business. An example of this could be a specific promotional programme for Alpha brands to achieve a target return on investment.

Collaboration

Collaboration Purpose and Choices

The outcomes Alpha would like from collaboration with chosen customers, and how they choose who to collaborate with, and how this may differ by customer type.

The subcategory of collaboration purposes and choices contains evidence that Alpha believes at the total organisation level collaboration with customers to be a key business enabler. Evidence of this is found in Alpha's public statements. The document review highlighted the Alpha Trading Statement presentation, which referenced collaborative activities such as 'sharper category strategies', 'ideal store rollout', and 'optimising price and promotions' as important in achieving their business results.

Category strategies and ideal store rollout are demand generation strategies and tools used by Alpha with their customers, to create better engagement

Table 4.2 Alpha research finding categories and descriptions

Category	Description	Subcategory	Description
Collaboration	Work that exists in order that Alpha works more closely with its customers	Collaboration purpose and choices	The outcomes Alpha would like from collaboration with chosen customers, and how they choose who to collaborate with, and how this may differ by customer type
	Both work with the customer (e.g., joint product development) and work developed for the customer alone by Alpha (e.g., market data analysis and reporting).	Collaboration work	The work Alpha undertakes to collaborate with their customers. This can be both joint work with the customer and work Alpha undertakes for the customer
		Non-collaboration work	The work the teams are undertaking purely for Alpha. It is work that has not been asked for by customers, but the Customer Team are undertaking it
		Collaboration barriers	Evidence that stopped collaboration work occurring, largely due to external (customer) factors
Power	The evidence of the influence of retailer power on the relationship and its impact on collaboration and/or value		
Value	Evidence of work aimed at directly creating value for Alpha	Value creation	Work that demonstrates value creation for Alpha, for example joint business planning
		Value capture	Work that provides evidence of value capture for Alpha, for example initiatives undertaken that clearly show with their ROI for the Alpha business.

with them, and deliver growth for the customer and Alpha. This senior level endorsement of collaboration was further evidenced when interviewing a Global Commercial Director, who stated that the Alpha approach is to seek collaboration with customers globally, even if, in some markets, the way that they collaborate is quite different:

> *I think that gone is the traditional school of thought that you have this adversarial customer/seller relationship, and I actually don't see that in any country in the world now, even the countries where we trade, so where we don't have very much category management, where we don't have very much shopper marketing, we still have a very different collaborative relationship.*

Another senior director also highlighted how in his/her view the industry now needs and values collaboration:

> *Smart retailers have begun to realise that manufacturers are a source of competitive advantage, in the same way, that the smart motor manufacturers, you know, when my dad was in the motor game in the seventies and eighties, began to realise actually long term relationships with manufacturers can have a big bearing on our success in markets that are beginning to slow.*

With collaboration viewed as an important strategy in their business, Alpha also has a clear understanding of what this means they should be seeking to achieve with their customers. The research indicates that Alpha recognises both personal relationships and business building proposals, which are important in enabling a collaborative relationship with their customers.

> *We tended to drive collaboration really on two fronts; the first is our ability to form personal relationships with (Customer X). So, we've spent a lot of time and effort getting to know the guys and girls on the other side of the desk, what it is they're trying to achieve … how we can help them to succeed …. the second is just the quality of our analytical thinking and the value of proposals that we make.*

Better Business Relationships

There were multiple references in the research to collaboration being used as the foundation to create a better business relationship between Alpha and its major customers. One Account Director referenced how he had looked to re-establish collaboration with the customer when taking on the role, and how he had focused on the personal relationship first in establishing the collaborative relationship.

> *I'm saying, look, I need, you and I need to work together to prove that there is a very, very close working relationship and a huge amount of trust of each other … we're going to take risks on each other, and that we're going to bias in each other's favour going forward. That's the conversation I then had with them, and that's where I wanted to get to.*

It is interesting to note that both of these references do place great emphasis on the personal nature of collaboration between Alpha and the major customers, and this theme will be explored in more detail later in this case.

Joint Business Plans

One tangible enabler of closer collaboration is a joint business plan that documents targets and activities that Alpha and its customer will work towards. The document review also showed examples of these plans, with clear activities and metrics aimed at formalising the collaboration between Alpha and its key customers.

One example of a business plan with a major customer showed there is a detailed breakdown of the sale and cost targets for the category in a question. There is then a breakout of the different investments Alpha is making in the customer, such as Promotion Markdowns (promotions that are discounting buying more than one pack), price reduction funding (reducing the retail price of one item at the shelf), and a general funding 'pot', which is a catch-all fund for manufacturer funding (this could include fines for late delivery, monies for securing extra space, etc.).

Within the joint business plan, it was also evident how Alpha balanced what they will deliver for the customer versus what they want in return. As an example, the joint business plan showed an exclusive product for that customer that Alpha had developed, and what additional benefits they wanted in return for supplying this product. These were mainly extended distribution (product placed in more stores) of other parts of the Alpha portfolio.

Collaboration Choices

When exploring how Alpha makes collaboration choices, it was evident that they do use a formal segmentation process to select who to collaborate with and how they should collaborate. The segmentation approach (Fig. 4.2) scores a range of factors under each heading in an effort to identify the different types of customer collaboration. The 'will' heading looks at metrics and evidence on how willing the customer has been in the past to collaborate, with 'skill' using similar analysis to understand what skills and resources the customer has in place to build a collaborative relationship; 'importance' reflects the size and growth potential for each customer, using metrics such as value turnover and value growth with the customer.

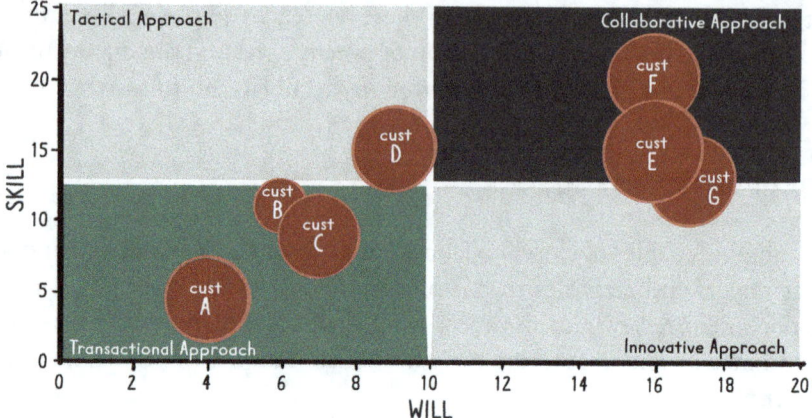

Fig. 4.2 Alpha customer prioritisation

The model in Fig. 4.2 highlights that Customers A, B, and C are high on both will and skill, and will receive a 'collaborative' approach from Alpha. Customers D, E, and F will have a 'transactional approach', with Customer G sitting in the 'tactical approach' quadrant.

The use of this model then influences how Alpha works with customers of different types and the resources that are invested in them. A customer who is deemed 'collaborative' will get a full range of support and resources from Alpha (category management, shopper marketing, dedicated insights as examples), whereas customers who are deemed 'transactional' will get none of these resources, and instead receive 'off the shelf' advice and recommendations, not tailored to their needs.

> *We do have a standard model, but we resource it differently depending on the strategic choices that we make about customers and channels. So, we run a strategy review every two years where we'll set out the contribution that we expect channels and customers to make to our success and then we'll line up our people and money, behind those strategic choices.*

What appears to give Alpha some confidence in its approach to collaboration is the reaction it receives from customers. The 'Advantage Group' survey is a customer satisfaction survey on a range of collaboration factors, completed by major UK retailers assessing their manufacturers.

It is evident from reviewing this document (Fig. 4.3) that customers are recognising Alpha's focus on collaboration, albeit with some issues raised.

In summarising collaboration purpose and choices, Alpha recognises the importance of customer collaboration in their corporate strategy. They

Fig. 4.3 Customer survey feedback

accomplish this with the help of tools and approaches such as ideal store and category management support for customers. They also recognise the importance of personal relationships by developing closer collaboration with customers.

Alpha uses joint business plans, containing scorecards and their own 'wish list' items, as a planning tool to achieve the collaboration. They select who and how they work with using a customer segmentation, based on 'will, skill, and importance'. The success of their approach has been seen in feedback from their customers, through the annual industry customer survey from the Advantage Group.

Collaboration Work

This is defined as the work Alpha undertakes in order to collaborate with their customers. It can be both joint work with the customer and work Alpha undertakes for the customer.

When the work of collaboration was explored in the research, there was a range of activities, from more strategic project-based work to more day-to-day tactical activity.

Global to Local Working

As a global business, Alpha has ways of working in place that aims to standardise work around a series of 'best practices'. This means at a local market level, tools, approaches, and training are available to support the work local markets undertake in collaboration with retailers:

> *There is a blueprint of the core elements, so we have one way of executing pre-and post-evaluation on promotions. We have a clear Alpha set of Trading Terms. We have a clear way of doing category management. We have a clear Alpha way of shopper marketing. So, we have capability blueprints that are more and more derived centrally, and then that blueprint goes out for markets to use within their customer practice. And obviously depending upon culture, market reality, customer preference, you may pull on one or two of those areas more than others.*

Category Management

When looking at the day-to-day collaboration activities of the commercial team, these would appear to be dominated by data analysis, especially where Alpha are 'formal' category partners or captains with a customer. The role of category captain or partner means Alpha employees are expected to undertake detailed and ongoing category wide analysis (not just of Alpha products) to make fact-based recommendations to grow the category with that customer.

What was noticeable in the research was that this work appears to be seen by Alpha as a means of supporting and establishing the collaborative relationships, with customers, rather than just a transfer of work from one party to another:

> *I think what generally helps in collaboration is we take away some of the burden from the retailer, and by that, I mean looking at data and drawing insights from the data, be that EPOS data, be that market data, be that formal sales data. So, I think we very much provide brainpower and resources which in many ways supplement retailers.*

This is then supported by more formal 'category management' work with retailers, where Alpha collaborates with retail customers to identify the best way to execute a tactical activity in the store, across all products. These tactical recommendations will cover the products to place in the range, the best way to display and merchandise the product, and how best to promote them. In some instances, retailers may also ask for pricing advice at a strategic level but will (for legal reasons) be responsible for final pricing decisions.

> *The work that I am involved massively in is category management, and the very basics of its sales fundamentals, range space all that sort of stuff. Making sure we have got absolutely the right assortment, range, segmentation to ensure that the shopper is delighted, and their demands are met.*

When looking more deeply into this work, it became evident that the work of category management that Alpha has been evolved in over recent years served as further indication of the importance of collaborative work in the business. Alpha has started to formalise the work, linking it to the joint business plan and created measures to ensure that the outputs of the category management work are tracked and managed:

> *Now we have moved into creating trade category plans that dovetailed into the joint business plan. So, you are looking at growing both your businesses with genuine shopper metrics.*

> *It's moved from individual event by event transactions to a much more joined-up approach with scorecards, not just on the finances but on how are we changing the shopper behaviours and are we effecting the right metrics that we want to do … if you don't have that level of collaboration, you will never get there, and you need to, but that takes time.*

Promotion Strategy

One example of this work that was cited saw Alpha work with Customer A to change the way Customer A promoted a non-food category. This saw Customer A moving away from an 'Everyday Low Price' strategy (EDLP) to a strategy that delivered greater value to Customer A and Alpha (A 'HiLo' promotion strategy), while still also delivering the value the Customer A shopper was looking for.

EDLP delivers an ongoing one price point to shoppers and is not supported by any promotion. The message to shoppers is 'this product is consistently a great value any time you shop'. The 'HiLo' strategy, in contrast, has a period of a low price (typically four to six weeks) where there is supporting messaging about 'great low prices', with then a period of a higher price, recouping the investment made in lowering the price.

> *It (the new HiLo strategy) worked for us because our average price per pack moved up, it also meant that we started focusing the high/low activity purely on (products, which we are trying to migrate the shopper into for two reasons; firstly, we make a better margin, but secondly fewer chemicals, better for the environment.*

In summary, this section indicates that Alpha undertakes a range of work when they collaborate with customers, from the more tactical day-to-day analysis of data, and tactical levers of range merchandising and promotion, to strategic category projects. The Alpha global team provides tools and support to help the Customer Teams do this work to an Alpha 'best practice' standard.

The collaborative work that is more strategic may involve more than advice and support for products categories that Alpha works on; potentially giving its retail customers wide-ranging advice on the total category. The work evidenced in the research appears to be focused on delivering benefit for Alpha, the Customer, and the Shopper/Consumer—the triple win—showing how Alpha believes that this balanced approach is the best way to undertake collaborative work with customers.

Non-collaboration Work

This is defined as the work the teams are undertaking purely for Alpha. It is work that has not been asked for by customers, but the Customer Team are undertaking it.

The research found limited evidence of non-collaborative work in Alpha, which may be a result of the positioning and overall direction of collaboration in Alpha. As stated earlier, collaboration is viewed as a fundamental part of the Alpha 'go-to-market' strategy, that it appears to influence all of the work done by Customer Teams.

One exception was the experience of the Customer B Customer Team, where due to the confrontational nature of the relationship, Alpha had begun to withdraw from collaborative work. The relationship was characterised as being very day-to-day and transactional, mainly due to barriers to collaboration raised by the customer (which are explored in the next section of this case). It was evident that Alpha would rather not collaborate with customers than get drawn into activities or actions they fundamentally disagreed with.

> *Are there any examples where we've collaborated and genuinely done something that you'd put down on your CV? The answer is probably not.*

In summary, the lack of evidence for non-collaborative work may be due to the fact that the overall emphasis of Alpha's philosophy is focused on collaboration as the 'way of working' in their business.

The only example where this wasn't the case was Customer B, and this was driven by customer resistance to collaborative working as opposed to Alpha undertaking 'non-collaborative' work as a choice.

Collaboration Barriers

This is defined as the work Alpha undertakes in order to collaborate with their customers. This can be both joint work with the customer and work Alpha undertakes for the customer.

The research uncovered a number of themes with regards to barriers to collaboration. The themes that emerged were focused on the Alpha resources that were needed to enable a successful collaboration, and those of the customer as the barrier to collaboration.

With regards to Alpha resources, as discussed earlier, Alpha operates a customer segmentation model to prioritise its customers and the resources they invest. However, even with that prioritisation in place, there can be challenges when a willing customer offers a collaboration opportunity despite the fact that the resources have been placed elsewhere.

> *What becomes a little bit trickier to manage is when a great opportunity comes over the wall from a customer that we have decided that we are going maybe have on a lower priority.*

Customer's Behaviour

Through the research a particular theme emerged regarding the difficulties in collaborating with one customer, Customer A. It was felt by some that the issue was institutional, that Customer A at its core doesn't truly value collaboration with its manufacturers.

> *I've said this to Customer A: I think they don't fully value the contribution manufacturers make to their success and, therefore, are much less likely to talk about fundamental business problems, to work with manufacturers to develop strategy, to build close-working relationships where manufacturers bring their best people and their best ideas .... I think that's deeply cultural.*

Even though that barrier was in place, it was recognised by Alpha that it would be important to try and overcome this collaborative barrier, if possible, since Customer A was a large customer. It is instructive that even when a large and significant customer such as Customer A is so challenging to work with, Alpha was still looking at ways of seeking collaboration.

> *I think we have to work very hard to prevent a drift towards doing business where it's easiest and losing our strategic share ... there is a tension there between Customer A (it) can be a hard nut to crack, but strategically they are a large part of the business .... I absolutely have to find a way of winning with them.*

However, it was clear that this is a big barrier to overcome with Customer A. The research suggested that Customer A shut down access and collaboration based on the fact that very clear quarterly scorecard metrics had not been met. It appears that Customer A saw these collaborative activities as less essential than Alpha did, to be traded against Alpha if the performance did not hit the target.

> *as a result of not hitting our financial targets, even if it's not my fault, and it's largely not my fault, it is then used against me that says, and we will now stop any supply chain development discussions, any category management discussions, any collaborative working .... So, it's actually almost used as ... it becomes a penalty to me for offering these things.*

This final point of 'penalty' was also raised as an internal barrier, wherein dealing with a confrontational customer like Customer A, consistent failure to deliver collaborative work and projects starts to disengage the internal Alpha team. The Customer Team also becomes wary of suggesting collaborative approaches to the customer (Customer A), as they fear they will be used as leverage against them.

> *the phrase that I used with my category colleagues is effective, they were providing the bullets for Customer A to shoot the commercial team with ... funnily enough, I'm not up for that, my job's hard enough without going in and going I want to do this and (Customer A) going no, your category team tell us it's the wrong thing to do.*

Trust

It could be argued that one of the reasons that customers other than Customer A were not mentioned as placing barriers to collaboration is based on the degree of 'trust' in the relationship. The concept of trust between Alpha and its customers was raised a number of times in the context of it being a key enabler of building a collaborative relationship.

One example was cited with Customer C where Alpha gave nine months or more of notice of impending price increases on their products. This is a frequent discussion between a manufacturer and retailer. The core issue being can the retailer raise their retail price to cover the cost of goods increase; if not, then who is going to 'pay' for the loss of resulting margin. These negotiations can be protracted and very difficult on large and important brands, such as those owned by Alpha.

Alpha believed that, in order to build trust and confidence, early notice could help both sides have more constructive, collaborative negotiation on this topic.

> *What does that do …? It diffuses the emotion further down the line … to be brutally honest, it makes getting cost price increases through an awful lot easier, because you don't hit that brick wall of emotion because the answer is, well, we have had the conversation already.*

In summary, the research in this area is suggesting that the customer largely drives collaboration barriers. Consistent with other findings in this research, collaboration appears to be seen as 'the' way of working for Alpha, so there was a lack of evidence for any internal barriers to collaborative work.

The barriers that were found related to customers, specifically one, who through their behaviour and actions, used access to their people, and collaboration on projects as a 'weapon' to be used when their demands were not met. In spite of this, it was evident, even in these situations, that Alpha aimed to find a route through to a better collaborative relationship.

Power

The evidence of the influence of retailer power on the relationship and its impact on collaboration and/or value.

The research findings were almost all focused on the retailer exerting power to restrict or stop collaboration, and one customer dominated this behaviour, namely Customer A.

A Shift in Attitude?

At a senior level, one respondent believes that due to the growth challenges in the major supermarket channels, retailers generally may be more willing to collaborate. It was recognised that, allied to this, was the need to understand the balance of power, and that this does have an impact on the level of collaboration that can be achieved:

> *Then you're reaching an interesting stage right now in the industry where we're beginning to see that the hypermarket/supermarket model has its limitations. New channels are emerging. ... I have noticed a greater degree of collaboration in the last three or four years. ... (Influencing) the extent to which, in this game, the balance of power has a bearing on the level of collaboration.*

Punitive Action

When looking at different retailers, the standout example is Customer A as evidence of using power in an obstructive and destructive way. The findings suggest that Customer A had no issue with halting any collaboration, and furthermore, any contact between them and Alpha if they were not getting the support (funding) they required.

> *The key barriers, if you take a customer like Customer A, and we talked earlier that very much one of their tactics is to keep you on the knife-edge. If you have a commercial dispute with them, and I mean just something minor, you might not have signed off the joint business plan, or they decide the margin on their category isn't growing where it should do, all bets are off. So that means that not only the commercial team, as in the account managers, the customer director, and the controller can't go through the door. They will cut you off as Cat Man; they will cut you off even though you were their category partner.*

This power was exerted across the Alpha business, so even if the dispute were, for example, in one category, Customer A would act across this and all other Alpha product categories, regardless of how well these other businesses were working together.

> *for instance, we might have fallen out in our category X business knowing the fact ... (then) half my category Y range was delisted the next week ... so, the hunting as a pack is really, really powerful.*

In contrast to Customer A, and how it used its power, one example was found in the meeting attendance of how through collaboration, Alpha did not receive a 'penalty' from the retailer but a reward.

> **Meeting Note**: Customer C asked Alpha to support a change in pricing strategy, and promised 'commercial neutrality', that is, it would cost Alpha no more to invest in the new pricing strategy. After executing the strategy, Customer C found that it didn't work, and Alpha had actually invested an extra £Xm. Customer C, as per their promise, returned this extra £Xm to Alpha.

In summary, the research in this area is suggesting that Alpha understands that the balance of power can influence the way collaboration is undertaken. The research evidence shows only one customer is leveraging this power, in a very obvious and challenging way.

What is interesting is that Customer A, in this instance, is not connecting the collaboration work and activities proposed by Alpha as ways to grow value, rather they are optional items to be used against Alpha. It contrasts with the research finding of work with Customer C, where through a collaborative relationship there is sufficient trust for Customer C to remain 'true to their word' and refund a substantial investment to Alpha.

Value

Value Creation

Work that demonstrates value creation for Alpha, for example joint business planning.

The findings in this area show a blend of relational and transactional value creation being used by the Alpha Commercial team.

As in other areas of this research, Alpha appears to have clarity at a senior, strategic level of what value creation is and should involve when collaborating with customers. It is interesting to note that the following example of both relational and transactional value creation was cited:

> We tended to drive collaboration really on two fronts; the first is our ability to form personal relationships with Customer A. So, we've spent a lot of time and effort getting to know the people on the other side of the desk. What it is they're trying to achieve, with a great deal about how we can help them to succeed. And the second is just the quality of our analytical thinking and the value of proposals that we make. So, you put those two things together, and I think that's world-class, right? No manufacturer knows more than you about how to grow our business, and they come forward with a series of great proposals, and by the way, they're fantastic to work with. Do those two things at the same time, and you're away.

This approach was seen as evidence in the customer business team meeting when discussing helping a buyer in Customer C through a short-term issue:

> **Meeting Note:** Buyer asked for personal support on issue X—it doesn't make immediate sense for us, but we are doing it, making a 'relationship investment to draw from the bank later'.

Alpha also appears to recognise that collaboration on sound business-case-driven proposals is a logical method for the creation of value, versus a transactional approach.

> *Well, in the end, if your approach is … business case driven, then it's in your economic interest to pursue collaborative projects, right? Because you realise more value through that route than you would through the muck and bullets of a transactional relationship.*

When exploring the value creation activities that Alpha use, as stated earlier some global blueprints and tools are available to local markets. One example is the 'Ideal store'.

This is a business planning approach that helps retailers understand what their total store, as well as total category, should look like. This advice covers the range, merchandising, price, and promotion tactics recommendations. This is an example of value creation beyond the Alpha categories and is also embedded in the commercial team's personal bonus system, to drive the behaviour in its team.

> *we've got very clear strategy … the targets that trigger the bonus of people in all of our markets in customer development will have an element of 'Ideal store,' which is a centrally-driven strategy … there's a real line of sight from strategy through to local marketplace and within that is a clear collaboration agenda.*

Category Management for Value Creation

When looking at the Customer Teams, the other work evident in the area of value creation is that of category management support. This is achieved through using formal category planning process with the retailer, to build detailed category level business plans. As in other areas, this is supported by toolkits to an Alpha format, such as a 'Customer Category Strategy'.

These toolkits are used to create a formal plan between Alpha and its customers. They include summary insights on how the category is performing, strategic drivers of growth to be reviewed and aligned with the customer, and tactical plans in an 'ideal store' toolkit, again to be tailored with the retailer.

It also includes a scorecard at the category level that looks to quantify the value created. This plan is then managed and implemented by the Alpha and Customer Team through the year.

However, Alpha does recognise the risk to value creation if they are pushed into more short-medium term activities by their retail customers.

> *I am more concerned that some of the other things that they're (retailers) doing at the moment undermine the value that's created in some of the medium-term initiatives that we're engaged in growing. Such is the pressure on short term sales that if you're not careful, you short-circuit in the minds of the shoppers' purchase decisions to, is it on end? Is it at a good price?*

This tension was also evident in the Customer Team meeting, where a focus on achieving the numbers for Alpha in the next quarter was a major area of focus and did not refer directly to aligning to the joint business plan or category plan.

> **Meeting Note**: Discussion on achieving numbers through the new promotional plan and focus on key brands and packs.

It was also recognised that having a focus on just achieving transactional value through the collaborative business planning process is ultimately not enough if the personal relationship with the customer is not good.

> *as my old boss ... used always say you can have all the JPB templates in the world you like but at the end of the day, if your relationship stinks, you don't move it forward. You've really got to have a strong, empathetic, factually based relationship.*

In summary, the research in this area is suggesting that Alpha is fully aware that there is a need to create relational and transactional value in their collaboration with customers. The research evidence shows that Alpha believes one type of value creation without the other is not the way they want to work.

It is evident Alpha has in place formal process and tools, such as JBPs, Category Business Plans and Scorecards to ensure they create a focus on the work they are doing and that it is tracked and measured. The research also indicated Alpha are aware of the tension between meeting the short-term value creation needs of the customer, but place faith in their approach to manage this discussion with customers, and avoid being distracted into short-term, potentially value destructive activities.

Value Capture

Work that provides evidence of value Capture for Alpha, for example initiatives undertaken that clearly show with their ROI for the Alpha business.

It was clear from the research that Alpha does have a focus on how to capture value from their collaboration work with their retailers.

As stated earlier, Alpha believes collaboration does generate more value for them than non-collaboration. A senior director in the global team was clear:

> *I think for Alpha, the value comes in expanding the dialogue away from the straight trading buyer/seller relationships, so it makes the relationship bigger which ultimately creates space to identify ways to grow the business which are much more horizontal than vertical ... therefore, the value you create is ultimately that you're able to sell more of your products to more people, grow your business but also achieve some of the other business KPIs on top of that.*

This was supported by a senior director in the Customer Team, who was clear that the work undertaken by teams was able to capture greater value for Alpha, but that there was tension on short-term demands that could inhibit the value created.

> *if you looked at our promotional ROIs and you were to compare that to the ROI that we would make in .... Category management, it's very clear in business terms that the transactional stuff is a lower value but has a greater short-term impact. So, in thin markets where you're chasing quarterly numbers, there is a significant risk that you compromise ROI to deliver the top (line).*

Value Measurement

This reference to ROIs indicates that Alpha do set specific targets and measure the value of their collaboration with retailers. This is done through a formal process, such as a Joint Business Plan, or Category Business Plan as referenced earlier. Again, from the research, it was clear that this ROI focus is present through the commercial team. One example was cited in work with Customer D:

> *Well, let me tell you when we do a piece of work, we would set ourselves a series of KPIs ... we tend to find that they are prizes worth going after.*

> *We were talking to Customer D on Friday about an opportunity to help drive the conversion of shoppers in the category X. It's £xm category and it's a £20m prize, it's worth going after. Now, bearing in mind the biggest innovation we'll do next year is probably incrementally £5m, I mean, in that context it's huge. And by the way that's*

£20 million of assets, brands that are already proven with good margins, as opposed to innovation which requires all of that advertising and promotional investment, probably with a three-year payback, and is a 7-1 shot.

This focus on ROI was also true of category projects and work that Alpha undertakes with its customers. As mentioned previously, this can be work that is not always beneficial to Alpha directly (Ideal store) but still has a set of KPIs to measure and track the value captured, for both Alpha and the retailer.

If you take our approach to category management every time, we engage in a category project, as I said, there will be an agreed set of KPIs that will be reviewed after twelve and twenty-four weeks. The same as shopper marketing, we'll set a clear ROI on that. Any supply chain development work that we do, again, there'll be a prize cost-saving.

There was recognition that some of the collaborative work is more difficult to place a value on, but still, it is tracked, even if it is regarding the number of projects or initiatives that are implemented with customers:

You would look for a result in the business performance because ultimately, at the end of the day, that's how you measure it … in terms of the more collaborative stuff like category management, like shopper marketing, you would evaluate it in terms of the number of activities you've managed to get away, but even that ultimately is measured by what was the business win as a result?

Measuring Shopper Behaviour

This measurement can be more focused, looking at how shopper behaviour changed in the ways that were planned and did this deliver the value back to Alpha and its customer.

Then it's a case of let's quantify this … when we see average pence per pack on the product move; this is what we expect to see. And then when we make it happen, we make sure that we are tracking it within an inch of its life to ensure that it's delivering against those (metrics).

There was evidence in the Customer Team meeting that this measurement and focus on value capture is working. Looking at Customer C the team cited how the collaborative work they had done had delivered enhanced business results and value they had captured.

> **Meeting Note:** "and that's essentially, we've run that model for the last two and a half years, and on the back of that we grew in the first year at 10%, we grew last year at 5%, and we have a JBP this year of 7%. And in the midst of that, we've been their Manufacturer of the Year for the last two years, and we are number one in their Advantage Group survey scores."

Personal Relationships

This delivery and tracking of value captured also enabled the Customer Teams to use the relational value they had created to manage difficult conversations if the value captured was not as planned.

> *I have had one example where I have gone back on an individual buyer: … he …. Wasn't engaging …. The relationship wasn't there. … I went back on that one and said all is well, but actually in this particular area this isn't working in the way that we're working everywhere else …. They nailed it, they went and had a word and low and behold the phone rings the next day, and he's back on these in the right place, so they do respond to this.*

In summary, the research in this area is suggesting that Alpha had a clear focus and tracking of the ROI of their collaboration activities. This is applied not only to joint business plan activities but also to category planning activities. The latter activities are recognised as sometimes being more challenging to measure, but this does not stop Alpha tracking them.

This measurement is being used to create a dialogue with customers that can not only demonstrate value created to both sides but also manage the discussion when Alpha are not capturing the value they anticipated.

The research is indicating this ROI measurement is not only being used to evaluate individual activities but also is fed into the business planning process to evaluate the strategic choice they are making by the customer (as evidenced earlier in their customer segmentation work).

Alpha Case Study Summary

In reviewing all of the evidence from the Alpha research, these are the main findings:

1. It is clear that Alpha has a clear focus, process, and approach to collaborating with their major customers. There is guidance and help from a global team to help the local UK team use standard tools and approaches to facilitate the choice of collaborative customers, and the plans and approaches that can be used (joint business plans, category plans, 'ideal store', etc.).
2. It is evident that Alpha has clarity on how they create and capture value from their collaboration with customers. The evidence showed the use of joint scorecards and the setting of ROI targets to understand what value has been created and captured. Further, the research showed that this is reviewed and managed by the Alpha teams.
3. The influence of power is present in the relationship, most clearly referenced with experience of Customer A. The research showed how one customer used his/her power position to shut down the collaborative efforts of Alpha.
4. It was evident that one customer saw collaboration as an 'add-on, nice to do' set of activities, versus a way of creating and unlocking extra value with their manufacturer.
5. Alpha appears to have a clear focus on creating and capturing value from their collaborative relationships. It's clear that the foundation of relational value may be a pre-requisite to successfully creating collaborative value.

Beta Case Study: A Fresh Food Business Looking to Collaborate Across Many Customers

After reading this case you will discover:

1. How collaboration between Beta and its customers works, but also how there is little evidence of value creation and particularly value capture.
2. A lack of clarity by Beta as to what collaboration is and does, and how it appears to open to personal interpretation in the Beta team as to what works and the approach they took with their customers.
3. How collaboration is potentially all 'one way', with an absence of what Beta received as a benefit from the collaboration.
4. The lack of formal process, plans, and targets between Beta and their customers making management of the collaboration challenging.

Introduction

Beta is a privately owned company, operating in a fresh food category, and has a strong brand in its product category. The key accounts team at Beta is responsible for managing the business-to-business relationship and is organised into five Customer Teams. Each major customer has a dedicated team allocated to it for the management of the joint business.

These teams comprise a Customer Controller, who manages the team, and is supported by a Customer Business Manager, a Category Manager, a Shopper Marketing Manager, and a Supply Chain Manager. Also, for some customers, a Beta employee is placed as an 'implant' into the customer's head office, to help with a range of tasks such as analysis of performance issues and opportunities.

Part-time Customer Team members include a Supply Chain Manager and a Retail Operation Manager. The structure of the team is highlighted in Fig. 4.4 and the individual work roles and responsibilities in the Customer Team are shown in Table 4.3.

In analysing the research findings, three main categories emerged as significant in answering the overall research question. These categories and their subcategories are characterised in Table 4.4.

The two high-level themes that have emerged are 'Collaboration', 'Power' and 'Value'.

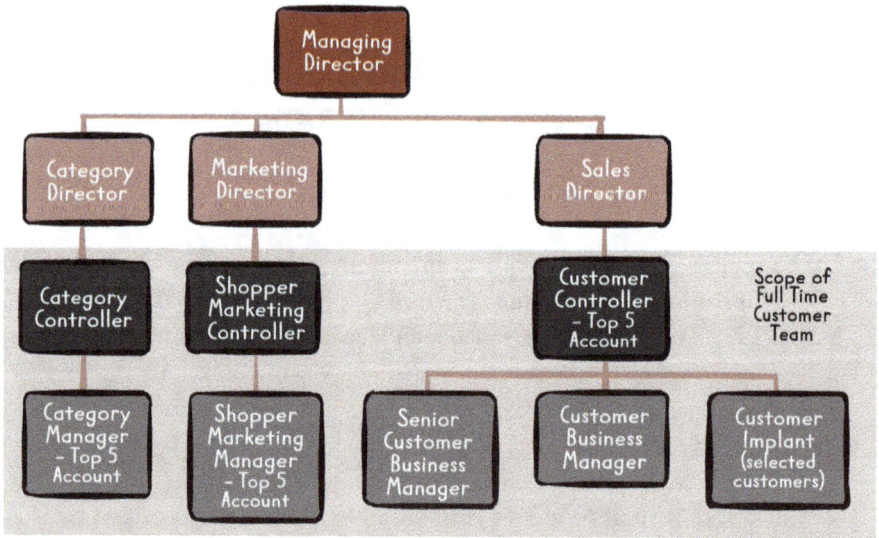

Fig. 4.4 Beta commercial team structure

Table 4.3 Beta Customer Team roles and responsibilities

Role	Responsibility in Customer Team
Full-time team member	
Customer Controller	• Overall management responsibility of the customer P&L and team management
Customer Business Manager	• Day-to-day responsibility for relationship and delivery of business plan with key customer contacts
Category Manager	• Provide total category insights and advice to the customer on how to grow the (customers) overall business
Shopper Marketing Manager	• Develop tailored marketing programmes for Beta's brands in the customer, working with the customers marketing team as needed
Customer Implant	• Undertakes analysis and reporting for the customer for their business, based in the customers head office, but paid for and provided by Beta
Part-time team member	
Supply Chain Manager	• Ensures the on time in full delivery of Beta products to the customer, working with customer supply chain operations
Retailer Operations Manager	• Delivers the in-store activation and display of Beta products in the retailer's stores, working with the retailer's store operations and retail management

Collaboration is the area of work that exists so that Beta works more closely with its customers. This may be work with the customer (e.g., joint product development) or work developed for the Customer Alone by Beta (e.g. market data analysis and reporting).

Value is evidence of work aimed at directly creating value for Beta. Value creation, for example, could cover work such as joint business planning, and work areas showing evidence of value capture for Beta could include evidence of initiatives undertaken with their ROI for the Beta business. An example of this could be a specific promotional programme for Beta brands to achieve a target return on investment.

Each of these high-level themes of collaboration and value will now be explored in more detail.

Collaboration

Collaboration Purposes and Choices

The outcomes Beta would like from collaboration with chosen customers, and how they choose who to collaborate with, and how this may differ by customer type.

Table 4.4 Beta research finding categories and descriptions

Category	Description	Subcategory	Description
Collaboration	Work that exists in order that Beta works more closely with its customers	Collaboration purpose and choices	The outcomes Beta would like from collaboration with chosen customers, and how they choose who to collaborate with, and how this may differ by customer type
	Both work with the customer (e.g., joint product development) and work developed for the customer alone by Beta (e.g., market data analysis and reporting).	Collaboration work	The work Beta undertakes to collaborate with their customers. This can be both joint work with the customer and work Beta undertakes for the customer
		Non-collaboration work	The work the teams are undertaking purely for Beta. It is work that has not been asked for by customers, but the Customer Team are undertaking it
		Collaboration barriers	Evidence that stopped collaboration work occurring, largely due to external (customer) factors
Value	Evidence of work aimed at directly creating value for Beta	Value creation	Work that demonstrates value creation for Beta, for example joint business planning
		Value capture	Work that provides evidence of value capture for Beta, for example initiatives undertaken that clearly show with their ROI for the Beta business

Collaboration purposes and choices had limited evidence in the research, and perhaps reflect a lack of clarity of what Beta want from collaboration with their key account customers. In one-to-one interviews, there appeared to be an understanding that collaboration was the 'right thing to do' as evidenced by an Account Manager:

> *I mean in the perfect world, other than the fact it does take a lot of resources because you have to spend a lot more time and a lot more people have to be in it, but in a perfect world you would want to have a working relationship, a collaborative relationship with pretty well all of your accounts.*

This was further supported by a leader in the sales team who reiterated that Beta would choose to collaborate with any of their major customers.

> *In a perfect world, you would want to have a working relationship, a collaborative relationship, with pretty well all of your accounts. I think it builds a depth of relationship, which means that you get through tough times a little easier and you can really enjoy the good times.*

Customer segmentation is a tool often used in this context, to develop a view on which customers collaborate with and guide the type of collaboration (typically from strategic to tactical approaches). There was no documentary evidence of customer segmentation in the research collected in Beta.

When exploring what resources are invested in each customer to enable collaboration, different interview respondents indicated that the more important customers, regarding size and scale, would be better resourced.

> *So, it would be not just providing them (customers) with market updates, which we might do for some of the smaller retailers, it would be going to them with bespoke pieces of research which we know will benefit them and spending our money on those pieces of research for them.*

Collaboration and Trust

When discussing what collaboration involves for Beta, there was a recognition that this requires the retailer to want to collaborate and that a degree of trust needs to be in place.

> *both parties have to have that mindset in place that they actually want to do this work together. … it understands that if you are to give up some of your margins for that retailer that actually you're either going to see some value and revenue come back from that, that rewards it and having the confidence that does that …. a collaborative relationship might mean that from a manufacturer's perspective we actually have to give up some profit margin, etc with that retailer …. we have to have confidence that what we're doing with them and what they say they're going to do will put that back in down the road.*

This theme was further evidenced with a recognition that although Beta may desire this collaborative relationship with everyone, the retail customer may not reciprocate, and in fact, it was in the retailers' hands as to if a collaborative relationship would be possible.

So, if I'm honest about it it's probably more driven by the retailer and their willingness to work with us than we drive it. So if we have a situation where we've got a retailer that isn't collaborating with us at the moment but then suddenly decided that they wanted to collaborate with us, then we would look to put plans in place and build a far more collaborative relationship and that could mean investing more money in that particular retailer which we would do because we know the willingness from them to work with us.

Lack of Clarity

There was also some evidence that in fact, the purpose of collaboration was not clear across the business. This was mentioned by one respondent as a function of the brand power and focus of the business, meaning some viewed collaboration as not always required, if you have a powerful brand:

I think one of the challenges for us as a brand is that …. People believe in the all-encompassing power of the brand and that therefore you don't necessarily need to have a collaborative relationship with that, because your strength is all in the consumer and in the brand.

This potential lack of clarity on customer collaboration also became evident when reviewing the key documents of the business. Customer collaboration or focus was not evident in the overall corporate strategy of the business. The strategies outlined in the documents were focused on the Beta brand and operational factors (Fig. 4.5).

Where customer collaboration is referenced are in the goals of the corporate strategy document. It is stated in that document that there is a goal to be *'No.1 for customers' as measured by Advantage Group*.

The Advantage Group survey is an industry-wide survey of retailer opinions of their manufacturer's performance, across a range of collaborative measures. It is reported back against a manufacturer's peers (the competitive peer set being chosen by the manufacturer).

The business has a separate commercial strategy document, which contained the strategies as shown in Fig. 4.6.

This commercial strategy shows evidence of work elements such as developing Joint Business Plans, and a customer contact strategy. The customer contact strategy is an internal plan that targets the development of cross-functional relationships between the Beta team and its customer's teams.

In summary, the findings from this section of the research are suggesting firstly that developing a collaborative relationship with any customer is the

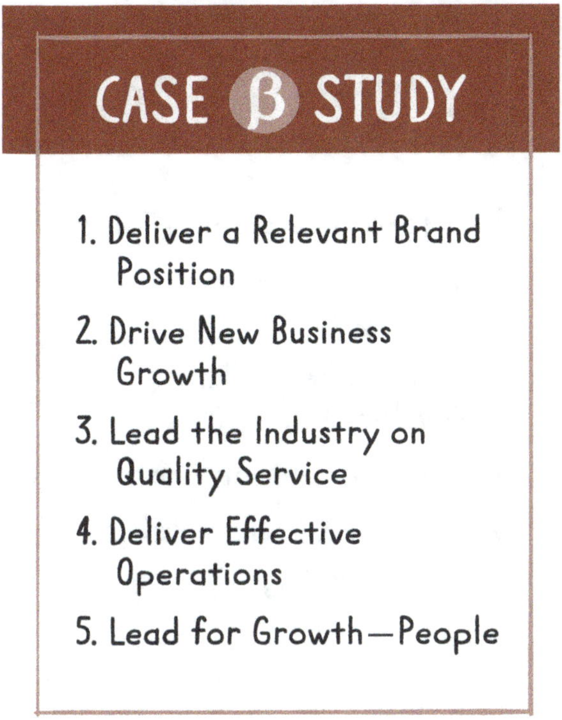

CASE β STUDY

1. Deliver a Relevant Brand Position
2. Drive New Business Growth
3. Lead the Industry on Quality Service
4. Deliver Effective Operations
5. Lead for Growth—People

Fig. 4.5 Beta strategy document

aim of Beta, with recognition that the decision on collaboration is ultimately with the customer. There is also evidence that as a major branded manufacturer, some in the business may not view customer collaboration as essential, as the power of the brand can be leveraged in its place.

The findings also suggest that the achievement of a joint business plan with a customer is the key measure of success versus any mention or evidence as to the quality and outputs of the plan. There were no references to the quality of the plan regarding what the plan should include, strategies, initiatives or metrics, timeframes, and so on. It appears that the presence of a plan is enough to meet the strategy set in the commercial strategy document.

What is evident from the document review is that Beta does have strategies in place that cascade from corporate to department to customer plan level. This could be evaluated as an indication that the planning process aims to connect the corporate direction directly to the plans that are developed with customers.

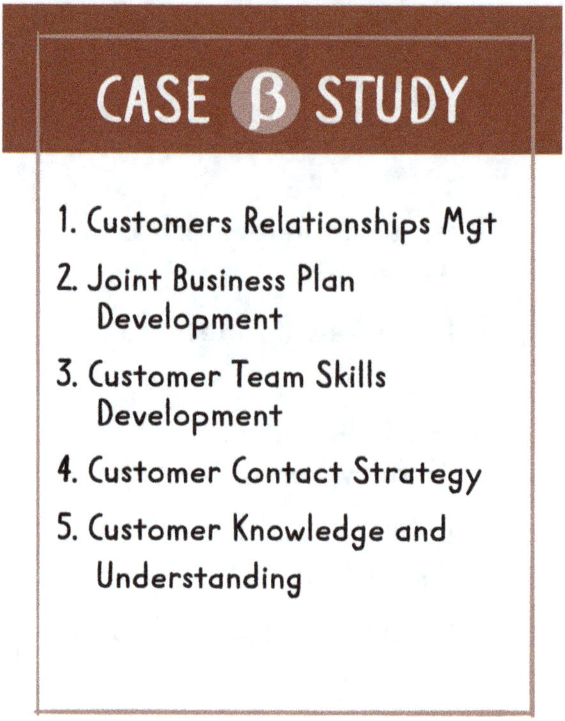

> **CASE β STUDY**
>
> 1. Customers Relationships Mgt
> 2. Joint Business Plan Development
> 3. Customer Team Skills Development
> 4. Customer Contact Strategy
> 5. Customer Knowledge and Understanding

Fig. 4.6 Beta commercial strategy document

As stated, there is no formal customer segmentation in place that is driving collaboration choices and work. However, from the interviews, it was evident that larger customers can receive more management focus and resources, with the implication being that this would equal a better return for Beta. There was no evidence offered (when asked) if this was the case.

Collaboration Work

The work Beta undertakes in order to collaborate with their customers. This can be both joint work with the customer and work Beta undertakes for the customer.

When the work of collaboration was explored in the research, a range of activities emerged, mixed between what could be characterised as strategic, longer-term work, and more tactical short-term work. There was also a split between work internal to Beta and external work with or for the customer.

Data Analysis and Reporting

In looking firstly at the collaboration work, that is work with or for the customer, the most common work theme that emerged in this area was the work of data analysis and reporting. This work was described as both internally and externally focused, that is work just for internal Beta reports and teams, as well as work directly requested by the customer.

The evidence from the interviews showed that the act of providing data and insights to customers is a major part of what is being termed collaboration in Beta and that this work can fluctuate depending on the demands of the customer at a particular time.

> *I think the nature of the fluctuating relationships within retail is such that you're happy when the works there. I mean category can be a little bit like, I've heard it described as standing on a beach and waiting for the next wave. .... You're just doing the basics, sending your monthly reports, and keeping an eye on the market and suddenly you'll get a request, and you're flooded ... Customer B's a classic example of that, there have been times when they haven't even wanted to talk to us, and there are times like now where they seem to be quite keen to engage.*

Providing Customer with Resources

Beta provides to two customers a dedicated resource ('implant' as referenced earlier) that sits in the retailer's Head Office, and their role is largely to deliver any analysis work and reporting required of them by the retailer.

> *The short answer is that we will deliver everything that Customer A ask us to do .... so, we will manage and create reports, and to do that we need to manage and organise their retail data, so their EPOS data.*

When examining why this is happening, it appears that the reason is not just that the retailers ask for it, but the retailer cannot or will not undertake collaborative work with Beta unless the resources are supplied:

> *They don't have enough pairs of hands. They don't have enough resource ... we're wanting to do things like store trials, etc, etc, and all the other stuff we want to do in the category, then he just said he doesn't have the time or the resource to do it.*

Category Management Support

One area of collaborative work that is more strategic is that of range reviews. Retailers periodically review and change their category range of products, and the space allocated to them, with an objective of better meeting their shoppers' needs, and improving overall performance.

Beta has been selected by Customer B to help in this process, which means Beta will be providing a range of analysis and recommendations, not just on their products but those in the total category. It was evident in the team meeting that Customer B did value this work. The discussion in the team meeting was around the Customer B objectives for this review (a 20% reduction in SKUs), and the team's view on the implications of this for Beta' business, and how they wished to try and influence the direction the review is taking.

To manage the Key Account Team, there is an internal monthly Customer Team planning meeting. At this meeting, the wider Customer Team referred to earlier meetings and focus on three main areas (Fig. 4.7).

In the Customer Team meeting attendance, it was evident that a large amount of time is spent on analysis, both on the category performance and on the retailer's performance within that, and if/how Beta is a cause of the performance changes.

It was observed that this analysis work was often looking for 'selling stories', that is ideas, themes, or evidence that could be presented to customers as to why Beta was helping the retailer grow, or why a competitor was causing a performance issue.

Hence, it could be interpreted as the team potentially looking for data to help 'sell' collaboration to the retailer. To that point, it was observed in the meeting:

> **Meeting Note:** More detailed analysis going on to show that Beta is being supported less by Customer B—other brands have increased support, and this is linked to Customer B performing less well in the overall category.

This was supported by one meeting participant who stated:

this analysis is being used to 'irritate' Customer B to work with us ... we need to remind Customer B on why they need to work with us and our brands ... this chart is an attempt to be a category in our Beta story.

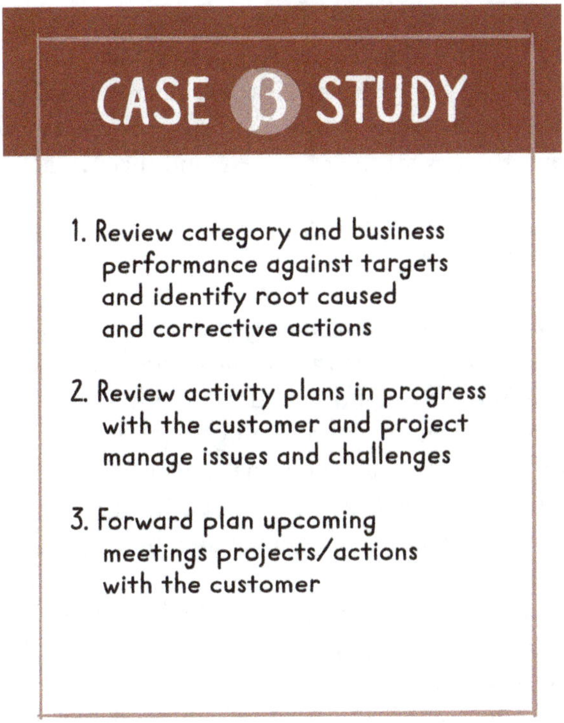

> **CASE β STUDY**
>
> 1. Review category and business performance against targets and identify root caused and corrective actions
>
> 2. Review activity plans in progress with the customer and project manage issues and challenges
>
> 3. Forward plan upcoming meetings projects/actions with the customer

Fig. 4.7 Beta Customer Team meeting objectives

When in this area of discussion in the Customer Team meeting, a substantial amount of time was also spent on working out how to message certain performance issues or challenges around the Beta brand performance.

> **Meeting Note:** It was evident that the attendees were focused on using data and analysis to position Beta in the best light to the Customer A and appear to be as collaborative as possible.

In summarising collaboration work in Beta, the first area is that of data analysis and reporting, that is provided to customers. The nature of this work is both ad hoc and linked to specific questions, and regular reporting to selected customers. Further, in Customer A this work is undertaken to be a dedicated Beta resource (implant) working in Customer A office to do this work.

The second area of work is that undertaken by the category team on range review and planning for customers. This work sees Beta help retailers understand how to make changes to their overall category range and how it is merchandised to improve overall category performance.

The final area of collaborative work is the regular internal Customer Team meeting. This sees the cross-function KAM team meet to review performance and identify opportunities for their business, and that of the customer.

Non-collaboration Work

The work the teams are undertaking purely for Beta. It is work that has not been asked for by customers, but the Customer Team are undertaking it.

The research found that a significant amount of non-collaborative work is focused on insights generation and reporting. It was evident that this work is largely to explain performance to an internal audience. At the Customer Team meeting, significant time was spent on Beta sales analysis in Customer B and discussion on how this would be presented and 'messaged' internally to colleagues in the business.

This focus on internal reporting was also evidenced in the detailed work and objectives that are set out in the sales strategy document, Fig. 4.8. It states its strategies as shown in Fig 4.8.

These strategies are focused on Beta, and their direction and objectives. There is no reference to the customer evident in the strategies and their detail.

Under each strategy are details on which each area focuses its measures, for example for 'Deliver commercial returns' (see Fig. 4.9).

There was no evidence found of any customer measures in the documents reviewed. As stated earlier, although the joint business plan is measured, it is the presence, not the content or quality, of the joint business plan that is being measured.

In summarising non-collaboration work, this covered the area insights reporting, which appeared to be mostly focused on internal reporting and analysis. The internal focus was also evident in the document review, with a focus on Beta's needs in the sales strategy and commercial strategy, versus clear references to customer's needs, or customer collaboration,

Collaboration Barriers

The work Beta undertakes in order to collaborate with their customers. This can be both joint work with the customer and work Beta undertakes for the customer.

The research in the area of collaboration also uncovered barriers to collaboration. The themes that emerged were largely external, that is, based around

> **CASE β STUDY**
>
> 1. Deliver commercial returns
>
> 2. Market share growth
>
> 3. Customer Relationships Mgt
>
> 4. Lead our team for Growth

Fig. 4.8 Beta sales strategy document

the retailer. There was evidence in the one-to-one interviews of the power effect in the relationship between the manufacturer and retailer. It was indicated the retailer could stop the 'collaboration' at any point if a trading 'dispute' arose.

> We have Joint Business Plans with a lot of our retailers … more and more I would say that we are seeing category being dragged into those discussions, in the sense of if things aren't going so well, then they will put the barriers up …. we won't be able to get them to answer the phone, and we might have meetings cancelled, no response to emails, that kind of thing.

Retailer Power Influence

Furthermore, it was evident that some retailers were purely focusing on a transactional relationship with those it has chosen not to collaborate with. The evidence suggested that this collaborative choice was, in fact, a

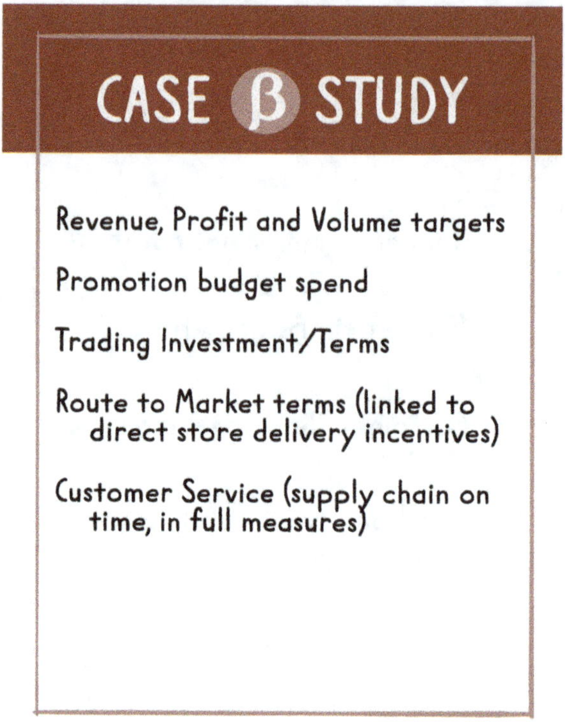

> **CASE β STUDY**
>
> Revenue, Profit and Volume targets
>
> Promotion budget spend
>
> Trading Investment/Terms
>
> Route to Market terms (linked to direct store delivery incentives)
>
> Customer Service (supply chain on time, in full measures)

Fig. 4.9 Beta sales strategy document detail

commercial, trading terms decision. This played out in a lack of access for the Beta KAM teams to that customer when a trading agreement had been signed with another manufacturer on more favourable terms.

> *At the moment, due to their performance, they are looking for relationships with whoever is going to help them with their performance the most, and that has meant it's gone to trading agreements, unfortunately … we have been affected by that in terms of our category relationship with X, where they have started working with one of our competitors a lot more. So, at the moment we get very little interaction with them at all.*

This theme also emerged in the Customer Team meeting, where it was claimed a category performance effect on the Beta business was as a result of the retailer supporting a rival brand.

> **Meeting Note:** Further analysis showing a competitor promotion using four weekly data and how this has coincided with Customer B losing share in the total market. Key inference is Customer B backing the wrong brand.

This was supported by attendee comment:

This is happening because we set out to beat Competitor Brand X … Customer B has allowed Competitor Brand X to buy the No.1 slot.

Customer Implementation Barriers

Another barrier or impact to collaborative work was cited as the retailer's willingness and ability to implement recommendations. It was evident that even if a retailer claimed to accept the insights and proposal from Beta, there was no clear path to implementation with some retailers, meaning the Beta team was wary of investing in further work, questioning the value of doing so if implementation was not guaranteed.

The trial stores outperformed the control stores quite considerably, and they didn't do anything with it; the actual areas that were tested they didn't roll out to any new stores … we will make recommendations to them … and then nothing will get done with it.

Linked to this theme was the retailer also placing a collaboration barrier if the work proposed does not help them to meet their objectives. In the Customer Team meeting, a discussion took place on whether or not to invest in buying additional data analysis from Customer B's own data provider.

> **Meeting Note**: The team believed it would provide new customer insights to unlock growth for Beta and Customer B and would cost circa £xk to buy. However, because this measure is not on the buyer's scorecard, they were actively discouraged by Customer B from doing this, as Customer B would not 'credit' Beta for this investment in their joint business plan.

In summary, the findings in the area of collaboration work and barriers are suggesting that collaboration work has a large focus on data analysis and insights. This can be at the request of the customer and is being cited as evidence of the collaboration. There was no evidence found as to the effectiveness of how these data and insights have been used to generate plans, actions, and deliver business results.

It was evident the retailer is willing to exert their power and withhold contact and dialogue until its trading and commercial demands are met, perhaps suggesting collaboration is a 'privilege' it grants dependent on day-to-day trading issues being resolved. It was also evident a retailer's ability to implement recommendations is a barrier to collaborative work in some instances.

Value

Value Creation

Work that demonstrates value creation for Beta, for example joint business planning.

The high-level findings from this analysis were firstly whatever value is being created appears to be largely relational value. Virtually all the examples given talk about the meetings and face-to-face interaction frequency as evidence of the value of collaboration.

> *We've had them off-site twice in the last six months. … That's the first time the category director had visited these offices with the buying team. … We had 12 people from Customer B attend, so from the senior buyer through to customer managers. So, it is collaborative.*

There was also some insight around the value in the relationship being better with different types of interaction with different customers. The way this was described again indicated that it was relational aspects, such as frequency and types of personal interaction that indicated whether greater or lesser value was being created in the collaboration.

> *Well, I'm currently enjoying a collaborative role with Customer A …. with Customer C it was pretty much a transactional relationship whereby it would be on the end of a phone, and certainly they'd phone me up and ask me for something and then I'd deliver it in. … It felt fairly distant from what I was doing. Whereas now I certainly … feel that I am phoned up for my opinion far more and my input and my experience and my recommendations, rather than just data or at presentations.*

Reference to the commercial strategy also indicates the areas that are about delivering improved relationships with Key Account customers (Fig. 4.10).

Joint Value Creation?

However, when reviewing key documents, there was no evidence of specific value creation measures, such as joint sales, profit, and so on. In the Customer Team meeting, the team did review the joint business plan that was in place and discussed the fact that Customer B could not deliver their side of the joint business plan, and how this would change their thinking for future joint business plans.

> **Meeting Note:** Detailed discussion around Customer B not able to deliver their commitments to achieve the joint business plan, and learnings on the next joint business plan negotiation—i.e., can Customer B deliver what they promise before Beta decides to invest in initiatives?

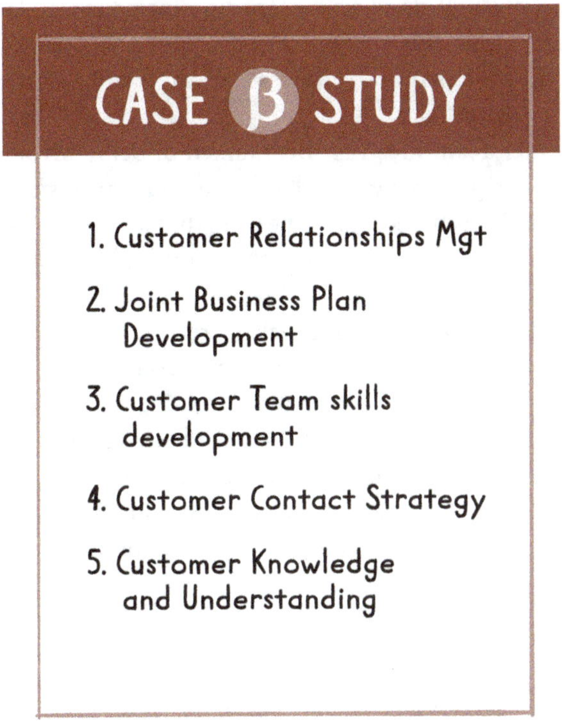

CASE β STUDY

1. Customer Relationships Mgt
2. Joint Business Plan Development
3. Customer Team skills development
4. Customer Contact Strategy
5. Customer Knowledge and Understanding

Fig. 4.10 Beta commercial strategy document

The description of the joint business plan in the meeting was one of a retailer business plan that Beta was required to 'hit' by making investments. The emphasis of the discussion was more on how to create value for the retailer, than any evidence of how value is being created for Beta.

The discussion also highlighted that Customer B was delivering few, if any, of the requests made by Beta in the joint business plan. The impression was this was a one-way plan, rather than a joint business plan, giving further evidence of the value creation discussion being centred on value to the retailer versus value to Beta.

Category Management Work

When looking for evidence of the work of value creation, the closest appears to be providing support to lead the range and space review work with the customer. This work is often a twice-yearly activity in a retailer, where they review all of the products in the category, and space they take and undertake changes they believe will improve category performance. Retailers often ask for manufacturer 'input' into this process; this input can range from the manufacturer providing their brand proposals to the manufacturer running the whole process for the retailer.

At the Customer Team meeting, Beta talked of being involved in one segment of the total category review, with other manufacturers taking ownership of the other areas. It was noted in the meeting that lots of detailed analysis had been done, but again they could not get meeting time with the Customer B team to review results.

In summary, the findings around value creation appear to be indicating that firstly the value that is being created is 'relational value'. The commercial strategy has specific relational goals in place to drive this behaviour, and it was evidenced in the interviews and meeting attendance of this being achieved.

What was not evident in any of the research were specific collaborative transactional measures, such as joint sales, profit, and so on, and the transactional value that was achieved as a result of the collaboration with the customer.

Value Capture

Work that provides evidence of value Capture for Beta, for example initiatives undertaken that clearly show with their ROI for the Alpha business.

In the research, finding strong evidence of examples of value capture occurring proved difficult. When looking at just the interviews undertaken, there were few references to value capture. Furthermore, where mentioned, value capture was largely talked about from the perspective of the retailer.

> *All they (the retailer) seem to be bothered about is the deal that's on the table, the price they are selling their products at compared to other retailers, the promotions that they are doing, and how much they can get out of the manufacturer that way, rather than how much they can actually benefit the category by implementing some of our recommendations. It just doesn't seem like it was much of a priority to them that they would follow it up afterward.*

Shopper Needs?

Where it was referenced for Beta, it largely related to new product launches and the listing of new products. This was also referenced as a challenge in value capture, with retailers viewing the listing of new products as a mechanism to enhance their margin position, even at the expense of meeting their shoppers' needs.

> *Clearly within retailers though there's always the money talks and money are always at the heart of every discussion. They try and break away from that and say, 'Well we're doing what's right for the shopper. It's all about the shopper. This is about the shopper', where really is it really about the shopper when you're saying you're not going to list product x in every store because I'm not giving you enough money? Even though the category team have told you that it's right, I've told you that it's right because I want to sell as much as I can, I'm not offering you enough money, so you're not going to do it.*

As discussed earlier, it is apparent in the document review that aside from the joint business plan no other plan or mechanism refers to value capture for Beta from their activities with their customers.

The summary of the findings in this area is that there appears to be an underlying assumption that through work such as joint business plan, category reviews, and advice, the value would be captured. One interview respondent stated:

> *Now you know we are selling more products in Customer A at the moment than we ever have. Now I can't prove a direct correlation between those two points, but I've got no doubt that broadly the category relationship we have in Customer A has a positive impact on the overall relationship with Customer A.*

In summarising value capture, the evidence suggests that, in Beta, it is unclear how this is happening. When discussed in the research value capture was mostly referred to with regards to the value the retailer is capturing. The documents in the business, such as the commercial strategy and joint business plans, did not refer to value capture for Beta, with no evidence of scorecards or other management tools.

Beta Case Study Summary

In reviewing all of the evidence from the Beta research, these are the main findings:

1. There appears to be strong evidence of collaboration between Beta and its customers. However, there is less evidence in the areas of value creation and particularly value capture.
2. The research suggests a lack of clarity by Beta as to what collaboration is and does. It appeared to be absolutely open to personal interpretation in the Beta team as to what works and the approach they took with their customers.
3. This case highlighted evidence that the collaboration is potentially all 'one way'. The research was striking in its absence of what Beta received as a benefit from the collaboration, aside from meeting time, and potentially benefit from better new product introductions.
4. The retailer appeared to 'grant' access to the manufacturer in the knowledge that this will gain them (the retailer) a more significant share of voice in the manufacturer, and thus greater investment.
5. The lack of formal process, plans, and targets between Beta and their customers would appear to aid this situation, where there is no evidence of any formal return being committed to by retailers for all the investments Beta is making.

Gamma Case Study: Managing Collaboration When Supplying Brands and Own-Brands

After reading this case you will discover:

1. How Gamma are unclear on the benefits of the collaboration work they do, and their focus appears to be more on achieving internal Gamma business and brand targets.
2. Gamma's collaborative work is focussed on the category team, and the work they undertake with and for customers, such as range review support and data analysis and own-brand-new product development.
3. The challenges of managing collaboration when supplying brand and own-brand products.
4. Joint business plans appear to be more internal Gamma plans than joint plans.
5. Gamma's desire to expand their business in other channels, such as discounters, has led to difficult discussions with their major retail customers as to the impact this will have on current customers' performance.

Introduction

Gamma are one of the largest manufacturers in their product category in the UK and are publicly owned. Their business comprises both branded products and the manufacture of own-brand products for UK grocery retailers.

It sells to customers across all channels of trade, but it is its relationship with its major retailer customers in the UK that is the focus of this case study, and the sales of both branded and own-branded products.

The key accounts team at Gamma is responsible for managing the business-to-business relationship and is organised into four main Customer Teams. Each major customer has a dedicated team allocated to it for the management of the joint business, including the management of the branded and own-brand business together. These teams comprise a National Account Manager, supported by a resource from Category Planning, Shopper Marketing, and Supply Chain. Figure 4.11 highlights this structure, and the work involved for each role is described in Table 4.5.

Gamma Case Themes

In analysing the research findings, three main categories have emerged as significant in answering the overall research question.

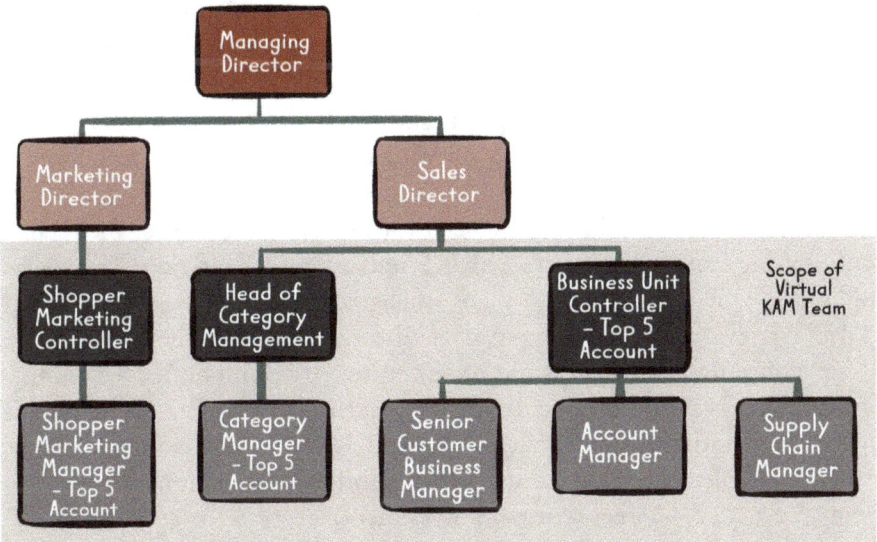

Fig. 4.11 Gamma commercial team structure

Table 4.5 Gamma Customer Team roles and responsibilities

Role	Responsibility in KAM team
Full-time team member	
Business Unit Controller	• Overall management responsibility of the customer P&L and team management
Account Manager	• Day-to-day responsibility for relationship and delivery of business plan with key customer contacts
Category Manager	• Provide total category insights and advice to the customer on how to grow the (customers) overall business
Shopper Marketing Manager	• Develop tailored marketing programmes for Gamma brands in the customer, working with the customers marketing team as needed
Part-time team member	
Supply Chain Manager	• Ensures the on time in full delivery of Gamma products to the customer, working with customer supply chain operations

These categories and their subcategories are characterised in Table 4.6

Research Categories Overview

The three high-level themes that have emerged are 'Collaboration', 'Power', and 'Value'.

Collaboration is the area of work that exists so that Gamma works more closely with its customers. This may be work with the customer (e.g., joint product development) or work developed for the customer alone by Gamma (e.g., market data analysis and reporting).

Power is evidence of the impact of retailer power specifically on Gamma's ability to collaborate with the customer in question and/or its ability to generate and capture value. This is evidenced with specific instances of the retailer withdrawing from collaborative activities and asking for funding over, above, and outside the formal business plans and agreed activities.

Value is evidence of work aimed at directly creating value for Gamma. Value creation, for example, could cover work such as joint business planning, and work areas showing evidence of value capture for Gamma could include evidence of initiatives undertaken with their ROI for the Gamma business. An example of this could be a specific promotional programme for Gamma brands to achieve a target return on investment.

Table 4.6 Gamma research finding categories and descriptions

Category	Description	Subcategory	Description
Collaboration	Work that exists in order that Gamma works more closely with its customers	Collaboration purpose and choices	The outcomes Gamma would like from collaboration with chosen customers, and how they choose who to collaborate with, and how this may differ by customer type
	Both work with the customer (e.g., joint product development) and work developed for the customer alone by Gamma (e.g., market data analysis and reporting)	Collaboration work	The work Gamma undertake to collaborate with their customers. This can be both joint work with the customer and work Gamma undertakes for the customer.
		Non-collaboration work	The work the teams are undertaking purely for Gamma. It is the work that has not been asked for by customers, but the Customer Team is undertaking it
		Collaboration barriers	Evidence that stopped collaboration work occurring, largely due to external (customer) factors
Power	The evidence of the influence of retailer power on the relationship and its impact on collaboration and/or value		
Value	Evidence of work aimed at directly creating value for Gamma	Value creation	Work that demonstrates value creation for Gamma, for example joint business planning
		Value capture	Work that provides evidence of value capture for Gamma, for example initiatives undertaken that clearly show with their ROI for the Gamma business

Collaboration

Collaboration Purpose and Choices

The outcomes Gamma would like from collaboration with chosen customers, and how they choose who to collaborate with, and how this may differ by customer type.

Collaboration purpose and choices showed evidence from both the document review and interviews on the importance Gamma places on customer collaboration in its business.

When reviewing the strategic planning documents used by the business, there is little reference to customer collaboration, with the focus of the documents being the brands of the company, and the channels they wish to operate in, and by definition that will include customers.

However, the evidence of these documents suggests that there is little recognition at the more strategic level of the importance of customers to achieve these ambitions. The three high-level strategies stated in the documents are growth, continuous improvement, and people plan (Fig. 4.12).

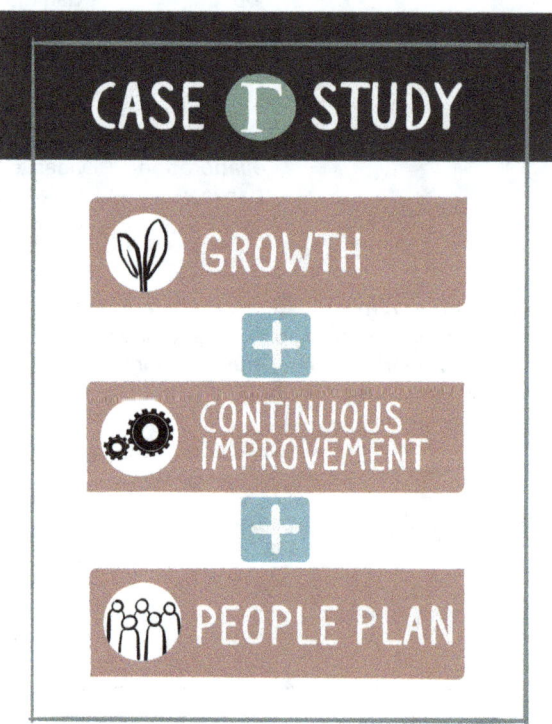

Fig. 4.12 Gamma corporate strategy document

When reviewing the documents at the level below this, for the growth strategy, this listed 'grow faster than the category', 'extend our brands', and 'grow international' as the objectives to achieve growth. Once again, this was all the detail the documents contained, and whilst customers are undoubtedly important in achieving these objectives, how Gamma would collaborate with customers to achieve them was not evident.

Lack of Focus?

This apparent lack of focus on collaboration and having the brands of the business as the priority was further evidenced in the interviews with the commercial team. As both a branded and own-brand manufacturer, Gamma at times has to balance sometimes conflicting needs with customers, and it appears that the brand, as far as Gamma is concerned, is their priority.

> *The business is a brand focused business, with an owner that wants to drive brands, we need own-brand, we need it for factories and for efficiencies and we understand the importance of it.*

Furthermore, it was stated that in the end money 'always wins' when working with customers. This last comment was in the context of the role of collaboration; the sense from the interviews was that collaboration was an exercise that was more 'nice to do' rather than a mechanism for creating value for Gamma and its customers.

When looking more deeply into the business, the commercial strategy document does provide more detail on how Gamma intends to deliver their strategic ambition. Table 4.7 highlights a summary of this document.

Under each 'Driver/Strategy' are a set of initiatives, and reviewing these, some of them do refer to customers, or channels (groups of customers). They also refer to activities that would assume some level of collaboration with customers to be required (Discounter Strategy and Online Strategy as examples).

However, as previously in the corporate strategy documents, what is not evident in these documents is a sense of how they will be achieved, and no reference to collaboration, what it is, and its level of importance to the Gamma business. The evidence in the documents and from interviews is suggesting that the work of the commercial team is being directed towards solely Gamma branded targets and goals, with little of the customer and their importance to help achieve them.

Table 4.7 Gamma commercial strategy summary

Strategic pillar	Initiatives
Growth	• Discounter Strategy • RGM expansion • Convenience Channel Strategy • Online Strategy
Continuous improvement	• Category Vision Next Phase • Category Captaincy • Brand X Activation
People and capability	• Commercial Team Training • Field Sales • Commercial Team Organisation Design • Recruitment Strategy

Whilst documentary evidence was lacking around collaboration, it was evident from some interviews that Gamma did collaborate and made choices on whom to collaborate with. This insight appeared to show that Gamma is willing to collaborate with any of their major customers who show a willingness to collaborate with them.

> *We try to collaborate with all customers .... we would work collaboratively with all our customers, and we'd love to be the lead manufacturer there, the first point of contact etc for all our customers.*

Whilst on the one hand the commercial team was indicating it was prepared to collaborate with any customer with the 'will', it was evident in interviews that the same team indicated a view that there is a potential 'peak' for collaboration with customers, beyond which customers gain at Gamma's expense.

> *There comes a point when the collaboration reaches its peak because ... and this is again a personal view, going beyond that level means that one set of shareholders gains at the benefit of the others.*

In finding that the importance and purpose of customer collaboration was lacking strong evidence, the one theme that was consistent was that of creating personal relationships with customers. When asked about collaboration, many interviewees talked of getting close to their customer contacts as examples:

> *I think overall the relationship I have with the buyer is absolutely key because we can manage our seniors ... if you don't get on you don't see eye-to-eye, or you can't at least*

have a laugh with them, remember what he did at the weekend and know that he's got a daughter. My buyers have all been a similar age, so we can go out and have a laugh. At the end of the day, it's a job and you have to remember that they are human beings as well, and that works.

In summary, the research around collaboration purpose and choices is indicating a lack of evidence in the strategy documents of the business of collaboration with the customer being important. A number of strategic initiatives would appear to be dependent on collaboration with customers, but the link is not made in the documents reviewed.

When talking to the Gamma team in interviews it was clear collaboration is taking place, indeed it was found Gamma would collaborate with any customer who wanted it. When this topic was explored it appeared the collaboration being referred to is the development and maintenance of personal relationships.

Collaboration Work

The work Gamma undertake in order to collaborate with their customers. This can be both joint work with the customer and work Gamma undertakes for the customer.

Collaboration work showed evidence of work split into areas of work from the category team, joint business planning, and own-brand development.

Category Team Work

When reviewing the work of collaboration in Gamma, the first area of focus is the work of the category team in providing insights, plans, and support to retailers to grow their business. This is seen as a very important part of the collaborative approach to Customer A.

In Customer A as category partners X (Category Manager) is equally as important to me in terms of the amount that we interact. So, the buyer will probably speak to X more than he speaks to me.

The category team in Gamma is there to provide help and support to retailers in areas such as developing range recommendations and merchandising plans, for the whole category, not just Gamma products.

> *For example, the range we have just landed, that lands in February next year .... so planning for that starts in June/July time, where you want everybody to get together and say, look this is what's wrong, this is what's broken with the category as a whole. How are we going to fix this? It's feeding in all the information that we have, all the information that they have, because that early stage is really crucial in terms of, they will have retailer specific knowledge, and they will know about their shoppers much more than we do.*

When talking to the category team directly, they were clear that their role was to provide this impartial advice, and that gaining the trust of the retailer was vital if they were to do their work:

> *I think the most important thing in my role is to be trusted by the retailer, ahead of defending my own-brands or own-brand, it's if they trust me then I get more influence, and I find out more.*

The work of the category team was characterised by the KAM team as largely ad hoc and driven by demands of the customer to meet their day-to-day needs and requirements. The sense was the category team was used as an extended resource to be called upon as needed for specific requests, versus aiming to achieving specific objectives or targets that had been arrived at through planning.

This was supported by a document used by the sales leadership to highlight the initiative of 'category captaincy outside Customer A'. The implication being it was the achievement of the captaincy, versus any objectives that the captaincy would achieve, was the important factor.

This initiative contains activities such as developing a category vision (a Gamma strategy document on how to grow the whole category). It also indicates a desire to be 'category captains' in customers other than Customer A, and finally a very specific product objective of creating more feature and display in store for their breakfast biscuit products.

When exploring further the work of the category team, there was evidence of documents and analysis provided by the Gamma team to Customer A as part of their work of being category captains. These documents are provided to highlight weekly and monthly market data updates, providing Customer A with facts on their performance. What was not evident in these documents were the insights and recommended actions Customer A should take as a result of the analysis, although this was indicated in interviews with the category team.

An example of the category captain report is highlighted in Fig. 4.13.

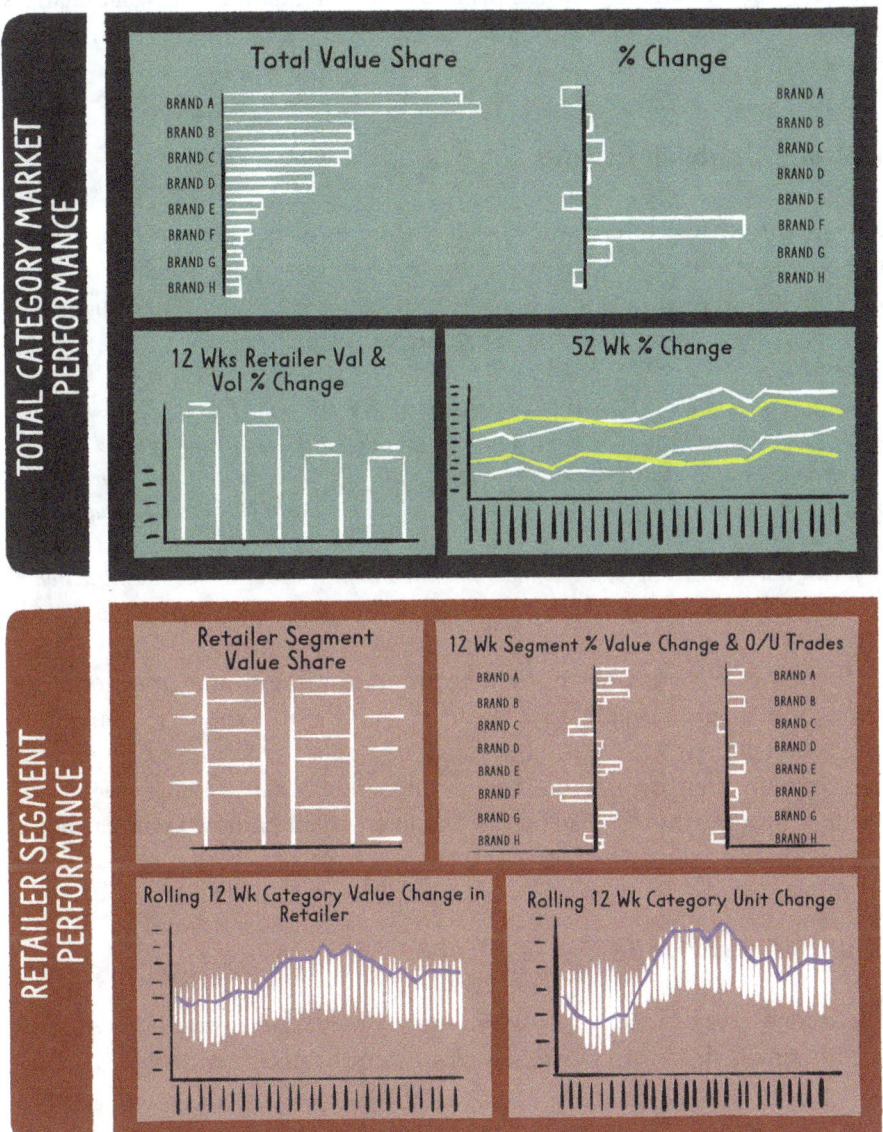

Fig. 4.13 Gamma category captain report

This fact sheet, provided to the Customer A buying team, gives Customer A a snapshot of their market share and change in the last 12 weeks. It highlights to them the change in volume and value, and against their key competitors. The report also shows a breakdown of the segment performance in the category (cornflakes, muesli, etc.). This report is then used by the Gamma category team to enable discussions and recommendations on what changes Customer A should make to their range, merchandising, or promotional strategy.

Utilising Customer Insights

However, from the interview below it can be seen that the category team is not only providing this advice to Customer A but bringing insight back from Customer A to their business, in order to help Gamma understand the implications to their business of what Customer A is thinking.

> *All they [Customer A] want is an honest category opinion, if you give an honest category opinion they will tell you more things, and that places a value far and above defending a 20% distribution or getting an extra five stores for a line or something. If I find out something, or if I get more of an understanding of how the retailer is thinking, or what the view is, at that retailer, higher up the chain about a certain product, a further category. If I know they are thinking about taking drastic action in one area, I can bring it back in here.*

There was also evidence in the KAM team meeting of this behaviour. The category manager brought back sensitive information about a competitor's promotional plans with Customer A, whilst under the terms of being a category captain for Customer A, this should not be shared. However, it was brought into the meeting, and a discussion emerged on how Gamma should respond to the issues it revealed.

Joint Business Planning

The second area of focus of work around collaboration is that of developing joint business plans with key customers. From the document review it is evident that joint business plans are seen as important but are not consistently developed across all customers. The creation of consistency in joint business planning was highlighted as an objective in the commercial strategy document.

This objective of consistency was also supported in the interviews, when asked about the Gamma process and approach for developing joint business plans. It became evident there is a lack of consistent process, or template for what is developed.

4 Collaboration in Action: Four Case Studies

I'd say there's no formal way of doing it (joint business planning).

When reviewing the joint business plans in more depth, it was clear that there was significant detail in them, but they were very internally focused. From the documents reviewed, there was no evidence in the joint business plan that they were jointly developed and did not include joint targets agreed with the customer. The Customer A version of the joint business plan contained the following areas:

1. An overview of the Gamma business performance at a total level, this was both branded and own-brand business supplied to Customer A.
2. An opportunity summary—these are the opportunities for Gamma in Customer A, to list new products, extend store distribution of existing products, implement new promotions for example.
3. Risks—similar to opportunities these were specific areas that Gamma business could be at risk, from product de-listings, loss of own-brand supply contacts, and so on.
4. Key priorities—these are the major initiatives or actions that Gamma would like to focus on with Customer A in the coming year. These include areas such as leading range reviews, maintaining category captaincy status, and so on.
5. Promotional plan—this area listed the proposed plan to promote Gamma and Customer A own-brand product in Customer A for the year, spilt by product type and month, the type of promotion mechanic (price down, multi buy), and the funding level proposed to Customer A.
6. Within the joint business plan, there were clear scorecard targets, however all of the targets related to the Gamma brand, or Customer A brand products that they are producing. The targets are related to levels of product distribution and gaining share of shelf relative to market share, for example. It is unclear in these documents on how these relate to the customer's (Customer A) strategies or needs, or in fact how they will be achieved.

This extract highlights the current and target store distribution for Gamma products, indicating the reasons why they should be increased in the 'comments' box. These reasons are focused on Gamma business needs.

Also contained in the joint business plan was a page that indicated a 'contact strategy'. This indicates the type of contact that is desired by Gamma with the Customer A team, and the objective to be achieved with each contact, the timings to meet them, and who in the Gamma team should be driving the meeting.

For example, the top-to-top meeting has an objective of ensuring the category director (at the retailer) is aware of Gamma key initiatives and the joint business plan. This is indicated as a half yearly meeting. This evidence once again highlights a Gamma view of what they would like, versus any evidence of how this fits into Customer A's needs or wants. This contact strategy does indicate a desire to create/maintain and develop relationships, which is evidence of the desire to create relational value.

Own-Brand Development

The third area of the work of collaboration centres on the Gamma teams' work on developing own-brand ideas and innovations. As a manufacturer of both brand and own-brand Gamma have to manage at times a conflict in the business. The business leadership appears most interested in their brands whereas the KAM team has to manage this, as well as their customer's (Customer A) needs and objectives to grow their brand.

> *The emphasis internally will always be on brand … our Chief Exec, is about driving branded sales.*

Gamma manages the own-brand business together, so there is no separate team or business unit to keep the business apart. This is reflected in joint business planning, where the two parts of the business are in the same plan. This brings about an apparent conflict for the account manager to manage:

> *Our joint business plan is very much joint between brand and own-brand, I think sometimes it gets lost and it becomes the poor relation … Customer A care more about their own-brand, it's pretty much 50% of what we do with them, and it makes them a lot more margin, so actually that is their focus.*

This tension is evident in the day-to-day work of the KAM team, where the internal pressure is to grow the brand, as it is more profitable to Gamma. However, the customer has the opposite objective which is to grow their own brand. For Gamma, strategically it appears the own-brand is a mechanism for filling factories with volume to create efficiencies, and the KPIs of the team are mostly brand measures, which drive this behaviour.

> *It makes me mindful of the way I collaborate because internally my KPIs are around brand more than own-brand …. and the business is a brand focused business, an owner that wants to drive brands, we need own-brand, we need it for factories and*

for efficiencies and we understand the importance of it .... We aren't great at doing bespoke own-brand.

As an own-brand manufacturer, Gamma are expected to innovate and develop the Customer A brand proactively. From the KAM meeting it was evident Gamma are doing this development, largely in the area of cost reduction. The reason for this appears to be that as Customer A drop the retail price of their products, they are looking to recoup the lost margin through a lower cost price for the product, and Gamma development teams search for savings in the recipes they use.

> **Meeting Note**: Own-brand seen as key pressure area for cost challenge—Gamma trying to improve other value-added elements on PL supply to defer focus on costs. Working on Customer A request to remove sugar from the Customer A Private Label range. Update on Private Label trials—and development work on Customer A brand developments—quality improvements/cost reductions/sugar reductions.

Also, evident in the KAM meeting was that the team was aiming to engage Customer A in a more strategic discussion on the development of own-brand products. The Gamma team recognised that the relentless focus on cost reduction is not a route to success for them and were discussing with Customer A a strategic review to look at where Customer A could develop more premium products, in order to increase the value for Customer A. There was no evidence in the meeting on Customer A's response to this, or how it fitted with their needs and strategy.

> **Meeting Note**: Customer A Brand Strategic Direction—aiming to engage Customer A on how to add value on the brands—proactive attempt to lead the agenda.

This was also supported in interviews, where it was evident Gamma are seeing providing good quality products as a key factor in anchoring the contacts, they have with Customer A.

We work really hard with our R&D team to continually improve the quality of our own-brand, so it is at least as good as the brand .... their aspiration, that their product tastes as good and is quality wise, it's good .... That's important to us because that adds value and collaborative relationship and that's being supportive ... if we didn't have that we wouldn't keep the business.

As illustrated earlier, there is a tension in this process, although it was evident Gamma do try and only supply products that are not directly comparable to brands, although it seems Gamma believe there are different shoppers for own-brand and brand, which should minimise switch between each product type.

> So, we make product x, but if we sell more of that it only affects (competitor brand A) … The only conflict you'd have would be on product B where we make own-brand competitor to our own-brand, but actually you tend to find in this category there's an own-brand shopper and a brand shopper …. So, if there isn't own-brand there, they're probably going to go for another own-brand product rather than the brand.

In summary in the area of collaborative work the first area of work was that undertaken by the category team. The category team provide insights and recommendations to customers on whole category. In the case of Customer A, they have been appointed formal category captains, which bring with it certain responsibilities for reporting and ways of working.

The second area of collaboration was that of joint business planning. However, in reviewing this in detail, it appears that the focus on the joint plans is solely about the Gamma business, and does not consider the customer needs, strategies, or targets.

The final area of collaboration is that of own-brand management and development. In this area Gamma are re-developing products and responding to retailers' needs, largely around pressures to reduce costs. This area is a cause of tension in the Gamma business, and they are making own-brand products that potentially conflict with their desire to grow their brands in that customer.

Non-collaboration Work

The work the teams are undertaking purely for Gamma. It is work that has not been asked for by customers, but the Customer Team are undertaking it.

When reviewing non-collaborative work, this points to Gamma undertaking activities that are purely for the benefit of Gamma. As discussed in the previous area of collaborative work, Gamma do undertake category work and own-brand work that is collaborative in nature.

However, it could be argued in the area of joint business planning, as referenced in collaborative work, the joint business plan is Gamma focused versus truly a collaborative plan. When discussed in interviews, there was no direct evidence from the Gamma KAM team that they recognised this as non-collaborative work, but the document review highlighted previously does show this as an apparent contradiction. That is, what Gamma call a joint business plan is in fact an internal business plan, with little involvement from the customer.

Collaboration Barriers

The work Gamma undertake in order to collaborate with their customers. This can be both joint work with the customer and work Gamma undertakes for the customer.

The research showed that supplying both own-brands and brands to the same customers created barriers and challenges for the commercial team.

The Gamma team have commercial agreements in place that combine own-brand and branded business, and this could cause issues when the retailer is looking to hit their own targets because the retailer will often look to their own-brands to drive profit (as they are often at a higher percentage margin than brands), potentially at the expense of branded sales.

Own-Brand Versus Brand Challenges

One example of this was cited where Customer A were looking to improve their margin delivery, and logically looked to grow their own-brand business kids' range (as it delivers a higher percentage margin). Gamma were resistant to this, as the opposite is true for them, and it also potentially harms sales of their brands at the same time.

> With Customer A because we do a lot of their x range, their it is on a permanent three for £x and stuff…we have to agree in advance what … we're prepared to fund on that because it's hard to margin maintain when their retails could be anywhere…. It's just too risky for us, we just have to say it's this amount of support and whatever you do outside of that is up to you.

Another barrier to collaboration appears to be linked to the drive for channel expansion by Gamma. In their corporate and commercial strategy documents, the focus is on increasing presence in discounters, as a growing channel. However, this has a double impact for the business in terms of collaboration. Firstly, the main retailers in this channel are not collaborative, and in fact force a transactional relationship in their dealings with manufacturers.

> *Some of our customers only wish to be transactional. Customer X for example they won't see you. ... They will write to you on a fax and that sort of thing, and then shout at you down the telephone and things like that.*

Secondly, as Gamma gain presence in these channels, it impacts on the major customers it does wish to collaborate with. This impact is felt in the pricing that the discounter sells the products, and the reaction of the major customer. Evidence was present of Customer A reacting to Gamma activity in discounters by demanding action and increased funding from Gamma as a result.

> *He's lowered the price of a lot of my products at the moment to hit his price basket targets—brilliant for me I sell more—he says, 'Can you help me fund it?' 'No, it's nothing to do with me what you retail your products at.'*

So, for Gamma, the management of other customers in new channels of growth is impacting and creating barriers to collaboration with current major customers. This management challenge is not referenced in any of the documents reviewed. One way Gamma seem to try and mitigate this issue is to claim they offer the same deals and support to all customers, but this evidence suggests it is not helping in their collaborative efforts with their larger customers.

> *The rules are pretty much, 'If you see it somewhere else you can have it.' We don't offer something to one retailer that we're not prepared to with another because you just trip yourself up and it will cost you a bloody fortune.*

Category Management Restrictions

A final example of collaboration barriers is evidence from interviews indicating how the category teams work and support could be 'traded away' or access stopped if a commercial trading issue arose between Gamma and its customers.

Further, this was not always a retailer stopping this access, but Gamma itself choosing to withdraw if what it considered unreasonable commercial demands were made. In interviews, a member of the category team indicated how they were not 'category captains' in one customer as a choice, as the customer had asked them to pay for the privilege.

> *We're not category captains and we've not chosen to be category captains. There's a commercial reason why we're not category captains.*

In summarising the findings of collaboration barriers, firstly Gamma face barriers relating to the supply of branded and own-brand products. Managing the retailers' demands and aspirations for their own-brands (e.g., in the area of margin and pricing) whilst balancing the impact on Gamma branded portfolio causes conflict in their business.

Gamma's desire to expand their channels of trade is also a cause for conflict with current customers. The channel of focus for expansion for Gamma are discounters, and as they build business in that channel, they impact current large customers' performance, who then create challenge and barriers for Gamma to respond to, especially in the area of margin and pricing.

The final area of barrier involves the category team. The research showed that this area of collaborative support was at risk of removal by the customer, if the customer decided Gamma were not delivering the commercial terms and support, they required. This finding is potentially indicating an area of collaborative work that is seen by some retailers as a 'nice to do' versus an integral part of creating joint value through collaboration.

Power

The evidence of the influence of retailer power on the relationship and its impact on collaboration and/or value.

Power had little emphasis placed on it in the Gamma research. The only direct reference to power was from a respondent indicating that the retailer could stop any discussions based on their commercial demands.

What is interesting from this evidence is how it again is based on achieving 'what Gamma wants' as opposed to how to achieve Gamma's needs in collaboration with their customer.

> *guess the raw commercial side of it which is … collaborative relationships are turned on and off as and when commercial issues arise and it's a tactic that clearly, you'd use if you were the buyer. So, they know that we need to land NPD, they know that we need to close off distribution gaps, they know that we want to execute our branded activity plans. Clearly, we're trying to align them to their strategies and their objectives, but ultimately if a commercial conflict arises, they can choose to put everything on ice.*

Value

Value Creation

Work that demonstrates value creation for Gamma, for example joint business planning.

Value creation highlights evidence of the targets and aspirations for brand growth in customers. As stated earlier, account plan documents show detailed targets for share, distribution, share of shelf, share of promotional activity. However, these are not joint targets, and there was no supporting evidence of how these would be achieved, or what actual value would accrue from achieving them.

The main finding on value creation related more to the creation of relational value. In interviews there were numerous references to gaining access to retailers and developing personal relationships as being the major focus of collaboration with customers.

> So, we say we want to have top to tops with our key customers a minimum of twice a year. We should be in regular contact with our trading teams, whether that's through phone calls, whether it's through emails, whether it's through formalised meetings. So, I suppose there is an understanding in the team that being with the customer and reinforcing our strategies, learning of any changes to theirs, is an important part of trying to work together.

Further, when finding evidence on what is measured in the area of value creation and capture, account managers cited being assessed on their 'Advantage Group' survey scores from their customers. This annual survey of buyer's rates manufacturers on various metrics that combine to show how customers view their relationship versus peers. It is not related to the business results achieved, so it is instructive that an account manager is measured by external benchmarks on how strong their relationship is.

> One of my KPIs now is to become a top five choice for Customer A in terms of our Advantage Group survey, so it's now an objective and that's new this year.

Value Capture

Work that provides evidence of value Capture for Gamma, for example initiatives undertaken that clearly show with their ROI for the Gamma business.

With regards to value capture evidence of this was limited in the research. As stated earlier, gaining access to retailers, and Advantage Group scores were used to indicate relational value success.

New Product Development

Where reference was made to value capture, it was in reference to Gamma developing new product formulations or approaches on own-brands that indicated transactional value creation for both the customer and Gamma.

> *Customer B were a long way behind their JBP margin target or … most of their margin shortfall was on own-brand products …. we're matching their prices on a pro rata basis against a competitor equivalent and as a consequence they dropped their retail prices … we discussed with them an initiative to develop different product that would enable them to match the competitor and then be able to return, so they're offering their shoppers a price matching against competition in different pack size and then their standard packs could be priced closer to where they needed to be to make their margin.*

This quote indicates that Gamma are willing to look at recipe costs/cost of goods in a creative way to help their customers achieve a lower price in the marketplace, which will also reward Gamma with higher product volumes. It is also interesting that Gamma were prepared to engage in the challenge of retail pricing when it related to retailer brand products, but not when it involved their brands.

It is perhaps instructive that these own-brand examples were the only ones that could be quoted of value creation when asked. It could be an indication of where Gamma management can most easily identify transactional value gains from collaboration, as opposed to being able to demonstrate any examples focused just on the branded part of the business.

In summarising value creation and capture the value creation evidence was largely about Gamma own business and KPIs, such as distribution targets, and so on. The value creation activities were largely focused on relational value, such as developing and maintaining personal relationship with the customer's teams.

As an own-brand manufacturer, there was evidence of Gamma value creation and capture activities with regards re-developing own-brand recipe, in order to reduce costs. This would lead to value capture for Gamma as well as the customer.

Gamma Case Study Summary

In reviewing all of the evidence from the Gamma research, these are the main findings:

1. The research in Gamma did establish generally that collaboration was undertaken, but not a strong rationale as to why or the benefits to the Gamma business.
2. There is a sense from the research that collaboration appeared to be viewed as a 'nice to do' exercise, that was done to please customers. There was evidence of scorecards and targets, but these were focused on achieving internal Gamma business and brand targets, with little evidence of how this linked to targets or scorecards for the customer.
3. Collaboration in the business was focussed on personal relationships; it is this that appears to be the main emphasis in the Gamma collaborative approach.
4. The work of collaboration appears to be more directed towards the category team, and the work they undertake with and for customers, such as range review support and data analysis and own-brand-new product development, but the research suggests this is a challenging area of Gamma to manage alongside its branded business.
5. Joint business plans appear to be more internal Gamma plans than joint plans. The contents are focused on achievement of Gamma's business objectives, and also have a customer contact strategy that indicates the desire to develop personal relationships across the customer's team.
6. Gamma's desire to expand their business in other channels, such as discounters, has led to difficult discussions with their major retail customers as to the impact this will have on current customers' performance, and how Gamma will (or will not) help mitigate any impacts the customer may suffer.
7. The research suggests that Gamma does look to use both relational and transactional approaches to create value in their collaboration. However, the transactional value is solely brand focused, not joint value. There wasn't any evidence of how their collaborative category management work, for example, performed, and what value was or was not created from it.

Delta Case Study: Own-Brand Supplier Transforming Their Collaborative Approach

After reading this case you will discover:

1. How the Delta business has undergone a significant recent change in its approach to collaboration with its major customers.
2. How Delta has made significant changes to their approach to collaboration, including its process and people, to enable a more collaborative joint business planning approach.
3. Delta have developed joint business plans of a longer-term (three years) horizon being taken with customers, with lead scorecard measures focused on customer growth (own-brand participation) and an underlying belief that achieving this will deliver growth for the Delta business.
4. The work of collaboration in Delta involves the Commercial, Category, and Product Development teams and appears to be broad in scope.
5. How power is shifting towards Delta, following many years of a very transactional and short-term relationship with its retailers.
6. How there is increased strategic importance of own-brands to major UK retail customers, which has enabled Delta to reset its collaborative approach.

Introduction

Delta is a business producing own-brand products for UK supermarkets and out of home food retailers. It is its relationship with its major supermarket retailer customers in the UK that is the focus of this case study, and how Delta manages its own-brand business with those customers.

The key accounts team at Delta is responsible for managing the business-to-business relationship and is organised into four main Customer Teams. Each major customer has a small team allocated to it for the management of the joint business. These teams comprise a National Account Manager, supported by a shared resource from Category Planning and Supply Chain. Figure 4.14 highlights the structure of this team, and Table 4.8 details the roles and responsibilities of the team members.

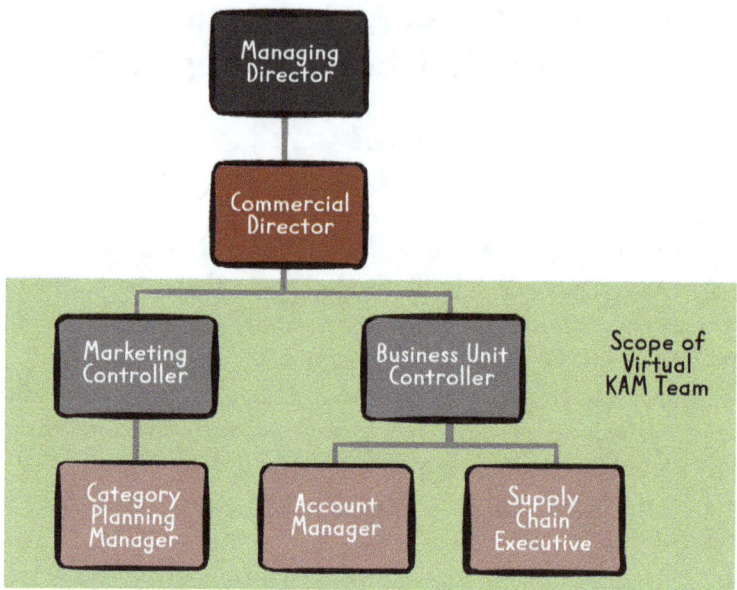

Fig. 4.14 Delta Customer Team structure

Table 4.8 Delta Customer Team roles and responsibilities

Role	Responsibility in KAM team
Full-time team member	
Business Unit Controller	• Overall management responsibility of the customer P&L and team management
Account Manager	• Day-to-day responsibility for relationship and delivery of business plan with key customer contacts
Category Manager	• Provide total category insights and advice to the customer on how to grow the (customers) overall business
Part-time team member	
Supply Chain Executive	• Ensures the on time in full delivery of Delta products to the customer, working with customer supply chain operations

Delta Case Themes

In analysing the research findings, three main categories emerged as significant in answering the overall research question. These categories and their subcategories are characterised in Table 4.9.

The three high-level themes that have emerged are 'Collaboration', 'Power', and 'Value'.

Table 4.9 Delta research finding categories and descriptions

Category	Description	Sub category	Description
Collaboration	Work that exists in order that Delta works more closely with its customers	Collaboration purpose and choices	The outcomes Delta would like from collaboration with chosen customers, and how they choose who to collaborate with, and how this may differ by customer type
	Both work with the customer (e.g., joint product development) and work developed for the customer alone by Delta (e.g., market data analysis and reporting).	Collaboration work	The work Delta undertakes to collaborate with their customers. This can be both joint work with the customer and work Delta undertakes for the customer
		Non-collaboration work	The work the teams are undertaking purely for Delta. It is work that has not been asked for by customers, but the Customer Team are undertaking it
		Collaboration barriers	Evidence that stopped collaboration work occurring, largely due to external (customer) factors
Power	The evidence of the influence of retailer power on the relationship and its impact on collaboration and/or value		
Value	Evidence of work aimed at directly creating value for delta	Value creation	Work that demonstrates value creation for Delta, for example joint business planning
		Value capture	Work that provides evidence of value capture for Delta, for example initiatives undertaken that clearly show with their ROI for the Delta business

Collaboration is the area of work that exists so that Delta works more closely with its customers. This may be work with the customer (e.g., joint product development) or work developed for the customer alone by Gamma (e.g., market data analysis and reporting).

Power is evidence of the impact of retailer power specifically on Delta's ability to collaborate with the customer in question and/or its ability to generate and capture value. This is evidenced with specific instances of the retailer withdrawing from collaborative activities and asking for funding over, above, and outside the formal business plans and agreed activities.

Value is evidence of work aimed at directly creating value for Delta. Value creation, for example, could cover work such as joint business planning, and work areas showing evidence of value capture for Delta could include evidence of initiatives undertaken with their ROI for the Delta business. An example of this could be a specific promotional programme for Delta products to achieve a target return on investment.

Collaboration

Collaboration Purpose and Choices

The outcomes Delta would like from collaboration with chosen customers, and how they choose who to collaborate with, and how this may differ by customer type.

Collaboration purpose and choices uncovered two major themes influencing collaboration purpose and choices in the business. These two themes were external market dynamics and an internal strategic shift in how Delta as a business works with its customers.

Looking first at the external perspective, in the UK Grocery Industry the major supermarkets have lost share, mostly to discount operators, and as a consequence they have come under increased pressure to drive footfall and halt sales declines. This has resulted in Delta receiving direction and requests from their major supermarket customers to help them achieve this aim, as these retailers see own-brands as a key factor where they can drive loyalty to their stores.

> *The bigger prize for them, and I think this is kind of where they buy into it, the bigger prize is if we can get more footfall, and we can differentiate, and people keep coming back and don't buy in Discounter A, or ... wherever, then that's going to be the benefit to them.*

Own-Brand as a Differentiator

The retailers' guidance to Delta seems to be that own-brands are a key competitive differentiator that can drive retailer loyalty. This focus on own-brand products is instructive, as major brand products are available in every retailer; this means retailers believe they need to shift their emphasis to the own-brand products in their stores to build shopper loyalty.

As a result of this, Delta is seeing the retailer cutting branded ranges and reducing their promotion and feature slots in store, to ensure the own-brands feature more prominently to shoppers. Delta also believes that retail customers are restricting access to branded supplier KAM teams, and refusing to build joint business plans with them, treating them in a more transactional way than in the past.

> *What we are also seeing is the removal of branded JBPs—moving to a very transactional relationship with brands as we offer them the Category support and advice they need.*

Delta also has heard evidence of the GSCOP (HM Government Grocery Codes of Practice, 2009) influencing this change of behaviour. The GSCOP code aims to curb a retailer's ability to make unreasonable funding requests of suppliers (typically requests for large 'one-off' sums of money), which has resulted in retailers moving their business negotiations more to cost price and front margin discussions (margin focus on cost of goods, as opposed to 'back margin', which is focused on rebates, promotional funds, and other similar mechanisms).

This has played more to an own-brand supplier's strength, as they typically do not have large discretionary funds to spend (back margin) but can offer above average category margins to retailers (front margin), so now appear more competitive to a retailer versus their branded competition when looked at in this new way of building category value.

Building Collaboration

For Delta, this now means they are in a competitive environment in which they see the benefit of generating closer and longer-term collaborative relationships with customers. With this new approach to funding and deals with their customers, they see that in helping these customers grow share and sales they will benefit significantly.

> *Brands are fighting like mad for more space, they invest for space—but then nothing happens, and the retailers gain nothing. … Customer A was telling us that brands have become commodities—brands are ubiquitous and not differentiated enough, so they see own-brand as a way to cut through this and offer their shoppers something unique and different—and we can help them with that.*

From an internal perspective, this backdrop has seen a significant investment in process and capability improvements to enable them to deliver this collaborative way of working. They have developed clear roles for their Commercial and New Product Development teams, and have added a category management expertise, to provide help and support to their customers to drive category sales and value.

Delta sees the commercial role of the manager as the customer interface, and the internal 'voice of the customer', to ensure other internal teams understand customers' needs. The commercial team also has ultimate responsibility for the profit and loss of the customer.

The category team is primarily responsible for understanding current category performance and uncovering insight to help improve the sales and profitability of the whole category for the customer.

The New Product Development team is expected to proactively develop and redevelop products, based on sound consumer insights, to build sales and profit of the products for Delta and the customer.

Delta sees closer collaboration as improving the security for their business in the medium term. Up until recent years, own-brand contracts were tendered annually or even more frequently by retailers, creating a never-ending cost price pressure on their business.

Their new approach has seen them move to a three-year joint business plan, which they believe creates a far more conducive environment for Delta to make the investments in product development and the people and resources required. It is evident they are also structuring their business plans towards mutual growth with the retailer so that they mitigate the risks of making large upfront investments without the payback from the relationship.

> *We have also added a business unit structure for major customers of a single account manager and category manager—so customers see much more resource from us. There is an on cost for us on this approach—we have had to invest upfront, but the business case means we will recoup this from the volume we will create to get the ROI.*

Delta has embedded this new approach by creating a joint business plan with both Customer A and Customer B. The JBP has a target for own-brand participation in the category for each customer. This is notable as it is a customer measure, focused on delivering the customer growth, and through achieving that target, will also benefit Delta.

This JBP is focused around two major customer range reviews. It is in these reviews that the retailer will review their current range of products and make decisions on removing products and adding new products. This activity will also look at the space allocated to the new range.

Delta, with their category management resource referenced earlier, can help lead and deliver this work in conjunction with the retailer. The plan example also shows the target economic delivery Delta is anticipating from the plan, and also the benefit to the customer, indicating a balanced approach to the joint business plan, with benefits to the retailer and Delta.

In summary, the purpose of collaboration and the choices Delta is making are being driven by external and internal factors. Externally retailers are looking to own-brand to help them fight for market share through increased shopper loyalty. As a large own-brand supplier, Delta is now being given greater access and collaboration opportunities by their retail customers.

Delta has responded by developing formal joint business plans with selected customers and undertaking significant internal changes to their ways of working and process, to enable this to happen.

Collaboration Work

The work Delta undertakes in order to collaborate with their customers. This can be both joint work with the customer and work Alpha undertakes for the customer.

When looking at collaboration work, as an own-brand supplier this has always traditionally involved product development expertise. As the retailer looks to expand their ranges, Delta has dedicated product and food development expertise (NPD team) to lead the thinking on where and how the retailer should build their own-brand products.

In addition, this team is also looking closely at the total cost of the product and exploring cost reduction opportunities across the whole supply chain. This means Delta can proactively engage the retailer in collaboration opportunities to gain shared value from making such changes.

> *We are always looking to show commitment and build trust—we proactively look to improve products and show them to customers, they don't ask, but we show them better, cheaper recipes to demonstrate our commitment, this works really well in building the collaboration—we all win and share the benefits, it's better business for all of us.*

Account Planning

This activity is one of a number of areas identified in the newly updated account planning process in Delta. The business has now established 'Commercial Standards' for its account plans, and the 'Commercial Levers' it wishes to see used with customers to drive mutual value.

It appears from customer feedback that this approach is meeting with positive feedback. The document highlights specific feedback from Customer B on how they are moving their strategic focus away from brands to own-brand, and how they are recognising Delta's new approach is of value to them, referencing that 'we are one business'.

This is highlighted in Fig. 4.15.

As discussed earlier, in a market context of intense competition and sales pressure, Delta's major customers such as Customer A have made significant cost reductions in Head Office headcount. This has resulted in further efforts from the retailer to 'outsource' work to collaborative partners such as Delta. This has always included product development work, but now extends to category management work and recommendations:

> *Another significant factor behind this change we are seeing is retailers have fewer resources—they are all cutting headcount in head office and need partners—they are effectively outsourcing things they used to do, and we are happy to collaborate with them in this way on own-brand—I think brands find this much harder to deal with.*

> *I think now, given where we're at, we've got a strong route in to influence what's happening now with the category.*

Increased Own-Brand Support Works

This is a changed dynamic; previously large, branded suppliers would be providing this level of resource and support. As brands (and branded suppliers) fall out of favour, the retailer is looking to their own-brand partners to provide this support.

> *We are told by ... Customer A and Customer B that own-brand is leading the agenda—we are now helping them manage the whole category, not just own-brand—using our category teams and insights teams. We have built a new category team to add these new skills and approaches, we are adding insights team—this is a transition for us as we add these new capabilities.*

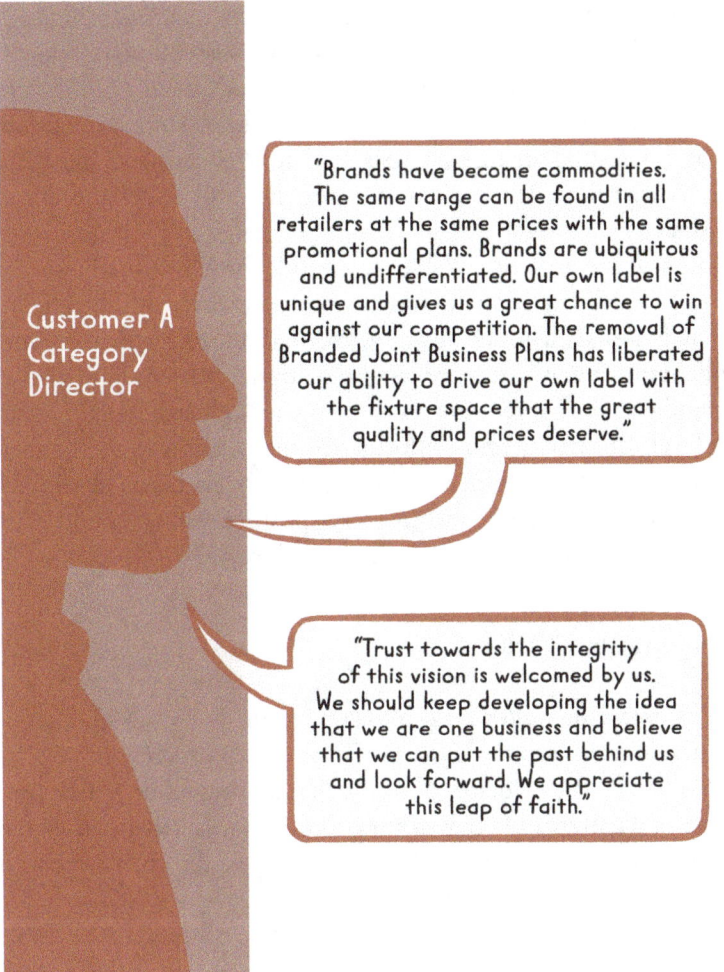

Fig. 4.15 Delta customer feedback

It appears this is also linked to 'trust', with no brands to sell, the retailer sees their (Delta's) advice as more impartial than that given by branded suppliers and consequently focused on their (the retailer's) shoppers' needs.

> *Our feedback from customers is a real distrust in brands at the moment—Customer A are now reducing the brand's space and opportunities to promote and giving more emphasis to own-brand—of course we win but so do they as they gain shopper loyalty.*

Delta now has evidence of the work it has done which has delivered growth for both the retail customer and Delta themselves. Their own analysis showed the impact of the joint business plan developed with Customer A. It is indicating that the result of this change has been an increase in own-brand participation (the number of Customer A shoppers buying own-brand products in the category) and a significant growth in value, which is ahead of the market for Customer A.

What is interesting in this analysis is that it is showing the benefits to Customer A as well as Delta, to demonstrate the value of collaboration to the Delta business.

In summary, the area of collaborative work for Delta firstly covers own-brand NPD, which traditionally has always been core work for Delta in this area. What is new is a much more formalised approach to this work, and wider collaborative work areas, covered in commercial standards and levers.

The standards and levers are now being introduced to the business as expected levels of activity and performance that Delta will see in their joint business plans with customers. These plans have been developed with Customer A and Customer B, and are seeing positive results for both Customer A and Delta regarding sales and market share growth.

Non-collaboration Work

The work the teams are undertaking purely for Delta. It is work that has not been asked for by customers, but the Customer Team are undertaking it.

There was very little evidence of non-collaboration work. This may be due to two factors. Firstly, of the new-found approach to a collaborative model, it appeared all work was striving to build and deliver the collaborative plan in the business. Secondly, as an own-brand business, Delta does not have lots of resources to focus on areas other than those that are important and valued by the customer.

Collaboration Barriers

The work Delta undertakes in order to collaborate with their customers. This can be both joint work with the customer and work Alpha undertakes for the customer.

When reviewing the barriers to collaboration, as discussed there has been a recent significant shift in how Delta collaborates with its customers. Internally this has meant for some people and internal teams a change in their attitudes to retailers.

> *(In developing a) … a three-year deal … is a bit of a leap of faith … and it's about taking everybody on the journey … because for us to really make this work properly, if we do increase volume … we need to get more efficiency out of the factory to allow us to continue … the whole business is involved in actually putting this deal to bed.*

Building Trust

In the past, when retailers were treating own-brand suppliers in a very transactional way, the relationship was characterised by a lack of trust and openness, with business freely taken away, and aggressive requests for additional funding. Internal teams are now having to reconcile that recent behaviour with a new approach to trust, partnership, and openness.

> *One of our biggest challenges is the branded suppliers have a bigger chequebook—we can't do that, and I know buyers can compromise their morals when they just need to … get the numbers in, I know because I did it.*

This internal challenge has also been seen in the need to change the skills and capabilities of the commercial teams. This move to collaboration has required significant investments in training and development for KAM teams, as well as changing personnel. Delta actively looked to recruit ex-retail experienced professionals into their KAM team to ensure they had a broader, more collaborative skill set in their team:

> *We have refreshed our roles and built new skills and capabilities—competencies and approaches—we have measured the teams against this new way of working … some people have had to leave, but we need the right skills to deliver this approach.*

It is also evident that not all major customers are moving to this new collaborative approach. Customer D was cited as still behaving in a very transactional way, with aggressive demands, and so on. Although this is a barrier to collaboration with that customer, Delta is seeing it as an opportunity to divert energy and effort to other customers and using this information with Customer D to try and encourage a change in approach.

There was also evidence of Customer C making requests to move to an open book costing relationship. Customer C see this as 'collaboration', Delta does not and is resisting this request. Again, as above, they are now looking to show what they can do as a collaborative partner to encourage Customer C to change their way of working.

> *Customer C want open book costing; we don't think it works and (will) just focus the relationship on cost prices …. we think there is a better way to collaborate than this, and we are resisting this with Customer C.*

In summary, the collaboration barriers in Delta are firstly internal. This is based on recent previous experience, where retailers were short term and confrontational in their approach, and for some this shift in approach is taking time to adjust to.

The second area of collaboration barrier is that not all retail customers are moving to this new approach. Customer D and Customer C were cited as retailers who were still behaving in a short-term transactional way. This was causing the business to have a complexity to manage with their customer-based, collaborative longer-term approaches, and short-term transactional trading relationships.

Power

The evidence of the influence of retailer power on the relationship and its impact on collaboration and/or value.

When reviewing the role of power in the relationship, there is evidence of a move of power back towards the supplier (Delta) in their major customers, Customer B and Customer A. As discussed earlier, the market context has elevated the importance and value of own-brand to these customers, and Delta is benefiting from closer collaboration and increased influence.

> *Where now … they want to exploit their brand because it's the point of difference, it's the only point of difference. Which is good for us, I will say now the balance of…. strength and influence are without a doubt with own-brand now.*

These customers are actively looking to Delta to collaborate and provide resources, ahead of much larger multinational branded supplier competitors such as Mars. Although this has not been seen by all customers, such as Customer D (see above), this move appears to have boosted Delta's belief in its power in its relationship with customers and is being leveraged not just with Customer B and Customer A but also in trying to change the relationship with more transactional customers such as Customer C and Customer D.

Value

Value Creation and Capture

Work that demonstrates value creation for Delta, for example joint business planning and work that provides evidence of value capture for Delta, for example initiatives undertaken that clearly show with their ROI for the Delta business.

Value creation and capture highlights how through the development of the joint business plans with Customer A and Customer B, Delta is creating and capturing value in these customer relationships. As discussed earlier, Delta is seeing how value creation activities around changes in the range and merchandising of the cooking sauces category have seen own-brand share and volume growth.

The Customer A Joint Business Plan shows the joint plan created with the customer to deliver benefits to the customer, and to Delta. The plan consists of the actions and recommendations to achieve this, including product development, category, commercial, and value chain activities.

Category Management

As discussed earlier, this plan example is focused around two major customer range reviews. It is in these reviews that the retailer will review their current range of products and make decisions on removing products and adding new products. This activity will also look at the space allocated to the new range.

In addition to this transactional value evidence, it was clear in the research that Delta places great emphasis on their relationships with their customers. Interviewing the Customer A Account lead, who is an ex-Customer A buyer himself, it is clear the importance and value of the personal relationship in developing their collaborative business:

> *My experience from Customer A is that you can trust own-brand suppliers' way more than brands—even with big and good branded suppliers there is always a lack of trust that they are doing things for their own and not your benefit I just try and be easy to deal with so that we build our relationship.*

In summary, Delta's change of collaborative approach with Customer A and Customer B is showing evidence of value capture. The value creation activities in their joint business plans are highlighting how work on the different commercial levers is creating value and capturing value for Delta.

An emerging finding, in this case, is that of own-brand suppliers having access to the retailer that is unavailable to branded suppliers, and this being a factor in the levels of collaboration that can be achieved. As an own-brand supplier, they have a high degree of access and collaboration as shown earlier, and through this can develop joint business plans that create and capture value in a way that seems closed to branded suppliers.

Delta Case Study Summary

In reviewing all of the evidence from the Gamma research, these are the main findings:

1. It is clear that the Delta business has undergone a significant recent change in its approach to collaboration with its major customers. The shift in the UK grocery retail market landscape has altered the nature and role of own-brand products for retailers and with it their willingness and ability to collaborate with suppliers like Delta.
2. Delta has clearly looked at this shift as an opportunity, and made significant changes to their approach to collaboration, including its process and people, to enable a more collaborative joint business planning approach.
3. There is evidence in Customer A and Customer B joint business plans of a longer-term (three years) horizon being taken with customers, with lead scorecard measures focused on customer growth (own-brand participation) and an underlying belief that achieving this will deliver growth for the Delta business.
4. The work of collaboration involves the Commercial, Category, and Product Development teams and appears to be broad in scope.
5. There are apparent barriers in bringing the whole organisation with the commercial team, and some evidence that not all customers are yet willing or able to work on this new collaborative approach.
6. It was evident that Delta believes power is shifting towards them, following many years of a very transactional and short-term relationship with its retailers.
7. Delta does look to use both relational and transactional approaches to create value in their collaboration. There is evidence of transactional value for both Delta and the customer through implementing changes as part of their joint business plan. It was also clear how Delta places importance and effort on creating the relational value with their customers.
8. There is a sense that the increased strategic importance of own-brands to major UK retail customers has enabled Delta to reset its collaborative approach. It appears that this is a step change from their experience of collaboration with these customers in the last five years or so.

Chapter Summary

- All four cases have developed deep insights into the 'why and how' of how they collaborate and create and capture value in collaboration with the retail customer.
- There are clear findings and themes that apply across all the cases:

  - Collaboration
  - Power
  - Value creation and capture

- Chapter 5 will review and discuss these cross-case themes and develop the high-level insights from all the case studies.

5

Collaboration Under the Microscope: A Cross-Case Analysis

The examination of the four individual case studies in the previous chapter highlighted the work of collaboration, the influence of power, and the challenges of value creation and capture, patterns often seen in the FMCG industry. In this chapter, we will dig deeper into those patterns, looking to understand their relationship to the theory and their broader implications/significance on practice. The comparative analysis offered here will help us in answering the following questions.

> To what extent is collaboration a joint activity between the retailer and supplier?
> - How are KAM teams being used to build collaboration?
> - What is the role of joint business plans (JBPs) in collaboration?
> - How is power influencing collaboration?
> - What is the ability of suppliers to create and capture value in the collaboration?

Introduction

The analysis offered in this chapter was undertaken following a process of reviewing the individual case findings, developing cross-case themes, and finally building assertions from this research. I would like to begin by firstly highlighting and comparing each business regarding the business characteristics, KAM team construction, and the research instruments and data collected.

As we have seen, the four case studies in this analysis have different characteristics, and it is important to compare and contrast before discussing the findings and assertions across each case. When firstly looking at the size of each business, Alpha and Delta have the largest turnover, an indicator of their business structure, in that they operate across multiple products categories, versus Gamma and Beta, both of which operate in single product categories.

Moving onto the KAM team itself, each of Gamma, Alpha, and Beta have the same team sizes of eight people, with Delta having five people in their KAM teams. Their characteristic as an own-brand supplier may explain the lower number of people in the Delta team, versus the other case studies being brands or both brand and own-brand suppliers.

Looking at the composition of these teams, all have roles in the areas of KAM Controller, KAM, and Supply Chain representation (full or part time). This is consistent with the theory in this area related to the core functions required for a KAM team (Gruen and Hofstetter 2010). However, there is a difference in the addition of an extra layer of management in KAM, namely, the presence of a Senior Account Manager in Gamma, Alpha, and Beta, but not in Delta. Again, it could be suggested that Delta as an own-brand supplier, operating from a low-cost model, has a simpler and cheaper management structure.

Category management resource is present across all companies. This is the work that suppliers provide to retailers to recommend assortment, merchandising, promotions, and other tactical solutions to grow the entire product category. As discussed, previously, this work is either seen as a positive effort to grow joint value (Lindblom and Olkkonen 2008) or a mechanism for retailers to exert 'expert' power over suppliers (Dapiran and Hogarth-Scott 2003).

All of the case studies except Delta have resources in the KAM team to undertake Shopper Marketing work. This role is typically responsible for developing and executing brand promotion and other activities that are tailored to the specific customer. It is understandable that Delta would not have this resource, as it does not sell any brands to its customers.

The role of the Customer Implant was only present in Beta and Gamma. This is the work done for the retailer, and typically is based in the retailer's office, but paid for by the supplier. In both of these instances, the Customer Implant works in Customer A, and it is a condition of being 'Category Captain' that these companies provide the resource.

The final role is that of Retail Operations, present only in Beta. This work is the management of day-to-day product orders specifically for that customer. In this instance, it is linked to the direct store delivery (DSD) supply chain that Beta operates for their products and is a feature of a large fast-moving fresh product category (Fig. 5.1).

5 Collaboration Under the Microscope: A Cross-Case Analysis

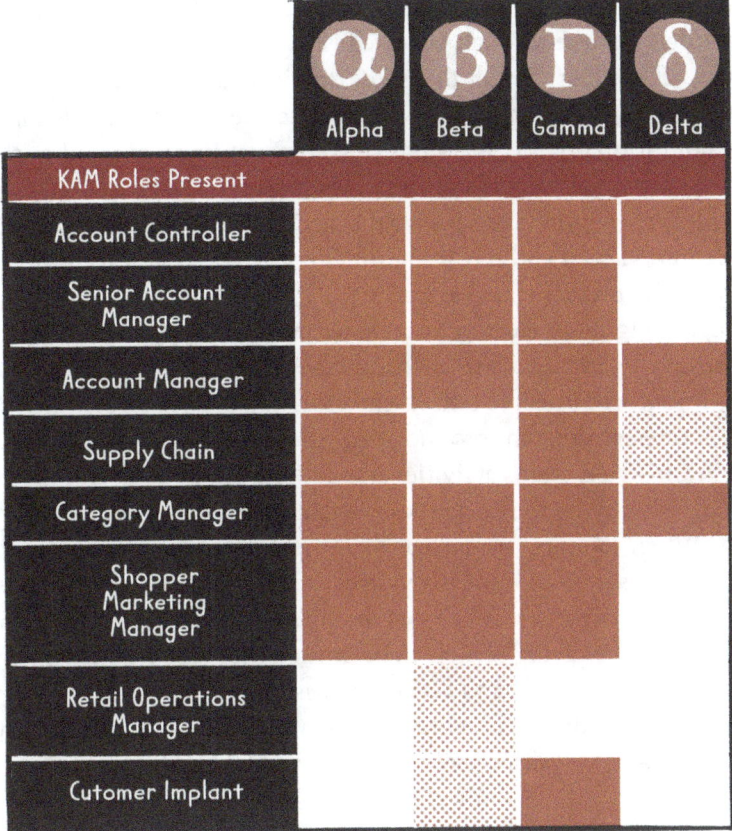

Fig. 5.1 Cross-case comparison—company facts and KAM structure

In regard to the size of the KAM teams, they are not proportional to company size, or the total number of employees. In all case studies except Delta, there is a consistent size of KAM team, with eight people. This is consistent with the research indicating seven as the average KAM team size (Marcos-Cuevas et al. 2014).

Cross-Case Comparison: Data Collection

Let's now explore the data collected in each case, comparing and contrasting it as a means of gaining insights that will assist us when we begin to compare across cases.

In comparing the data collected from each case, Table 5.1 highlights the types and detail of the research collected (Fig. 5.2).

Firstly, it is evident that all three research instruments are utilised in each case, except meeting attendance in Delta. The reason for this was that Delta did not hold formal KAM meetings since the team was so small as to allow issues to be managed daily as they arose with team colleagues.

The interviews undertaken reflect the size of teams, with similar numbers of people interviewed and recording times collected, again except in the case of Delta for the reasons stated above.

When looking at the meeting attendance research instrument, Alpha stands out for having 25 attendees present for the KAM meeting used in the research. This large number of people reflects the cross-category nature of the team, as they sell across five different product categories, meaning many teams have an interest in the KAM team's activities and actions discussed in this meeting. It is also indicative of the multiple roles in each category that need to attend this meeting. When looking to manage five categories in one customer, lots or people/functions need to be involved in activities, decisions, and actions. One outcome of a meeting of this size was that the KAM meeting was much more of an 'information' giving session than in the other case studies, which were more focused on decisions and action discussions.

When reviewing the documents accessed and reviewed, it became apparent that many differences existed across the case studies. Firstly, it was evident that

Table 5.1 Alpha findings: collaboration purpose and choices

Theme	Finding	Evidence
Collaboration purpose and choices	• Leadership direction and support is required to create a focus on collaboration	• Corporate strategies indicate the importance of customers and collaboration to their business • Senior managers endorse collaboration as the way Alpha works
	• The purpose of collaboration is a blend of business results and personal relationships	• Joint business plans were cited as evidence of Alpha's collaboration purpose • Customer segmentation is a methodology for choosing who to collaborate with and how to manage the collaboration • Advantage Group (customer survey) is used to gain feedback on the success of the collaboration, both containing personal and transactional elements

5 Collaboration Under the Microscope: A Cross-Case Analysis

	Alpha	Beta	Gamma	Delta
Data Collected				
Interviews People	5	7	7	3
Interviews Mins	141	292	267	97
Meeting Attendance People	24	6	5	0
Meeting Attendance Field Notes Pages	9	13	14	0
Documents Reviewed Total	12	12	12	3
Document Type Strategic Direction				
Corporate Strategy		■	■	
Commercial/Sales Strategy		■	■	■
Account Plan		■		
Joint Business Plan		■	■	■
Category Plan		■		
Business Review		■		
Document Type– Information/Guidance				
Industry Customer Survey	■	■		
Commercial Roles and Skills Framework		■	■	■

Fig. 5.2 Cross-case research comparison

Delta and Gamma have fewer strategic management documents in use, such as commercial strategies, sales strategies, or KAM plans. They are both involved in the supply of own-brand, which may be a factor in having a streamlined approach to planning documents.

Alpha has the fewest number of documents over all the case studies (three), although these would potentially be replicated across some product categories in the business. As discussed in the case study, Alpha does 'mandate' a global toolkit and approach to the management of customers, so this could be seen as a conscious decision by Alpha to streamline their approach to manage documents and reports.

Beta had the most documents in use by the KAM team, cascading from corporate strategic plans down to account plans and business reviews. When looked at more deeply in the case, it was evident that the corporate to commercial strategy documents had little evidence of customer needs or collaboration. These documents also did not contain numbers, so there were no targets to achieve.

When looking at category plans developed with customers, this was only evident in Alpha and Delta. For Alpha, this does appear consistent with their collaborative and 'category' focus, a way of working that was referenced in detail in the case, and the use of a mandated global toolkit. For Delta, this was a relatively new document, referenced in the case as work with Customer A and Customer B specifically. It was also somewhat of a hybrid category plan/account plan document, containing both category direction but also specific targets for Delta's business with that customer.

Joint business plans were present in all case studies, although the contents and focus do differ in each. For example, the Beta JBP is a number-focused plan with little evidence of insights or strategies to achieve them. In contrast, the Alpha document has extensive evidence of insight and strategies leading to the scorecard in the plan.

However, in all case studies, the description of these plans as 'joint' business plans (JBPs) may be a misnomer. All of the case studies self-described these plans as 'JBPs', but there was little evidence of customer involvement in developing them. They were all largely internal documents with no evidence of customer involvement.

The only exception to this was a customer scorecard in the Customer A and Customer B JBPs for Delta. In fact, Delta had the most detailed numbers-based JBPs, for both the customer and Delta. Again, as they are an own-brand supplier, perhaps this is reflective of their need to be close to the customer, and perhaps an indicator of access they can gain as an own-brand supplier.

The industry 'Advantage group' survey was present in two case studies out of four. This survey asks retailers to rate their suppliers on a number of attributes, including their collaborative skill and work. For Beta and Gamma, this was cited as an internal scorecard target for the KAM team, that is, 'improving our Advantage Group score', and is perhaps an indicator of the high level of customer collaboration focus in these case studies.

This review has highlighted similarities and differences in the company characteristics, and data collected across each case. The following section will highlight in more detail the themes that emerged for each case; this will enable us then to compare and contrast across cases later in this chapter.

Theme-Based Findings Per Case

The themes in each case were derived from the coding and approach outlined in the methodology chapter. These are nodes that emerged during coding and through a process of iteration in the themes that are developed and used to identify and organise the findings in each case.

In developing the themes per case, a process was used to refer back to each case in turn in order to identify the emergent finding and supporting evidence. The findings per case are presented here as tables per case, highlighting the findings emerging with the evidence points.

In summary, the themes identified were:

- Collaboration purpose and choices
- Collaboration work
- Non-collaboration work
- Collaboration barriers
- Power
- Value creation
- Value capture

Alpha Findings and Evidence: A Multinational Multi-category Supplier Demonstrating a Global to Local Approach

In reviewing collaboration purpose and choices, Alpha has formal (corporate strategy) and informal management support for taking a collaborative approach with customers. In the collaboration, Alpha does have a customer segmentation tool to help select collaborative partners and use joint business plans to enable collaboration. They also use the industry 'Advantage Group' survey to measure the success of their collaboration, this being a blend of relationship and business result measurement.

Alpha's collaboration work covers a broad area of category management, trading terms, and shopper marketing work with customers. A major focus is providing data and insights to customers for the whole category, supported by other category management work such as range and space recommendations (Table 5.2).

Non-collaboration work in Alpha does not have a lot of evidence, and where it does exist was limited only by the customer stopping collaborative activities due to trading disputes (Table 5.3).

Table 5.2 Alpha findings: collaboration work

Theme	Finding	Evidence
Collaboration work	• The work of collaboration covers trading terms, category management, and shopper marketing	• Alpha has global toolkits to guide on what work should be done and how
	• Day-to-day work of collaboration covers data analysis for the customer to uncover opportunities	• Alpha category captaincy with Customer A demands they do this work
		• Also cited as work done with other customers
	• Category management work (range, merchandising, price, and promotion recommendations) provides a mechanism for deeper collaboration and alignment on strategies to grow the joint business	• Alpha uses a pwrocess to create joint strategies, tactics, and a joint scorecard to measure success

Table 5.3 Alpha findings: non-collaboration work

Theme	Finding	Evidence
Non-collaboration work	• Non-collaborative work is less evident and is only limited by the customers', not the suppliers', willingness to work together	• Alpha cited an example of Customer B closing down access and collaboration due to a trading dispute in one category, across all categories

When looking at collaboration barriers, Alpha looks to overcome any barriers placed by the customer. Internal barriers were evident, with the conflict between parts of the KAM emerging as a conflict area (Table 5.4).

Power was evident in the Alpha case, with an example cited of Customer B shutting down collaboration across their business when in a trading dispute with Alpha. However, there was evidence of the top four retailers' power overall reducing, as they face an increased threat from discounters (Table 5.5).

Evidence in Alpha suggests that value creation is a blend of both personal relationship development and transactional value from collaborative activities. Alpha cited that the retailers' short-term requests for funding are factors that are undermining their ability to create value from the collaboration (Table 5.6).

5 Collaboration Under the Microscope: A Cross-Case Analysis

Table 5.4 Alpha findings: collaboration barriers

Theme	Finding	Evidence
Collaboration barriers	• Regardless of the challenges, Alpha looks to collaborate with their customers, even when barriers are placed in their way by those customers • Internal barriers may be in place that hinder customer collaboration	• Alpha cited Customer B example (above); they still looked for ways to collaborate with them • Alpha cited internal category teams providing support to Customer B that then placed pressure on the trading team

Table 5.5 Alpha findings: power

Theme	Finding	Evidence
Power	• Power of top four may be reduced as new channels (discounters, online) begin to take market share and business from them • Customer B as market leader has used its power position to stop collaboration	• Alpha is noticing a willingness to increase collaboration to improve business and counteract the new channel 'threat' to their business • Alpha example of shutting down discussions under trading dispute, and terms were met

Table 5.6 Alpha findings: value creation

Theme	Finding	Evidence
Value creation	• Value creation is seen as a blend of relationship development and tangible business proposals	• Alpha citing the example from the senior director—the importance of personal relationships • Ideal store and category management were cited as tools used to create value
	• Retailers' short-term requests and actions on pricing and promotion are seen as undermining value creation	• Alpha citing the example of promotion and pricing changes by Customer B and Customer A

Finally, reviewing value capture, Alpha sees this as a medium- to long-term activity, with joint business plans used to manage and measure the value capture. That said, it appears that Alpha did find the actual value capture hard to measure and cited relational value as a way to unlock or facilitate the capture of transactional value (Table 5.7).

Table 5.7 Alpha findings: value capture

Theme	Finding	Evidence
Value capture	• Value capture is seen as a medium- to longer-term activity through collaboration and is challenged by short-term retailer demands and behaviour • Joint business plans are used as a mechanism of tracking and managing value capture • Value capture can be hard to measure • Relational value can be used to leverage the transactional value	• Alpha director citing belief in category management activities as providing better ROI for alpha than promotions. But retailer places greater emphasis on more promotional activity and investment • Alpha citing Customer C example of retailer 'repaying' on a gap in the JBP • Alpha example looks for 'is the business growing' as an indirect indicator that the collaboration is working • Alpha citing example of using the relationship to address the lack of collaboration and commitment to JBP

Beta Findings and Evidence: A Fresh Food Business Looking to Collaborate Across Many Customers

In Beta, although not documented, collaboration does appear to be an unstated aim of the business. Beta appears to see that their brand strength in their product category does give them some choice in whom to collaborate with, although the leadership of the business stated they would collaborate with anyone who desired it. The research with Beta also highlighted the view the collaboration was in the customer's gift, and that they needed to trust that benefits would accrue from the collaboration (Table 5.8).

The work of collaboration in Beta is focused on category management support for retailers and is being used to 'sell' the idea of collaboration to some customers. It was also evident this team's work has an internal element, where the data and insights are used to create a positive message about Beta brands with the customer (Table 5.9).

Concerning non-collaboration work, this was in the main internal data and insights development and reporting. Further, the lack of customer measures and scorecards in documents in the business appeared to be indicative of Beta's inability to measure and manage collaborative work, so the business potentially finds it difficult to know what collaborative or non-collaborative work is. Also, the retailers using Beta brand competitors against them was cited as non-collaborative work, in that the Beta team had to focus on developing arguments and defend against these threats (Table 5.10).

5 Collaboration Under the Microscope: A Cross-Case Analysis

Table 5.8 Beta findings: collaboration purpose and choices

Theme	Finding	Evidence
Collaboration purpose and choices	• Collaboration is an unstated aim in the business	• Beta claims 'it is the right thing to do' • Beta claims they would collaborate with any customer that wanted to
	• Brand strength can be seen as a mitigating factor in needing collaboration with customers • The ability to collaborate is in the customer's gift and involves 'giving up' investment in the short term and hope it returns in the medium to longer term	• Beta's comment on brand strength and consumer connection with the brand • Beta's claims that it has to trust the retailer will reciprocate with increased returns later in the collaboration

Table 5.9 Beta findings: collaboration work

Theme	Finding	Evidence
Collaboration work	• Category management (range, space, price, and promotions recommendations) work is core to collaboration • Category management work is potentially being used to sell collaboration and its benefits to customers	• The Customer Team meeting focused on data review and category management work progress • Beta citing example of looking for arguments in data to convince Customer B of certain recommendations • Time spent on how to 'message' data and insights to Customer B in a positive light

Table 5.10 Beta findings: collaboration purpose and choices

Theme	Finding	Evidence
Non-collaboration work	• Internal data reporting and analysis is driving the non-collaboration work	• Beta cited work done to explain Beta brands and competitor category issues to an internal audience
	• A lack of customer measures in strategy documents indicates that collaboration and customer focus are missing	• None of the Beta strategic documents includes targets or measures linked to customers and collaboration
	• Retailers use rival brands as leverage with Beta to improve trading terms	• Beta's competitor example and Beta's perception that this was Customer B mechanism to gain increased support from Beta

Table 5.11 Beta findings: value creation

Theme	Finding	Evidence
Power value creation	• No references	
	• Meetings and access are seen as the main way that value is created in the collaboration	• Beta evidence on meetings/on-site visits as the main value creation activities
		• Customer A/Customer C as examples of value creation because of the frequency of contact
		• Customer relationship management as a strategy in the commercial strategy document
	• Joint business plan being used as the main mechanism to create alignment on value creation activities	• Beta cites JBP—BUT not clear it is joint, or that customer has signed on to its targets and activities

In the research, power had no references from Beta. With regards to value creation activities, meetings and access to retailers were cited as the main activities they see as creating value in the collaboration. Joint business plans were also cited as a mechanism for value creation, but in reviewing this document it was not clear what value creation activities were to Beta, or in fact whether those activities were jointly created with customers (Table 5.11).

Value capture had little evidence in the research. The example cited relates to how they drove customer value, not value capture for themselves, with the only reference being to the potential value of listing a new product in the retailer (Table 5.12).

Gamma Findings and Evidence: Managing Collaboration When Supplying Brands and Own-Brands

The research in Gamma indicates that they do not formally make choices on who they collaborate with, or what the purpose of collaboration is. When referencing collaboration purpose, Gamma stated that collaboration is about building relationships with the customer (Table 5.13).

When reviewing collaboration work in Gamma, this was focused on the work of category management. The category team was seen as an important resource for the KAM team, and this was work seen as done FOR the retailer. Joint business plans were in evidence but were not joint and not used consistently across customers.

5 Collaboration Under the Microscope: A Cross-Case Analysis

Table 5.12 Beta findings: value capture

Theme	Finding	Evidence
Value capture	• Value capture is customer-based not supplier-based with no measurement in place	• Beta citing example of customer being deal driven and the value being created for the customer but not for Beta • No indication of value to Beta • Only in the listing of new products did Beta have an idea on value (linked to brand focus as a supplier?)

Table 5.13 Gamma findings: collaboration purpose and choices

Theme	Finding	Evidence
Collaboration purpose and choices	• Collaboration and customer needs were not present in strategic documents of the company	• Corporate strategy is brand focused—No PL references (when PL is a large part of their business) • 'Business is brand' focused comment • The commercial strategy calls out customer activities but not how collaboration will work to achieve them
	• |No prioritisation of customers—we will collaborate with anyone	• Interview feedback with commercial director
	• Collaboration purpose is seen as relational	• Interview feedback on relationships with the buyer is key

The supply of both brands and own-brands provided evidence of collaborative work in own-brand development, but also showed how conflicts could arise between business priorities when supplying both areas to a customer (Table 5.14).

Non-collaborative work was not cited often in Gamma. The only evidence was around the joint business plan (as discussed earlier) where it was seen by the KAM team. This was more work done for the retailer than work done with them in a collaborative way. It listed the actions and investments Gamma were to take for the customer and held no evidence of the return and value to Gamma (Table 5.15).

Collaboration barriers in Gamma were related to the business being a supplier of both brands and own-brands to their customers. This caused a challenge in which areas to prioritise when aiming to meet the customer targets.

Table 5.14 Gamma findings: collaboration work

Theme	Finding	Evidence
Collaboration work	• Category teamwork is seen as core to collaboration work with customers	• Customer team cite that category team has more access and time with the buyer than they do • Range review work example
	• Category team needs to be trusted to be impartial with their collaboration with the customer	• Quote on not seen to be defending own business versus what is good for the category
	• Category teamwork is viewed by KAM team as ad hoc work and work done FOR the retailer	• Seen as an extended retailer resource
	• Category teamwork focused on reporting and analysis and category management recommendations	• Customer A category captaincy and documents showing the reporting done
	• JBPs seen as important but not consistently used with each customer	• Called out in commercial strategy but no process in place • Not jointly built or agreed to by customers
	• Own-brand development is a collaborative activity that involves constant management and innovation to manage the retailers' cost challenges	• Examples cited of cost engineering with Customer B
	• Supplying both brand and own-brand products creates a tension internally in managing the sales and profit impact in each with the customer	• Meeting and interviews cited challenges faced

Table 5.15 Gamma findings: non-collaboration Work

Theme	Finding	Evidence
Non-collaboration work	• JBP could be seen as non-collaborative work in that it is FOR gamma and does not involve the customer or their needs	• Document review shows lack of customer involvement and joint development

The other area of barrier was Gamma supplying discounters with their branded products, which was badly received by their major multiple retailer customers. This resulted in threats for price discounts and the shutting down of access to the category teams (Table 5.16).

Power had limited direct reference in the Gamma case, although evidence was found (as mentioned above) of the retailer shutting down access and

5 Collaboration Under the Microscope: A Cross-Case Analysis

Table 5.16 Gamma findings: collaboration barriers

Theme	Finding	Evidence
Collaboration barriers	• Own-brand and brand supply approach creates barriers to collaboration internally and with customers • Channel expansion (into discounters) creates barriers to collaboration with existing multiple customers (seen as a threat to them) • Category teamwork is stopped by retailers when they have a trading dispute	• Example of Customer A challenge on profitability and how to achieve this • Examples of price pressures applied when Customer A saw Gamma products in discounters • Example of Customer A shutting down access • Linked again to collaboration as 'nice to do'—not valued by customers?

Table 5.17 Gamma findings: power

Theme	Finding	Evidence
Power	• Retailers turn off access (collaboration) when short-term trading needs/issues are not met	• Interview respondent describing threat from retailers

Table 5.18 Gamma findings: value capture

Theme	Finding	Evidence
Value capture	• Value capture was only evident in own-brand supply that was linked to product design and cost reductions	• Evidence cited on Customer B example

making price demands when they saw Gamma brands in their discounter competitors (Table 5.17).

Account plans and joint business plans were cited as evidence of value creation activities, although as discussed earlier these were internal plans. The relationship and the customer perception of it were also cited as value creation.

Value capture was only evident when referring to own-brand examples. The activities here were around cost reduction and product reformulation, which resulted in value capture for Gamma, as well as the customer (Table 5.18).

Delta Findings and Evidence: Own-Brand Supplier Transforming Their Collaborative Approach

The purpose of collaboration is clear in that they see a role in developing own-brands that helps retailers differentiate themselves from their competition. Delta has made investments in the way it works and collaborates to achieve this, coupled with the development of three-year joint business plans with selected customers (Table 5.19).

The work of collaboration in Delta is focused on the development of own-brands, supported by newly introduced category management resources to help retailers with plans for growing the whole category. They have benefited from the retailer viewing own-brand suppliers as more trustworthy and better placed to provide this support than branded suppliers (Table 5.20).

There was no evidence of non-collaboration work in Delta. When reviewing collaboration barriers, the largest was internal teams believing the retailer had changed and would deliver on this new way of working. Recent experience of Delta was being treated in a very short term and transactional way by the retailers, so this shift to a longer-term collaborative relationship will take time to embed (Table 5.21).

Table 5.19 Delta findings: collaboration purpose and choices

Theme	Finding	Evidence
Collaboration purpose and choices	• Collaboration purpose is using own-brands to help retailers differentiate and create footfall versus using brands	• Evidence of new requests and strategy from UK retailers in their attempt to fight off discounter growth • Branded support being removed to make space for own-brand ranges • GSCOP effect as a move to front margin from back margin helps own-brand suppliers
	• Delta corporate invested in skills and capabilities to move to a new, more collaborative relationship with customers	• Evidence of commercial roles and standards, documents, and tools • Added category resources to support customers (taking role from branded suppliers)
	• It moved to three-year JBPs to gain the increased security of a contract	• Move away from annual tendering of business • JBP with Customer A and Customer B

5 Collaboration Under the Microscope: A Cross-Case Analysis

Table 5.20 Delta findings: collaboration work

Theme	Finding	Evidence
Collaboration work	• Core work is NPD and range development for own-brand products	• Look at total cost of supply • Embedded in the new process
	• Commercial levers were developed to help Delta KAM team identify areas of focus in collaboration with customers	• Supported by tools, new ways of working, and approach
	• Retailers were outsourcing work to Delta—category support	• Customer A and Customer B headcount reductions driving new requests • Own-brand supplier trusted more than a branded supplier

Table 5.21 Delta findings: non-collaboration work and collaboration barriers

Theme	Finding	Evidence
Non-collaboration work	• No evidence	
Collaboration barriers	• Internal barriers were the biggest issue—internal teams not believing the retailer will change their ways of working (from being short term and confrontational)	• Some customers still tactical—Customer D and Customer C cited

The power theme in Delta is one of the suppliers gaining greater power in the relationship. As the retailer is struggling in the market and has identified own-brand as a key method of improving customer loyalty, they are offering Delta more opportunities to collaborate and build joint plans as a means of achieving this (Table 5.22).

Value creation in Delta is achieved by the development of a joint business plan with Customer B and Customer A. This plan details how the two parties will create value. Identifying the scorecard targets to achieve this category management work is central to this plan and the value creation activities (Table 5.23).

As above, value capture is facilitated through the joint business plan. The plan details the Delta targets for the plan, and what value they will achieve as it is implemented with each customer (Table 5.24).

Table 5.22 Delta findings: power

Theme	Finding	Evidence
Power	• Power is the greater empowerment of supplier over retailer to help them with their strategic challenges—the reverse of branded suppliers	• Retailers asking for help, support, and collaboration

Table 5.23 Delta findings: value creation

Theme	Finding	Evidence
Value creation	• JBP shows clear evidence of value creation activities and targets (capture) for supplier • Category management activities (range, space, price, promotion) are at the heart of value creation activities	• JBP in place for both major retailers • Linked to trust of own-brand supplier? • Also linked to move away from branded suppliers doing this work

Table 5.24 Delta findings: value capture

Theme	Finding	Evidence
Value capture	• There is a clear scorecard in JBP plan for Delta and retailers	• Clarity and targets not seen in any other case in this scorecard

In summary, this section has highlighted by case the themes that have emerged from the research. These themes have also been supported by the points of evidence in each of the cases. In the next section of this chapter, we will look across each theme, comparing and contrasting them in an effort to develop assertions from the cases. This process will also identify any potential gaps in knowledge and new research propositions that may further advance knowledge in this field.

Cross-Case Theme-Based Findings: Four Cases, Common Findings

Each of the themes was reviewed across all of the cases, to identify the proposed findings across all the case findings. The process to achieve this was a detailed review to extract common areas of findings. These were then developed into the initial findings and reviewed once more against themes in each case.

In summary, the research findings are provided in Table 5.25.

5 Collaboration Under the Microscope: A Cross-Case Analysis

Table 5.25 Cross-case theme findings

No.	Cross-case theme findings	Overview
1	Collaboration is a 'one-way' activity, with the supplier pushing for and 'selling' the idea to retailers	Collaboration should be a joint activity between a supplier and customer; this research indicates that the customer largely directs and 'receives' the collaboration activities
2	Suppliers are using KAM teams to manage their relationships with customers	Research indicates KAM team structures are best placed to manage the supplier to customer interface; this research indicates those structures are being used in each case
3	Collaboration work is focused on providing insights and category management recommendations	Category management activity is the main work cited in each case as evidence of the work of collaboration. Its effectiveness is under question from some of the case studies and some literature
4	Where joint business plans are not jointly developed with the customer, they focus more on a supplier's desires and targets than what they will achieve together in collaboration with a retailer	While literature cites joint business plans as an important enabler of collaboration, this research highlights the plans are often not jointly developed with customers and not accepted as a joint plan by customers
5	Power has a pervasive presence in supplier-retailer relationships, although its influence varies	Power is 'the atomic particle of all business-to-business relationships'; it was in evidence in all the cases in this research
6	Value creation is more likely to be relational than transactional	The research highlighted that in each case most of the value creation activities cited were linked to creating and maintaining a personal relationship with the customer
7	Supplier value capture lacks evidence	There was very little evidence of value capture for the supplier from their collaboration with customers. The only exception was the own-brand supplier, Delta
8	Own-brand suppliers have a greater ability to help customers differentiate and have closer collaboration than branded business	The evidence in the Delta case highlighted the different work and collaboration it was able to achieve relative to the other cases in this research

Summary and Implications of the Cross-Case Analysis

Finding 1: Collaboration Is One Way

In summary, the first research finding is collaboration appears to be a one-way activity, with the supplier using or 'selling' the idea to retailers. This is generally supportive of the literature on the desire for collaboration as indicated by Millman and Wilson (1995) but challenges the literature in two areas.

Firstly, collaboration choices not being made through the use of account segmentation, challenging recent findings by Guesalaga et al. (2018), who highlighted the importance of account selection in KAM planning. The second challenge is the absence of the use of ECR as an enabler for collaboration, rather than being central to collaboration in the industry, as previously found by Kotzab and Teller (2003).

Finding 2: KAM Teams Are the Norm for Working with Retailers

The second cross-case finding is largely supportive of the literature, in that suppliers are using KAM teams to manage their business. This confirms a considerable body of previous literature (e.g., Ryals and Rogers 2007; Brusset and Agrell 2017). The findings extend previous research by Hartmann et al. (2017) and Arnett et al. (2005), who described a general KAM team composition, by highlighting how differing sizes and compositions of KAM teams are present with different company types and supply arrangements.

Finding 3: Collaboration Is Dominated by Insights Development and Category Management

The third finding was that of collaboration work largely being the provision of insights and category management recommendations, and this is largely supportive of prior research (e.g., Desrochers et al. 2003). This finding does extend the literature on relational conflict into the grocery market context, building on Stanko et al. (2007) who carried out their work in the industrial machine manufacturing, electronic equipment, transportation equipment, and hospital industries.

Finding 4: JBPs Aren't Joint Plans Between the Retailer and Supplier

Looking at the fourth finding, there was evidence that the joint business plans are not jointly developed but are in fact internal supplier account plans. This finding is supportive of the need for an account plan for successful KAM implementation highlighted by Ryals and Rogers (2007), and also supportive of the benefits of the plan to the supplier being hard to identify (Ryals and Rogers 2007).

Finding 5: The Influence of Power Is Everywhere

The fifth finding is that power is universally present, across all the case studies. This largely confirms literature on power, and how retailers dominate suppliers in the UK Grocery Industry, as identified by researchers such as Maglaras et al. (2015), Fernie (2014), Blois (2009), and Hingley (2005). The findings extend research in this area by demonstrating that not only do customers dominate suppliers, but HOW they do this in practice, which closes a gap previously identified by Hingley et al. (2015) who stated that detailed knowledge on how power is used in this industry was lacking.

Finding 6: Value Creation Is Challenging and Often Based Just on Relationships

The sixth finding is that of value creation, and this finding is generally supportive of the literature, with Jiang et al. (2016) and Baumann et al. (2017) arguing the importance of creating contacts and relationships with customers. This finding challenges the literature with regards to relational value, revealing that this is the creation of a relationship rather than value created through joint activity, as found by Möller (2006).

Finding 7: Evidence of Value Capture Is Hard to Find

The seventh finding is that value capture from a supplier perspective lacks evidence (except in Delta). These findings in which financial value capture was rare largely challenge the literature, such as that by Songailiene et al. (2011) who argued that financial value capture should be evident in the collaboration.

These findings extend literature on the complexity of value capture into a new market context from that previously explored, for example, by Biggemann and Buttle (2012) whose research was conducted in industrial markets such as can makers and photocopier manufacturers.

Finding 8: Own-Brand Suppliers Can Create Closer Collaboration

The final finding was that own-brand suppliers appear to have a greater ability to help their customers differentiate than a branded business. This finding on own-brand suppliers challenges the theory in this industry. It specifically challenges the notion that it is larger suppliers who have most to gain from category management activities (Akçura and Ozdemir 2019).

So, what does all this mean for the future of collaboration? How do we address these issues and challenges, and manage them in the context of the wider issues and challenges discussed in Chap. 2, and the theory of Chap. 3? This will be the focus of the final chapter, 'A New model of collaboration'.

References

Akçura, M.T. and Ozdemir, Z.D. (2019) Data-driven manufacturer-retailer collaboration under competition. *Enterprise Information Systems*, 13(3), pp. 303–328.

Arnett, D.B., Macy, B.A. and Wilcox, J.B. (2005) The role of core selling teams in supplier-buyer relationships. *Journal of Personal Selling & Sales Management*, XXV(1), pp. 27–42.

Baumann, J., Le Meunier-FitzHugh, K. and Wilson, H.N. (2017) The challenge of communicating reciprocal value promises: buyer-seller value proposition disparity in professional services. *Industrial Marketing Management*, 64, pp. 107–121.

Biggemann, S. and Buttle, F. (2012) Intrinsic value of business-to-business relationships: an empirical taxonomy. *Journal of Business Research*, 65(8), pp. 1132–1138.

Blois, K. (2009) Equity within business-to-business relationships. *Journal of Marketing Management*, 25(5–6), pp. 451–459.

Brusset, X., and Agrell, P.J. (2017) Intrinsic impediments to category captainship. *Journal of Industrial and Management Optimization*, 13(1), pp. 113–133.

Dapiran, G.P. and Hogarth-Scott, S. (2003) Are co-operation and trust being confused with power? An analysis of food retailing in Australia and the UK. *International Journal of Retail and Distribution Management*, 31(5), pp. 256–267.

Desrochers, D.M., Gundlach, G.T. and Foer, A.A. (2003) Analysis of antitrust challenges to category captain arrangements. *Journal of Public Policy and Marketing*, 22(2), pp. 201–215.

Fernie, J. (2014) Relationships in the supply chain, in Fernie, J. and Sparks, L. (eds.), *Logistics and Retail Management: Emerging Issues and New Challenges in the Retail Supply Chain*, London: Kogan Page.

Gruen, T.W. and Hofstetter, J.S. (2010) The relationship marketing view of the customer and the service dominant logic perspective. *Journal of Business Market Management*, 4(4), pp. 231–245.

Guesalaga, R., Gabrielssona, M., Rogers, B., Ryals, L.J. and Marcos-Cuevas, J. (2018) Which resources and capabilities underpin strategic key account management? *Industrial Marketing Management*, 75(May 2018), pp. 160–172.

Hartmann, N.N., Wieland, H. and Vargo, S.L. (2017) Converging on a new theoretical foundation for selling. *Journal of Marketing*, 82(2), pp. 1–18.

Hingley, M. K. (2005) Power to all our friends? Living with imbalance in supplier-retailer relationships. *Industrial Marketing Management*, 34(8), pp. 848–858.

Hingley, M., Angell, R. and Lindgreen, A. (2015) The current situation and future conceptualization of power in industrial markets. *Industrial Marketing Management*, 48, pp. 226–230.

Jiang, Z., Shiu, E., Henneberg, S. and Naudè, P. (2016) Relationship quality in business-to-business relationships—Reviewing the current literatures and proposing a new measurement model. *Psychology & Marketing*, 33(4), pp. 297–313.

Kotzab, H. and Teller, C. (2003). Value-adding partnerships and co-opetition models in the grocery industry. *International Journal of Physical Distribution and Logistics Management*, 33(3), pp. 268–281.

Lindblom, A. and Olkkonen, R. (2008) An analysis of suppliers' roles in category management collaboration. *Journal of Retailing and Consumer Services*, 15(1), pp. 1–8.

Maglaras, G., Bourlakis, M. and Fotopoulos, C. (2015) Power-imbalanced relationships in the dyadic food chain: An empirical investigation of retailers' commercial practices with suppliers. *Industrial Marketing Management*, 48, pp. 187–201.

Marcos-Cuevas, J., Nätti, S., Palo, T. and Ryals, L.J. (2014) Implementing key account management: Intraorganizational practices and associated dilemmas. *Industrial Marketing Management*, 43(7), pp. 1216–1224.

Millman, T. and Wilson, K. (1995) From key account selling to key account management. *Journal of Marketing Practice: Applied Marketing Science*, 1(1), pp. 9–21.

Möller, K.E.K. (2006) Role of competences in creating customer value: a value-creation logic approach. *Industrial Marketing Management*, 35(8), pp. 913–924.

Ryals, L.J. and Rogers, B. (2007) Key account planning: benefits, barriers and best practice. *Journal of Strategic Marketing*, 15(2), pp. 209–222.

Songailiene, E., Winklhofer, H. and McKechnie, S. (2011) A conceptualisation of supplier perceived value. *European Journal of Marketing*, 45(3), pp. 383–418.

Stanko, M.A., Bonner, J.M. and Calantone, R.J. (2007) Building commitment in buyer-seller relationships: a tie strength perspective. *Industrial Marketing Management*, 36(8), pp. 1094–1103.

6

The New Model of Collaboration

So here we are, at the point where all the challenges and opportunities before us come together. We have discussed a wealth of trends, ideas, and examples. We have seen research from four different cases on what the 'real world' activities are in collaboration, and how those businesses collaborate to create and capture value. All of this is important, but what matters is how we now act based on this knowledge. The question before us is this—'What steps can we take next towards creating more meaningful and effective collaboration between retailers and suppliers?'

What I am proposing are areas of focus for us to consider as industry partners. Many of the solutions are supplier focussed, but retailers could adapt and use most of these as well. We know there is so much common work in collaboration between the two parties.

These are my thoughts on starting this crucial debate. They are not offered as a definitive one-off answer since all of you work for businesses of different sizes, scale, and ambition. Rather, they are offered with the intent of inviting you to engage in a new way of envisioning collaboration—a collaboration that is effective and meaningful for all the parties involved. By thinking about how you might apply the ideas and prompts that follow to your particular business, you will become better positioned to invigorate and transform the collaborative efforts you are engaged in.

I do not think that the solutions in the areas we have discussed will be found in a vast new set of tools and processes (I know this is heresy coming from a consultant!). What we need more of is a *willingness to face the issues and challenges before us*, and to *change our mindset* towards an alternative approach. I would like to suggest that you look at my ideas as a basis for doing just that—as prompts to help you develop creative solutions in these areas and vehicles for taking a leap of trust that will allow you to face these sometimes uncomfortable areas.

I believe this is a discussion we, as industry, need to have right now. Here are my ideas to start that conversation.

We have seen that there are multiple dynamics that are transforming the relationship between the retailer of the supplier, and they have now come to a crunch point. Let's summarise the current status for retailers, suppliers, and consumer/shoppers, and why there is now the need for an alternative approach (Fig. 6.1).

- Retailers
    - Retailer growth is slowing, and costs are increasing.
    - Omni-channel is providing incredible complexity and cost challenges, alongside new opportunity areas.
    - Retailers are looking to pass on these pressures to suppliers, jeopardising the work of collaboration in the future.

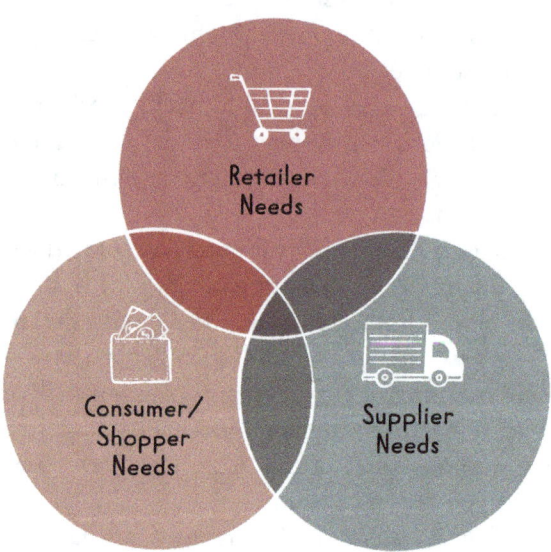

Fig. 6.1 Triple Win needs. (Source: Adapted from Shepherd 2014)

- Suppliers
  - Suppliers are consolidating to increase costs efficiencies with decreasing effectiveness.
  - Globalisation of supplier commercial functions is creating efficiencies but causing challenges locally.
  - Supplier category management work is changing, within the suppliers, and between themselves and the retailer.
- Consumers and shoppers
  - Consumer choices and habits are transforming across many product categories.
  - There is a danger of commoditisation of some categories as the retail experience and offer declines versus other alternatives.
  - Younger consumers and shoppers have very different habits to their predecessors and could cause another major shift in industry dynamics.

A manifesto for change in the industry

The Future Landscape: Foundation Principles

So, having discussed all the challenges that we're facing, some of them substantial, how can the industry move forward? It feels like now is the time we need to be honest with each other as retailers and suppliers—honest about what we need in terms of value, which can shape our collaboration in the future. The aim must be collaboration to deliver value growth for both parties, not just one at the expense of the other. If we don't do this, then the industry will continue to struggle to address the issues it faces.

I am proposing the following three principles, which will underpin the new model and tools that follow (Fig. 6.2).

Principle 1: Partner Choice

We cannot collaborate strategically with everyone, and nor should we. There are typically only a few truly collaborative partnerships we should focus on. This means we need to build a robust and honest segmentation of customers and suppliers, that is lived and not just a paper exercise. From a supplier perspective, this means a fresh approach to understanding which customers to collaborate with, and how that collaboration will work. For retailers, the same

Fig. 6.2 Foundation principles

principles apply for supplier segmentation, just mirrored in terms of the analysis that they will do. The important principle here, based on the research findings, is not just undertaking the segmentation exercise, but really living the implications that come from it.

Principle 2: Honesty and Transparency

There is a need to move to a collaborative relationship based on honesty and transparency. One factor clear in the research was a misunderstanding or lack of understanding from the supplier about what the retailers' actual needs were and the time scales that they were working on. In addition, sometimes, suppliers themselves were unclear on the value they were looking for and how they would generate and capture it. There needs to be much more openness and transparency on identifying the objectives of both the retailer and the supplier from the start.

Principle 3: Trust

Building on honesty and transparency is the principle of trust. Both retailer and supplier need to be in a position where they trust that each party is aiming to meet the other's needs. It was clear in the research that this trust was often missing, resulting in a combative and sometimes secretive relationship, with each side not willing to collaborate fully.

It's a common truth that retailers and suppliers are both trying to grow their business. They're both trying to achieve this growth by better understanding and meeting their mutual consumer and shopper needs. To achieve this, mutual trust needs to be in place. There needs to be this recognition from retailer and supplier that they are in a better place if they help each other, versus competing, as currently appears to be the case.

The Future Landscape: Opportunities for Growth

If these are our underlying principles for a new future of collaboration, what then are our opportunities for growth. They are (Fig. 6.3):

1. Value creation and capture
2. Category management transformation
3. Mastering power

Opportunity 1: Value Creation and Capture

Value creation and capture have two areas of opportunity to improve for the retailer and supplier in their collaboration. These opportunity areas focus on both transactional and relational value creation and capture.

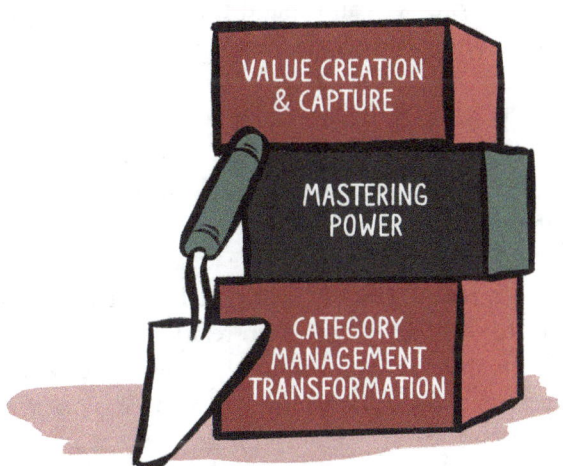

Fig. 6.3 Opportunities for growth

New Technology

I believe a key part of future value creation will be the adoption and utilisation of new technologies. In recent years, we have seen a rapid growth of technologies that can transform the work that is core to retailer and supplier collaboration. What areas can this new technology help in? The first is in the automation of day-to-day tasks, particularly area of data reporting and insight generation, and in category management tools such as range and space planning, as well as pricing and promotion planning.

Automation is now available that can gather multiple data sources, clean that data, and develop management reports. Some can now generate a high level of quality insights which can directly link into category management activities. These new tools are getting more powerful and provide a way to develop a single source of truth for both the retailer and supplier to collaborate around.

The benefit to both the retailer and supplier is that this automation can significantly reduce the amount of headcount that is needed to create these reports and develop insights. Moving to use technology in these tasks will reduce the amount of 'people bias', so rather than the insight development being that of the supplier or the retailer, it's a 'third party' developing the insight. This can help enable a more solid basis for developing joint business plans.

In addition, new technology can help support us in the day-to-day communication between the retailer and the supplier. Retailers and suppliers have already taken this approach in the areas of order management, order transfer, order capture, and so on. We can expand this into covering off some of the day-to-day transactional discussions between an account manager and a retailer.

The recent challenges of COVID-19 have forced a remote model of communication between a retailer and supplier, be that through email or video conferencing and calls. Some retailers have reported the impact as positive, with the benefit being more efficient interactions between retailer and supplier, and this could be a precursor to more areas of work transformation.

These changes can reduce costs and potentially increase transactional value creation. Whilst they may seem to worsen relational value, they could in fact allow the people involved to spend more time on higher value, higher order tasks. In my experience, the valuable time in collaboration is face-to-face creation of initiatives and ideas, where the human element of the co-creation builds more powerful solutions and creates agreement from both sides.

Relational Value

The research clearly cited the personal relationship between the retailer and the supplier as an area of value creation. This relational value clearly depends on the people involved on each side of the relationship, and the nature of that relationship between the different people in the organisation. Taking a Key Account Management approach means that there are often many people across both the retailer and the supplier who are interacting with each other, and they typically need coordination through the Key Account Management team and through the buyer in the retailer's case. As discussed, I argue that these interactions are best focussed mostly on the joint creation of ideas and initiatives.

In addition, I propose we develop the Key Account Manager as a role. I would like to see the key account manager lead as a facilitator of developing the joint business between the retailer and supplier. This is not new and is a foundation of KAM theory. However, the research showed that this focus on facilitating the relationship is not happening consistently, or at a high enough level between the two businesses.

Introducing new technology to remove many of the lower order tasks that currently take up a sizeable amount of time and energy from key account managers and their teams should release time for KAM leadership. This will enable more time to be spent ensuring the role focuses on facilitating the joint working between the retailer and supplier.

Opportunity 2: Category Management Transformation

The most important work in the research that delivered collaboration was that of category management. In light of its heightened importance, how do we transform category management? I argue that the fundamental questions posed by category management are as valid as ever. Dr Brian Harris built the 8-step process as a sound strategic planning process. The questions in each step are as valid today as ever. However, how we answer them, and who does the work, needs to change in the future. I propose improvements to the work and the process of category management later in this chapter in an effort to bring up to date the category management process. At the strategic level, I think there is an improvement to be made that can change the way we work in category management in terms of our collaboration with retailers.

I am also advocating the combination of the two areas of 'category manager' and 'key account manager'. As sales management practice has developed, there has been an emergence and development of 'consultative selling' (Rackham). This selling approach proposes starting with understanding your customers' needs and working back from that to facilitate your organisation to deliver against those needs. It is a world away from old-school selling, which is a focus on product features and benefits and trying to match and sell those to customers.

Opportunity 3: Mastering Power

It's clear from the research that the power dynamic between the retail and the supplier has a massive impact on the current nature of relationships, and the ability for each party to create and capture value. The way the power dynamic is managed needs to change if we are to transform the way we create and capture value in collaboration.

As discussed, the search for cost reduction has fuelled the drive for never-ending consolidation. In order to mitigate that power, each side is running out of road in terms of its ability to consolidate further to meet the needs for the future of the industry. What we need now is honesty in our discussion about the power issues, or, in some cases, we just need to initiate that discussion for the first time.

Each side needs to recognise that both parties will hold power and that the power is not there to be used destructively but is more around how to combine the strength of each side to better grow the business for each other.

What does this mean in practical terms? Well, in one respect, it means that when deciding on which partners to select, we recognise the power of each side, and we manage the implications. For example, smaller suppliers with fewer resources may need more help and support than a larger, more powerful partner. We need to recognise that power differences exist and that the power isn't there to be used as a weapon against each other, but rather as a force for change and growth when combined.

This also means that where there isn't a mutual benefit, where the power dynamic is likely to be destructive, the most productive way to work together may be in a transactional relationship. This isn't a bad thing. It's more that it is a more appropriate way of working, and recognises that there are barriers in place, so a collaborative partnership at that moment in time probably isn't the best way to work together. As we saw in the research, too often suppliers carried on trying to collaborate, even when the retailer was exerting their power to make short-term demands that were undermining the relationship.

The New Model of Collaboration

In order to capitalise on the opportunities highlighted and move to a fresh approach for the industry, I am proposing a new model of collaboration. This model builds on what exists in the industry, but also proposes some additional steps and enhancements for others. Figure 6.4 highlights the model.

The model provides a high-level framework and is designed to be a starting point for a discussion. Because it cannot provide all the details needed for each organisational situation, it would need to be adapted to reflect the unique needs of a particular business.

What do each of these steps involve?

1. Omni-channel mindset—mapping our target customers and their shopper journeys to inform all the planning we do as a commercial organisation.
2. Collaborative partner selection—who we choose to work with and how.

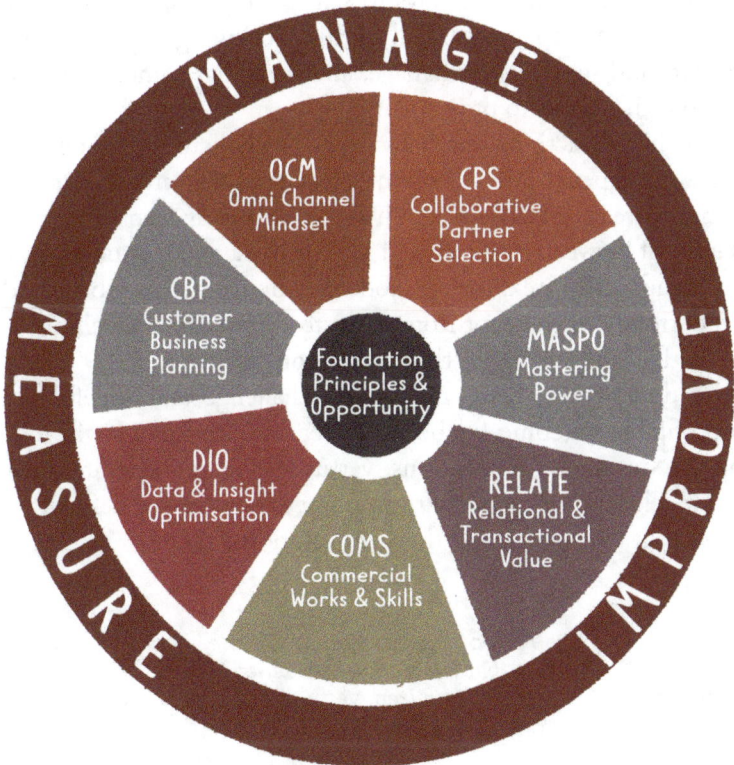

Fig. 6.4 The new model of collaboration

3. Mastering power—what is the status of power in our relationship and what does it mean for collaboration?
4. Relational and transactional value—what is the value we seek and how do we capture it?
5. Commercial work and skills—what will be the work and skills to enable the new future?
6. Data and insights optimisation—how can we transform the way we develop and use insights in our collaboration with partners
7. Customer business planning—how do we enhance how we plan and activate together in collaboration?

1. OCM: Omni-Channel Mindset

Over the last ten years, the landscape for FMCG retail has changed beyond recognition, with the explosive growth of online retailing, and other digital channels leading us to today's environment of 'omni-channel' retailing. This growth is not just in different ways to sell to shoppers, it's also a means to communicate with them as well. All of this is bringing added complexity to both retailers and suppliers to manage, and with that comes increased costs, and therefore challenges to profitability.

What is the impact? Research by Bain is predicting a potential 150% growth in weekly penetration of online shopping across many global markets over the next three years. This research also estimates an impact for grocers on their margin of between -11% and -15%, clearly a major issue for profitability. Even though there are different models for online delivery, be they delivering from current store base, or from dark stores dedicated warehouses, all are margin dilutive, and the fix for this is not short term.

So, what do you do to better manage the challenge, and hopefully move to a more profitable outcome for both retailer and supplier? I will focus here more on the demand side solutions, versus the supply side areas (different delivery models, etc.). A good starting point is how do we define the omni-channel, so that we can develop the right solutions.

> *The synergetic management of the numerous available channels and customer touchpoints, in such a way that the customer experience across channels and the performance over channels is optimized.* Verhoef et al. (2015)

Omni-channel is founded on the 'synergistic management' of multiple channels. Given that the two major thrusts of this definition are those of 'experience' and 'performance'. The first step is to understand for your target shopper (s) the journeys (experience) they have for buying your products/services, and then measuring their behaviour (performance). Understanding this for the target shopper groups is foundational to all that follows. We operate many processes for planning in commercial organisations; I argue that this mapping needs to be the new foundation to everything that follows.

In 2012, I was part of a cross-industry group that worked with ECR Europe to develop thinking around this need to respond to the omni-channel challenge. We developed a framework (playbook) on managing the consumer and shopper journey (ECR Europe 2011). One of the central recommendations in that report was using the need to understand the consumer-shopper journey, and what their needs are at each step. From this understanding, we developed and deployed the relevant strategies and tactics.

I highlight the models in Figs. 6.5 and 6.6.

The aim of this model is to represent in one place how specific target consumer/shoppers navigate their journey. The example shown is a fictional example for mums of smaller families on a bulk grocery shopping with

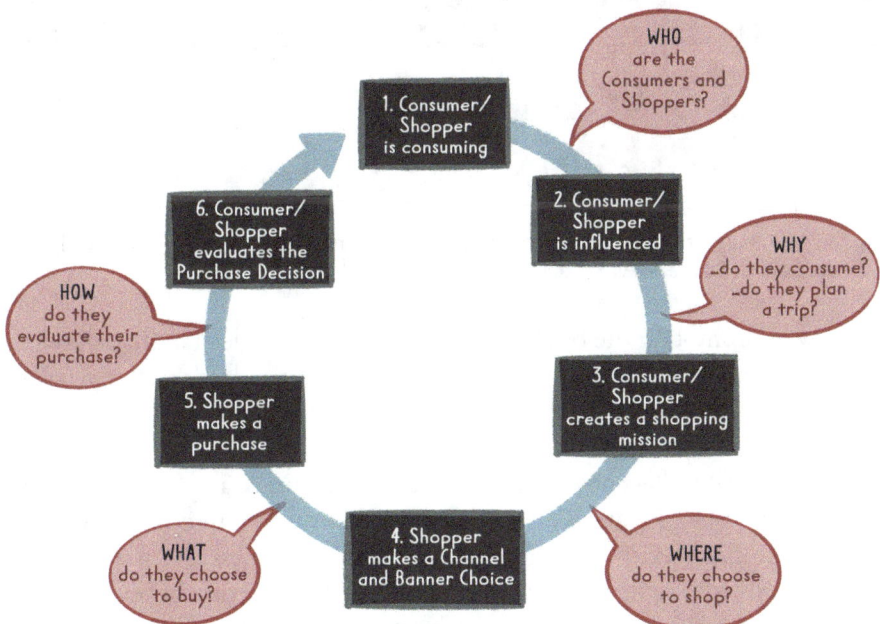

Fig. 6.5 Consumer and shopper journey overview. (Source: Adapted from ECR Europe, CS&J Framework 2011)

C&SJ INSIGHTS SUMMARY FOR:	MUMS OF SMALLER FAMILIES, BULK GROCERY SHOP IN B&M OUTLETS, SOFT DRINKS (FICTIONAL)						
JOURNEY STEPS/ LEAD QUESTIONS	DECISIONS MADE TO BUILD JOURNEY	WHAT THEY DO/SPEND		KEY REASONS/ MOTIVATIONS	HOW CAN THEY BE INFLUENCED?	WHAT ARE THE KEY OPPORTUNITIES?	OPPORTUNITY VALUE? (€)
		ALL CATEGORIES	FOCUS CATEGORY(IES)				
1. Consumer/ Shopper is Consuming 2. Consumer/ Shopper is Influenced	What are their Consumption Behaviors & Motivations?	Focus is on the Take Home Soft Drinks category.	N/A	- Household consumes 163 litres of soft drinks - Average 12 drinking cc'ns per week - 38% of home meals involve a soft drink - 25% consumption by kids	- "Quench thirst" = •1 - "Keep kids happy" = •2 - Mum is gatekeeper for kids	- Key meal types more likely to drive soft drinks consumption e.g. xxxx - When it's gone it's gone, soft drinks not a driver of trip planning	- Increasing number of meals where a soft drink is consumed from 38% to 42% would be worth +10% growth with this segment	€6m in the market

Fig. 6.6 Consumer and shopper journey opportunity mapping. (Source: Adapted from ECR Europe, CS&J Framework 2011)

C&SJ BUSINESS PLANNING SUMMARY	
TARGET SHOPPER SEGMENT:	Young Mums of Smaller Families
TARGET CONSUMER/SHOPPER JOURNEY:	Bulk Grocery Shop in Brick & Mortar Hypermarkets with a focus on buying Meals for the Family at Retailer X
HIGH LEVEL SHOPPER STRATEGY:	Convert Young Mums to shop at Retailer X using Soft Drinks
TARGET CATEGORIES & PRODUCTS:	Primary: Quick and Easy Family Meals, Secondary: Soft Drinks
TARGET BEHAVIOUR CHANGE:	Increase conversion at Retailer X of Target Shopper, Increase Conversion of Soft Drinks increasing from A to B will be worth €Xm

JOURNEY STEPS/ LEAD QUESTIONS	OPPORTUNITIES FROM C&SJ INSIGHT MODEL (To guide Business Planning Choices)	TOUCH POINTS	BUSINESS PLANNING: MARKETING PROGRAMME/TACTICAL IMPLICATIONS						
			SHOPPER MARKETING COMMUNICATION	CATEGORY MANAGEMENT TACTICS				OPERATIONAL TACTICS Inc. Customer Service	JBP IMPLICATIONS
				ASSORTMENT	MERCH	PRICE	PROMO		
1. Consumer/ Shopper is Consuming 2. Consumer/ Shopper is Influenced	Increasing number of meals where a soft drink is consumed from 38% to 42% would be worth +10% growth with this segment	CONSUME Stimulate Consumption	TV and Press Advertising using the Big Night In theme - showing great meal times as a family with a Soft Drink						JBP focus on large pack mix shift for Retailer X

Fig. 6.7 Consumer and shopper journey activation mapping. (Source: Adapted from ECR Europe, CS&J Framework 2011)

strategy of promoting the buying of soft drinks. This understanding allows us to identify the opportunities, the size of them, and then leads to the development of activities (strategies and tactics) that will address the opportunities (Fig. 6.7).

This approach offers a way to structure our consumer and shopper understanding and plan the omni-channel activity. However, it undoubtedly introduces more complexity into the business planning process and requires new insights and work to develop the plan. This complexity exists in both the way the retailer and supplier collaborate to share insights that each party holds, as well as within the supplier.

Why is this the case? The planning tools combine areas which would traditionally be the responsibility of marketing teams in a supplier (consumer insights, advertising tactics) as well as others that are the responsibility of category management and sales (shopper data, in-store activities). In addition, it also requires the addition of retailer-specific data. I propose that this challenge is opening up opportunities into how to better organise the work of a supplier. These opportunities exist in the work of the commercial team, and the creation of 'one-demand' group, and in the data and insights that fuel the omni-channel understanding. I will explore both themes more deeply later in this chapter.

Retailers are well aware of the value of the insights they are now developing. As far back as 1994, when Tesco developed its Clubcard, it started leveraging the value of this data by selling it to suppliers. This trend has continued. Walmart, which always saw data as a fundamental driver of retailer and supplier collaboration, has now stated their intent to sell their data for the first time (Neff 2021). This trend will continue, as retailers look to monetise any area of their business they can, in order to mitigate the increased costs of omni-channel management (Kamel et al. 2020).

Omni-Channel Insights Focus on Future Value Creation

What does all this mean? I propose that access to the right data and insights to develop a deeper understanding will become a new focus of collaboration between suppliers and retailers. This will be the area that both sides need to make central to their collaborative work. We can now automate much of the traditional 'work' of collaboration, especially in traditional category management areas and in the management of data and insights (I will discuss later this in this chapter). However, what cannot be replaced is the skill of those with a high level of expertise regarding retailers and suppliers who need to translate these insights into the 'so what' and 'now what' of directing the business through the ever-changing omni-channel dynamic.

The value of data and insights will increase for both retailer and supplier, and, as a result, the sharing of these data sets is a large area for value creation for both sides. When looking for collaborative partners, it will be vital that we factor in the access and expertise with data into making choices on who to collaborate with. This will also be an area that naturally holds less conflict since the principal aim is enhancing consumer and shopper understanding on both sides. This can then be the cornerstone of the joint business plan. Said differently, 'who can give me access to the best data and insights' will become just as important in the collaborative work as who can offer the greatest sales potential for my products.

Retailers are clearly keen to sell this data, and, even more so, sell marketing programmes that result from the insights. I propose retailers should think hard about the barriers to collaboration they could build with these plans. I believe there is an opportunity for retailers to 'invest' with their suppliers, allowing low/no cost access to some data sets, that will enable more productive and greater value creation with each other.

In Summary

- Omni-channel understanding and planning is the foundation of all the work of collaboration that follows between retailers and suppliers.
- The demand for additional work and insights can fuel positive changes in the collaboration work.
- Omni-channel insights will be a key value creation area for retailers and suppliers in their collaborative work in the future.

2. CPS: Collaborative Partner Selection

Most of us are aware of the principles of segmenting customers and suppliers in order to prioritise who to work with. However, as we have seen from the research, there are challenges to be addressed in how well this is working. I identified two significant questions that need to be addressed. First, what method can be used in the segmentation that will accurately reflect the level of priority for a customer, not just from a financial perspective, but also in terms of the customer's motivation and ability to collaborate successfully? Second, how do we actually follow through on the segmentation's outputs, and 'live' the direction it is giving us?

Partner Segmentation Methodology

Classically, when developing a segmentation, when looking at measures of priority or importance, we look at a basket of metrics, such as:

- Sales
- Profit
- Margin
- Growth potential

These are all useful, but when examined in isolation, it becomes apparent that they do not build in an understanding of the reality of collaboration in terms of the 'how'?

Looking specifically at suppliers, retailers will differ in their motivation to collaborate. Their organisational approach to collaboration can drive this, some being set up for collaboration, believing it to be core to their business. Walmart would be a good example of this.

Sam Walton's Ten Rules for Building a Business

1. Commit to your business.
2. Share your profits with all your associates and treat them as partners.
3. Motivate your partners.
4. Communicate everything you possibly can to your partners.
5. Appreciate everything your associates do for the business.
6. Celebrate your success.
7. Listen to everyone in your company.
8. Exceed your customers' expectations.
9. Control your expenses better than your competition.
10. Swim upstream.

The more they (suppliers) know, the more they'll understand. The more they understand, the more they'll care. Once they care, there's no stopping them.
   Source: Walmart Corporate Website

Others are less motivated. Either strategically collaboration isn't important for them, or, at the category level, their business does not see the value of collaboration. Where could this be the case? In commodity product categories, a retail customer may see the primary way to work with suppliers is purely transactional; lowest prices and lowest costs, with any other 'work' outside of this is a distraction.

It's important we understand this motivation level. It's also important that we ally this to an understanding of the ability of the customer to work together on the collaborative ideas that are generated. As discussed, many retailers have reduced headcount and resources at the head office level, so whilst they may like the idea of collaboration, they do not have the resources to commit to it. An example of one solution would be the supplier providing the resources (as discussed previously) for reporting and insights.

My proposed base-line questions for this segmentation approach are:

- What is the partner's level of **commitment** to collaborate relative to other customers?
- What is their **capability** to collaborate relative to other customers?

When we combine this with the more traditional sales, profit, and margin-type analysis, we can develop a more powerful segmentation (Fig. 6.8).

Collaborative customers are the most appropriate partners for full collaboration. They have the highest levels of commitment and capability to work together. They are deserving of an investment of people, data, insights, and other resources to unlock the potential of the collaboration.

Light-touch customers, although important, are not showing the commitment and capability to collaborate. We should manage them with more focus on day-to-day issues and activities, with fewer resources and investments into any collaborative work.

By contrast, test-and-learn customers are committed and capable, but currently less important. They are ideal candidates for a limited test-and-learn approach, where if they do not work as well as expected, the business risk is lower. Transactional customers are clearly those that should have the least investment and resources to manage them, as they neither have importance to the business, nor a broader significance.

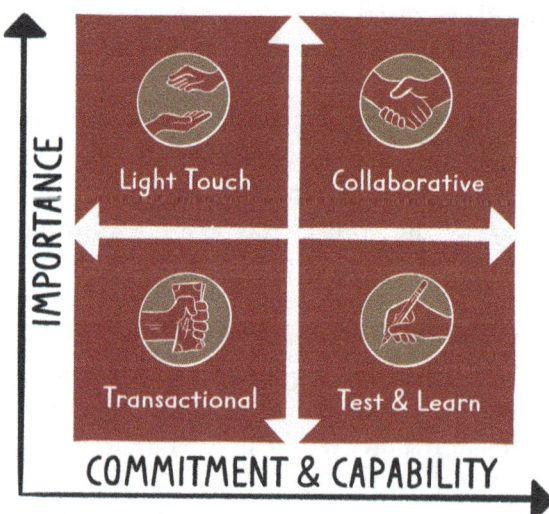

Fig. 6.8 Partner segmentation

Utilising this approach for customer segmentation provides a more realistic view of where collaboration versus a transactional relationship is appropriate. This is just the first step, though. The second issue uncovered in the research was 'living' the implications of the segmentation. Let's recall that the research showed that, even when suppliers decided on their customer segmentation, they would then ignore them, causing issues further down the road in terms of conflict and wasted investment in customers.

What does 'living' the segmentation mean? I propose it's being clear on what work you will, but just as crucially, will NOT do with that customer. This can be an uncomfortable place for a supplier organisation, especially if a customer makes requests that are outside what they have decided for them in the segmentation.

I would go back to our foundation principles, honesty, transparency, and trust; these are discussions to have with partners on the most appropriate ways of working, and if needed, what would need to change in the relationship for the ways of working to change?

In Summary

- Partner selection is crucial to identify the most appropriate ways of working between the two organisations.
- The commitment and capability of a potential partner are equally important as financial metrics for developing a partner segmentation.
- The partner segmentation should drive the work of the partnership—what we will and crucially will not do together.

3. MASPO: Mastering Power

The influence of power, as we saw in the research, is pervasive in the industry. It can often be the unseen 'atomic particle' (Dapiran and Hogarth-Scott 2003) in the relationship. Seen or unseen, it is having a dramatic impact on the collaboration between retailer and supplier, and rarely is this impact one used for the good of both parties.

The research showed many examples of where power was used to leverage a demand on suppliers, often short term, and often accompanied by punitive actions at the same time until they met the demand. This cannot be viable behaviour into the future if the industry is to grow together. There is a difference between negotiation and threats to business, and we need to address this if we are to thrive and grow together as an industry.

The big question is how! It's a behaviour that is well understood, but hard to address, even when called out by government enquiries or adjudicators. The step I am proposing is to pause, and better understand what the power dynamic is, as well as its implications, before driving further down the road of collaboration.

Building on the previous segmentation step, I would propose an analysis that checks the proposed level of collaboration against the power dynamic between the retailer and supplier, using the 'power–benefit matrix'. Figure 6.9 was adapted from the work of Cowan et al. (2015).

As we can see, in the MAPO Matrix, an Exploitative Relationship is one where the retailer is highly coercive, and the supplier is getting below-expected business results. The supplier is working with this retailer probably due to lack of options and will probably experience a very transactional way of working. It's doubtful in these cases that a collaborative approach would work, even if it were appropriate. The commercial benefits in this relationship are often skewed to the retailer, and the supplier may be constantly looking to leave/change the relationship to improve the benefits.

When looking at a 'Tolerable Relationship', we can see that it is but a small step on from the Exploitive Relationship, so the business benefits are what the supplier is expecting, or greater. In other respects, it exhibits very similar characteristics to the Exploitative Relationship, in terms of lack of collaboration and looking for routes to change/leave the relationship.

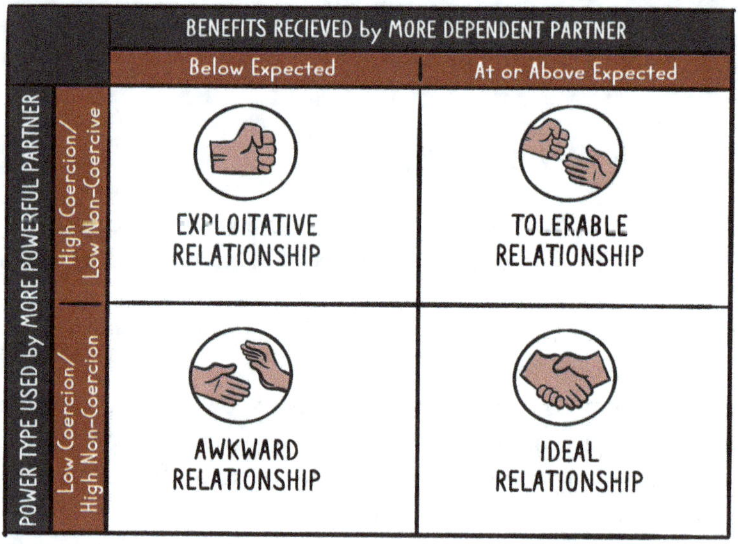

POWER TYPE USED by MORE POWERFUL PARTNER	BENEFITS RECIEVED by MORE DEPENDENT PARTNER	
	Below Expected	At or Above Expected
High Coercion/ Low Non-Coercive	EXPLOITATIVE RELATIONSHIP	TOLERABLE RELATIONSHIP
Low Coercion/ High Non-Coercion	AWKWARD RELATIONSHIP	IDEAL RELATIONSHIP

Fig. 6.9 Mastering power matrix. (Source: Adapted from Cowan et al. 2015)

The 'Awkward Relationship' is one where commercial and business results are low. This can mean that they often base the relationship on the personal (relational) benefits rather than business benefits and it may be one where the supplier can increase the business returns through negotiation.

The final and perhaps most elusive relationship is the 'Ideal Relationship'. Here, there is a mutual agreement on dependency, and both the personal and business relationships are strong. Collaboration in these situations is appropriate. The only 'danger' may be too much dependency on each other.

Mapping the current situation into this analysis can be very informative as it speaks to the potential for success for the proposed way of working identified in the partner selection step. This analysis maps the power dynamic onto those choices and gives guidance on what may be the reality versus the intended theoretical way of working (Fig. 6.10).

What this means is that even if we identify a strategic relationship as such, should we actually aim to develop that strategic relationship with the customer? The power dynamic may tell us right now that this approach will have a low chance of success. How do we deal with this? I propose we go back to our foundation principles of honesty and transparency. We could discuss together why the current power dynamic is causing the challenge and identify how to fix it. Or we could accept it isn't changing right now and decide that we shouldn't collaborate together right now.

Using the two analyses together gives some powerful direction on the level of collaboration that could be appropriate. It highlights that in the FMCG market currently, with the balance of power being where it is, the opportunity for a truly collaborative relationship may only exist in a select set of circumstances.

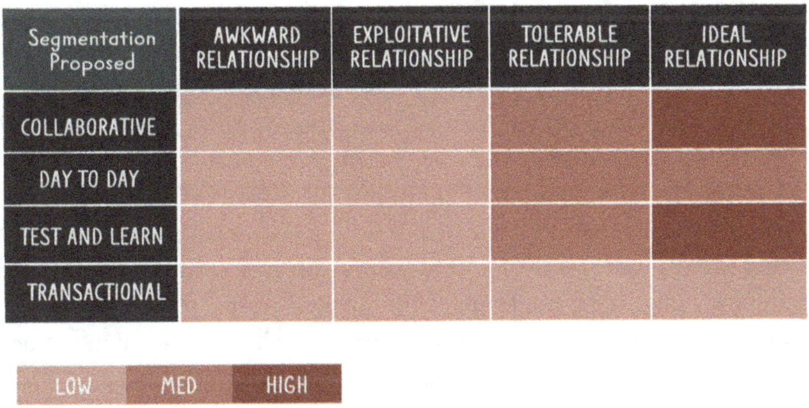

Segmentation Proposed	AWKWARD RELATIONSHIP	EXPLOITATIVE RELATIONSHIP	TOLERABLE RELATIONSHIP	IDEAL RELATIONSHIP
COLLABORATIVE				
DAY TO DAY				
TEST AND LEARN				
TRANSACTIONAL				

LOW | MED | HIGH

Fig. 6.10 Mastering power—proposed collaboration × power status

All the steps we have covered in the process have implications for the work and skills of the teams involved, and this is the area we will cover next.

In Summary

- The influence of power in the relationship is always present, even if unsaid, and can have a profound effect on the success of collaboration.
- Utilising a simple analysis can map where the power dynamic sits right now in the relationship, and what this means for the potential success of a collaborative relationship.
- The need to 'live' the outcome of the power analysis is as important as doing the analysis itself.

4. COMS: Commercial Work and Skills

We have seen in the discussion so far, some far-reaching effects on the way collaboration between retailers and suppliers can change into the future. This is bound to have a significant impact on the work of supplier commercial teams. The current work and skills model is based on an operating model and way of working that is at least 20 years old and doesn't look significantly different in terms of approach. Yes, titles have changed, headcounts have been reduced, but largely the same sales and marketing structures exist.

Even as new disciplines have emerged, such as category management, shopper marketing, or more recently RGM, they have often been incorporated into either team, or created a lot of debate on where they should sit and what roles are needed. In fact, I believe the time is right to look again at sales and marketing as a whole. The way that commercial teams (sales and marketing) are now asked to operate is so different from where it started. The sales team is increasingly the buyer and user of retailer-specific data and retailer-specific marketing solutions. RGM is setting pricing and promotion strategies for brands. The time is right to relook at the whole commercial teams work and skills.

Before moving onto proposed solutions, all organisations need to create structures based on the work that needs doing. As we have seen, this work is changing rapidly and is only going to be transformed further into the future, as technology takes a greater share of the work of teams.

If we look into the commercial organisation and how the work may change, we can identify areas for transformation. Clearly, this is a prediction, and not all the themes proposed here may come to pass. However, what is certain is that there is a rapid change underway at all levels in commercial organisations in the FMCG industry and the response to these needs to be swift and decisive if we are to avoid the challenges and dangers discussed earlier in this chapter (Table 6.1).

Table 6.1 The changing nature of commercial organisations' work and skills

Work/skill area	From	To
Collaboration	• One-off activity/event-based collaboration • Focus on tactical and short-term activity • Reporting and insights focussed	• Joint value creation collaboration focus • Clear strategic direction to frame short-term activity • Action and implementation focused
Sales	• Brand selling focussed • Admin and reporting emphasis • Multiple short-term negotiation events	• Category-centred selling approach • AI taking the admin and reporting burden • Increased focus on strategic negotiation and embedding collaborative value creation activities
Category management	• Short-term focus on responding to customer questions and requests • Category insights reports as the mechanism for thought leadership • Developing category 'stories' for KAM teams	• Omni-channel perspective allied with a medium- to longer-term focus on the 'what' and 'so what' to drive category growth • Category strategy activation focus to deliver medium- and longer-term growth • AI taking the tactical 4P development tasks • Enabling the KAM team to collaborate and adjust with speed
Revenue growth management	• Analytic and reporting focus • Brand focus without customer and category context	• AI taking the analytic and reporting burden • Category and customer focus with brand integration • Medium- to longer-term focus on the 'what' and 'so what' to drive category and brand growth • Enable an integrated RGM—category management approach to customers
Category and shopper insights	• Ad hoc briefing and analysing research • Developing insights reports	• AI taking the analytic and reporting burden • Focus is supporting the 'what and so what' of insights as inputs into collaboration and category management activities • Insights team lead the development of AI/ML capability in the commercial function

What are the overarching themes of this model? I am proposing that overall collaboration moves from an 'event based' activity to one that's focussed on joint value creation. Further, that freed of the short-term activity focus, more emphasis can be placed on directing the collaboration into medium-term value creation activities.

I am proposing that the sales function becomes more strategically focussed, with day-to-day tasks and analysis taken over by automation solutions. In addition, that the negotiation focus which is currently often dominated by multiple short-term events is replaced with an increase in focus on strategic negotiations that embed joint value creation plans.

Category management needs to change emphasis from being more a reactive function, both for customers and internally, to a thought leadership area. This can again be enabled by technology taking away the people-intensive areas of 4P development and reporting. This can create space for the thought leadership work that category teams are best placed to deliver.

RGM needs to evolve to create and embed the work into the category and customer needs. This can enable a more seamless link with brand and category teams, so one approach is seen by customers in an integrated way. And finally, the work of insights teams are transformed through automation to re-focus the efforts of teams on the future thinking related to 'what' and 'so what' questions.

Role of the Commercial Team: One Demand Team

The need now is to have one demand management function in a supplier. If we are to capitalise as an industry on the omni-channel opportunity, we must reflect the change and follow the omni-channel consumer and shopper. Recent research by Kantar (Szahun and Dalton 2021) showed that only 17% of brand leaders surveyed felt like they were organised for e-commerce.

The current organisation approach of structures in silos is placing barriers to getting to the right understanding of the 'what and why' of the omni-channel, never mind the development of plans that would allow us to address the opportunities. Having teams split across functions creates a barrier between expertise and data that puts in place obstacles to developing and executing the right solutions.

Suppliers can learn from retailers. Their sole focus is on their shoppers, and how do they understand and meet their needs. They align every other team with this goal. In suppliers, it's often the marketing/brand function that leads, which creates a different starting point and perspective for planning.

I recall from my time in Tesco that Terry Leahy, then CEO, would tell us to focus on *'following the shopper, and work out how to make money later .... be first and the customer rewards you for doing it for them .... be second, and the customer thinks you are doing it for yourself'*. This simple but clear direction aimed to keep the commercial organisation focussed on what was important: shoppers!

A move to a combined 'demand-generation' group will remove barriers, and make the teams involved, consumer-shopper, and customer focussed in an integrated way, versus right now being in separate silos. In addition, with the complexity of the customer base increasing all the time for suppliers, cost pressure will inevitably drive a rethink on how best to efficiently manage this area of the business.

What this looks like for individual business will clearly vary but having one team under one leader will enable the silos between sales and marketing to be broken and ensure better integration of newer functions such as RGM, as well as the re-establishment of the work of category management and shopper marketing.

Category Management Transformation

As the research made clear, category management activities are in fact the major mechanism of collaboration between the retailer and supplier. It is essential that this work continues. However, I'd like to propose that we change the way we develop and deliver this work. As discussed, the '8-Step' process is still relevant and the questions it asks are as important as ever. However, at this point in the industry's evolution, there are benefits to adapting these questions and rethinking who answers them. These changes will give the category management of the future a better chance of delivering its undoubted benefits (Table 6.2).

In this alternative approach, the category management strategy and associated toolkits still need to be developed by category expertise.

There are two significant changes in this proposal related to the work itself and who does the work. I propose that overall, the 8-step process re-focuses on an omni-channel level versus a customer level. This is undoubtedly a challenge, but one that needs to be met if we as an industry are to understand, manage, and better meet the needs of shoppers in the future. Single category silo thinking is not going to be good enough anymore.

In the overall process, I am also proposing an additional step of building the omni-channel path to purchase at the start of the process. This should be

Table 6.2 Category management process transformation

CM step	From	To	Who?
0—Omni-channel path to purchase	• Not present	• Foundation is shopper-consumer segmentation and mapping path to purchase	• Category Strategy Team
1—Definition	• Consumers define and shoppers segment the category • Practical reality is applied to a 'manageable' definition	• Consumers and shoppers define the category based on its widest understanding • New omni-channel reality leads to much wider definitions	• Category Strategy Team
2—Role	• Within retailer analysis of relative importance of categories	• Omni-channel analysis shows importance of categories across a much wider perspective	• Category Strategy Team
3—Assessment	• Category assessment based on supply and demand past opportunities	• A wider omni-channel assessment of the opportunities with more emphasis on predictive analytics and future state mapping	• Category Strategy Team
4—Scorecard	• A balanced set of targets by retailer	• Shopper-led targets set first at omni-channel level	• Category Strategy Team
5—Strategy	• Demand strategies developed by retailer	• Demand and supply strategies encompassing omni-channel and movement between channels	• Category Strategy Team
6—Tactics	• Demand tactics developed per retailer	• Demand and supply tactics encompassing omni-channel and movement between channels	• KAM Team
7—Implementation	• Plan per retailer	• Plan by omni-channel and tailored to each retailer	• KAM Team
8—Review	• Retailer POV	• Omni-channel POV	• Category Strategy and KAM Team

Source: Adapted from ECR Europe (1997)

the foundation of all thinking that follows and guides any decisions on how to develop growth plans.

In terms of who does the work, as we have discussed, my proposed approach is that the category team develops the strategic thinking elements of the 8-step process. Practically this refers to the work from Step 0, the omni-channel PTP down to Step 5, category strategy. I would propose then that the KAM teams take responsibility for the tactical development and execution (Steps 6 onwards), utilising new automation technologies as much as possible to streamline this work. As we have seen, in some retailer situations, the retailer themselves will do this work alone and won't require detailed input from suppliers anymore.

I know from talking to suppliers that this is a cause for concern. They argue that they know the details of the category and most of their work is currently in these tactical areas. They shouldn't be concerned. In my experience, it's not in the tactics that the greatest 'wins' occur; it's in the insight and thinking that developed the right strategies for growth. Focussing category teams in this area will pay back way more in mutual business growth than analysis of large amounts of sku level data to produce detailed range and space plans.

I designed this proposed approach to reorientate the category function into where it can add the most value—namely, focussing on the 'so what and now what' and creating a future of growth for themselves and their customers. When I speak to retailers, the collaborative help they need is understanding and planning for the future, creating a plan for growth, and delivering them competitive advantage.

This takes a high degree of skill and capability, and one that category teams in suppliers are well placed to deliver. This is not to lower the importance of the work category management teams, more to focus their energies on where they can create greatest value (future thinking and growth strategies) and reduce their focus, and cost, in what are currently highly people-intensive activities (data management, insights generation, and category tactic development). When I spoke with Brian Harris in 2021, he re-enforced this, saying that *'you need bright people to make category management work .... you cannot automate the creation of great strategy'*.

Category Management and Revenue Growth Management (RGM)

The emergence and growth of RGM work and teams has been the major focus of many suppliers in recent years. Its work that focuses on value creation, which is based on the research, is a positive step to identify and measure real 'transactional value' creation activities. Its challenge is often one of perspective; it is driven from a brand perspective rather than a category perspective.

RGM uses its own analytics to understand the levers of value growth (more people, more often, spending more) and apply the findings from this analysis to proposals for the price, packs, promotion, and investment of products. The work and focus of RGM is most often based in the 'Brand' as its brands that are being sold. Whilst this is logical, brands exist in wider products categories, and, to achieve success, RGM must fit into and help support category growth as well as brand growth to be successful. I think it is vital that we integrate this work into category management activities for RGM to work effectively into the future. Why do I say this?

Retailers do not care about brands! This is always a contentious discussion in my consulting work with large suppliers. What retailers do care about are brands that can drive category growth for them. If a supplier is developing viewpoints on RGM proposals that start with the brand, even if they then bring in retailer understanding, they aren't looking at a wider category perspective.

I believe, a category perspective is vital if the RGM strategies and plans that are developed are to be accepted by the retailer. In my experience, having a rounded and total category perspective in any commercial debate will develop new and positive ideas. If we take a narrower perspective of just the brand, this is much harder to achieve. A one demand team will help enable this, as will a wider omni-channel perspective to category management.

I recently discussed the current challenges in RGM with a former global lead for RGM capability in a supplier. Their view was that the work of RGM is still not consistent across the industry, and too few business link RGM across the commercial function. Further, in their view, RGM is more of a 'capability' than a function, meaning its philosophy and approach can be embedded across multiple teams in a commercial organisation. For me, this indicates the direction in which RGM needs to head.

Some companies I have talked to are already making this move. However, for some it seems to be driven by a desire to reduce costs, where heads in category teams are swapped for RGM resources, but the work isn't being integrated in any great depth. This is a mistake. Integrating category management and RGM work should come first, as the structure follows from this. I will discuss this in more detail later in this section.

Category Management and KAM

As discussed, I am proposing the delivery of this work, for highly collaborative accounts, be 'category-centred selling', which is the approach used by KAMs. They become responsible for providing 'one source of the truth' on the growth opportunities for their customers, and how they create and extract value from them. Some of these opportunities may not involve the suppliers' brands, but they are the one voice for the customer.

Category management and category strategy are a fantastic foundation for a consultative selling approach. Understanding the customer and their category needs should be the starting place for having ANY sales discussion with the customer. Where possible, we then place the supplier's brand as the solution to meeting that category needs, and therefore customers can clearly see how this will build their business (Fig. 6.11).

My proposal is that 'category-centred selling' becomes the norm for the industry. This approach to sales places the category insights and opportunity at the foundation of the sales story. The brand is presented as the final solution to realise a category opportunity for the customer. Through the removal of the day-to-day administration tasks, and through the increased use of technology, we can truly focus the category-centred salesperson on their customer and their needs and helping them grow by using their brands and their resources.

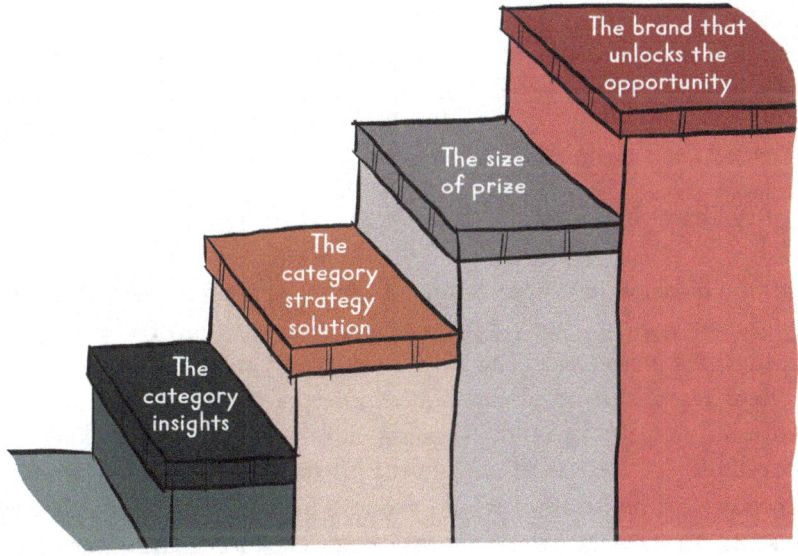

Fig. 6.11 Category-centred selling approach

There is, of course, a big decision to be made by the supplier about which customers you truly want to collaborate with in this way, because clearly not all customers are equal or offer equal levels of opportunity for growth and development. Similarly, from a retail perspective, not all suppliers are of equal importance and deserve the strategic attention that a collaborative approach, such as this one, would require.

What this would mean for category management is that the category manager resource in a supplier would only focus on the more strategic, medium- and longer-term opportunity development, using insights into how to grow the category into the future. The 'Category Strategist's' role would be to be the future thinker, not the backwards reporter of market data and trends. Automating this work through the adoption of new technologies will change their role in predicting the future landscape of the category and how to get there. These are people who the retailer can call upon, to talk to about where the categories are headed and what big strategic initiatives and changes are needed to build the business.

This alternative approach can then enable the streamlining of the category management organisation and focus it on the 'Why' and 'How' of category opportunities. This is where value is identified and created to step change the category growth, rather than a sizeable number of resources focussed on reporting and second-guessing past trends. Not only is this level of analytic resource costly, the gains for both retailer and supplier are often small, typically involving incremental changes to assortment, promotions, and so on.

How will this change the role of KAM? The approach does not require a radical shift, but rather one that is more focused on the skills and capabilities of the KAM teams to broaden their outlook to one that centres on category perspective.

Category Team Structure

A common question in my consulting life revolved around where to place the category management teams, as part of sales, or marketing, or as its own function with equal importance? For what is a relatively small decision, it was one that often created the most debate in commercial re-organisations! With my wise consulting head, I would always say 'it can sit anywhere, so long as the work and roles are clear and linked to the organisation, and that is true'.

However, for the future, I would propose for this fresh approach, which proposes that we separate the work for category management into two areas. The work of creating category strategy should be part of the marketing

Fig. 6.12 Commercial structure high level

function. It's this area that usually holds the insights that drive strategic thinking and is also where the strategy of the business comes to life from a consumer perspective. Placing it here would also link consumer (marketing) thinking to shopper (category management) thinking (Fig. 6.12).

In addition, this would also enable closer linkage of category and brand opportunities. My experience has shown me that 'great' category management works as hard internally in a supplier as it does externally with customers. What I mean by this is that rather than see category management as purely customer-facing work, it's a powerful way to look at the suppliers' brands in the category's context, and then innovate and develop from there. This approach means that once a new product idea gets to market, its category benefit is clear.

This can be executed by then having a 'golden thread' running through the launch of a new product for example. It's category insights that identify a category strategy, with a value attached. The brand launch or activity can then be shown to be the solution to a category opportunity (Fig. 6.13).

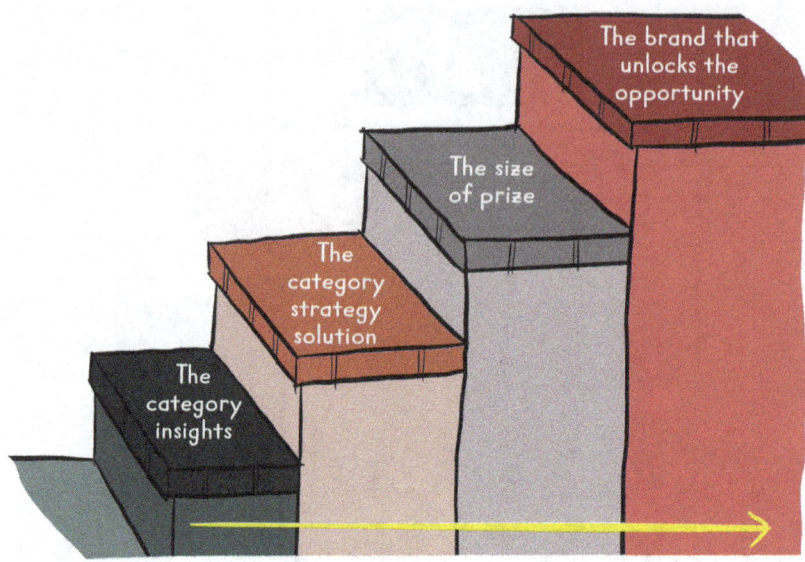

Fig. 6.13 Golden thread category-centred selling

We have seen that several largest suppliers have global teams that develop a lot of their category strategy thinking and accompanying 'toolkits' to support local teams in the work. This is valuable, but I believe it should be able to adapt to enable more local tailoring and responsiveness. This could be achieved by ensuring that the areas of omni-channel insight and thinking, and how to develop tactics, are ones that are locally developed.

Local markets are best placed to understand their customers' omni-channel path to purchase and incorporate it into their category growth planning. In addition, I propose that the work of tactical development is always local. This means that local teams can be more responsive and adapt to local needs. Without this, larger suppliers run an increasing risk of being challenged by smaller local brands, which are able to be much more responsive and flexible to retailers' requests (Fig. 6.14).

Commercial Teams Skills Development

The world of skills development has recently seen incredible change driven by the absence of face-to-face training workshops. Until the COVID-19 pandemic, e-learning, remote self-learning, and other blended methods were in use by my clients but weren't truly being embraced. There seems to be an inbuilt bias that 'face to face' is always better, more interactive, a better

Fig. 6.14 Global to local organisation

experience, and so on. Forced to change because of COVID-19, many businesses are rethinking their approach.

The world of learning has changed rapidly in other sectors, and the idea of 'learning in the flow of work' (LIFOW) is one which is developing rapidly. Bersin (2018) developed the idea of LIFOW, and it essentially makes available the resources and tools to 'do the job' at the fingertips of learners. Rather than attend event-based courses, or online courses that merely replicate a 2-day workshop in 10 hours of e-learning, this is providing the bite-sized task specific materials to learners at the moment they need help with a specific task.

This has the potential to further revolutionise the approach to the work of retailers and suppliers. Through creating high-quality materials and tools, the focus can be on doing the task better, with support, rather than 'how am I going to find time for this training course', and 'how will I apply the many things I learned on the course'. Research tells us this is a way people want to learn. They do it all the time now at home. Think of the times you have searched for a video on how to fix a household problem on YouTube. This is the same!

There, of course, needs to be additional support, be that coaching, or in-person events, but these are on top of always having the learning available when the learner wants to access it. This approach is going to be useful in our industry, where there are often many complex and technically challenging concepts to understand and use. For example, if we just consider the area of customer business planning, its approach, data, and analysis required, and so on, can take two days of face-to-face training. Having 'always-on' support for this task will unlock time and money for the company and help the learner complete their work more quickly and effectively (Fig. 6.15).

Fig. 6.15 Commercial skills development

In Summary

1. The work and skills of commercial teams are changing and need to be reflected in the commercial organisation of the future.
2. Moving to a combined sales and marketing function—one demand team—can streamline the work of commercial teams and remove barriers to collaborative working.
3. Category management needs to transform its approach to take account of the omni-channel world it now lives in.
4. The work of category management should split between the more strategic, how-and-why work, and the more practical, tactical work.
5. Category management and RGM need to be combined to create linkage and synergy in the strategies they develop.
6. KAM teams can undertake more of the tactical and implementation work of category management.
7. Category teams are best situation in marketing structures, to enable greater brand-consumer-shopper alignment.
8. Commercial skills development will be transformed by taking a learning in the flow of work approach—the right tools and support, always on, when you are doing the work.

5. Data and Insights Optimisation

If we look at any example of collaboration, business plans, category management protects, the underlying foundation to all of them is the availability and use of data and insights. So why do we need to take a fresh look at this area if its importance is a given? There are three areas of challenge and opportunity that I propose we need to address if we are to move to a new, more productive collaborative model in the industry.

Data Overload

The first is data abundance. We live in a world now where the amount of data available is creating huge issues for those looking to work worth it, and extract value. Yet, we hear from retailers and suppliers of the challenges of making more informed decisions. How can this be the case with a never-ending increase in data available?

One reason is the lack of structure in how I see we are using this data. I have led and worked on countless category management projects, and the part of the process that would take the most time, and cause the most work, was the Category Assessment stage. This was because it took a long time just to organise the data. We wanted to get access to, then gather the data, chart it, and then extract insights. One way we looked to help smooth this process is the use of business questions.

I am a genuine believer in the first port of call should be setting the business questions you are trying to answer before looking for any data. This can also apply to reporting. What business questions are we regularly trying to report on? I too often see the opposite approach, which is 'let's report on everything we have access to', resulting in a mass of reports and charts produced monthly or more frequently, that few are looking at. I spoke to one supplier recently who said they had dropped report packs one-by-one from their monthly updates, to see who complained, and to judge whether to stop producing them. And so far, there were no complaints!

AI and Machine Learning

So, if we have business questions as the focus as our first thought, we can then look at how we answer them, and what the answers are. This is an area that automation can and will take on more and more of a role in our industry. There are many solutions that exist right now that can make this a streamlined and efficient process and that do not need armies of analysts to do the work. These solutions can trawl databases across a business, assemble the best data for answering the business question, and chart it appropriately. Further still, AI solutions now exit to add commentary and insights to these charts, spoken by an 'AI analyst if you wish!'

The benefits of this move are many, but the major ones I expect are first headcount savings in the analysts needed for collecting and charting data. This will then free resources to focus on the 'So what and do what' of the data, which is the area that is often the weakest based on work I have done in the industry. The other benefit is that rather than spending so much time on 'hindsight' of data, what happened, how do we explain it, it should free up more time to focus on the predictive business questions—'where are the opportunities ... how do we solve them'.

Using a business question-based approach supported by technology should also create more value, with better insights into the shopper and their needs and in identifying future trends. Suppliers spend most of their data budget on continuous data, measuring share, sales, and so on, as well as on buying retailer-specific data sets. We have an opportunity here to streamline this whole area. An expert who set up a whole new data set to focus on the shopper explained to me:

> The continuous data sets have absorbed enormous sums of available investment cash (not least because retailers want to make money from these in their own right), but this cost really only drives relatively minor efficiency plays. Category people tell me they want more true insights about shoppers to uncover step change opportunity, but they don't have any significant budget left for it. Head office (often global) CPG brand insight functions invest in exploration around consumer needs, but rarely in the shopper space. I get asked often "what's the point of that—only retailers can truly execute against 'shopper'".
> Roger Jackson—MD, Shopper Intelligence

Value Creation from Insights

This builds on another area of opportunity, that of value creation, from insights. The real value in collaboration is the merging of data into insights and opportunities that identify value creation for both parties, versus endless reporting on what has happened. We often focus this type of reporting on the tactical level, where the solution often only creates a small impact anyway ('change this sku for that', 'swap this promotion for that', 'more space of this product and less for that'). Too little time in my experience is spent on looking to the future in a way that is founded on this shopper and consumer understanding and that will navigate us towards growth opportunities. Technology can be one enabler to change this dynamic.

We also know that the omni-channel challenge demands more insights and creates increased complexity. If we are to manage this effectively, just adding more analyst resource working in the same way always have won't be sufficient (or costs effective). We need an alternative approach to how we manage the end-to-end process of data and insights.

We have an opportunity now, based on the technology available, and being used extensively in other industries, to transform this area of collaborative work that currently swallows up an enormous amount of resource in terms of time and money. The streamlining of this area unlocks many benefits in terms of quality and type of insight focus, and it will enable closer and more valuable collaboration into the future.

We have seen that retailers are recognising the value of their insights and moving from selling data to selling access to powerful shopper journey knowledge and advertising and promotion solutions that can be activated along that path, so-called Retail Media Networks. Whilst that is clearly valuable to retailers, suppliers are being faced with a costly challenge. They are being asked to buy more and more data and retailer-specific investment packages.

The collaboration opportunity is to understand the value of combining insights from both parties. The technology now exists that will allow us to achieve this in a relatively simple way, and the power of both sets of data can realise more benefit for both sides. I believe this area is one of the main focus areas for creating and capturing value thought collaboration for both sides. If suppliers do not step up their approach and expertise in these areas, they face being overwhelmed with complexity and cost in their attempts to collaborate with retailers in the future.

Moving towards a new model for learning, as we have discussed, can support this change. Learning in the flow of work (LIFOW) will place the right resources and tools in the hands of the teams using the insights, right at the moment they need them. It can emphasise 'how do I do this work now' versus learning endless process, tools, and made-up case studies to build the skills, which the team member then must translate themselves into the work they are doing. Let's be honest—this is just a very inefficient way of giving people the skills they need to do their job to the best of their ability.

In Summary

1. Data abundance and new sources are driving the need for a business question-based approach to data and analytics.
2. Technological solutions are vital to streamline and simplify the data analytics task, saving time and money.
3. Data and analytics will become the key part of value creation in collaboration into the future.

6. RELATE: Relational and Transactional Value

The reason we are in business is to create and capture value. Value creation can take on several forms, but its transactional value is what we are looking for. We collaborate as we believe we create and capture more value through collaboration than if we didn't collaborate at all. So why are we in such a tough place as an industry, where we are unclear what this value really is, and how we create and capture it?

The research findings in the entire area of value creation and capture provided us with significant insights. As we know, those findings split value creation and capture into two areas of relational value and transactional value. Relational value was found in those elements of contact that the supplier has with the retailer which they place great value on, while transactional value was evident in the actual accrual of money from the collaboration.

Relational value has challenges in terms of how it's measured. This is especially true in the light of recent events, where the challenges of COVID-19 meant that face-to-face interactions were unavailable, and retailers and suppliers did all of this communication electronically. Anecdotal evidence suggests that this is a situation that retailers are happy with as it creates more time for them to focus on the work they need to do, versus spending many hours in interactions with suppliers.

This is a challenge to the way of working and the creation of our transactional value that suppliers need to address. I propose that this change can be a positive thing. It's arguable that the relational value suppliers were creating and capturing for themselves just through interaction and meetings was actually creating the same amount of value for the retailer. I know from my personal experience working in a retailer, spending so much time with a lot of suppliers really added little value to my work.

From a supplier perspective, there appears to be an inbuilt assumption that more time spent with a retailer in face-to-face interactions was, in quotation marks, a good thing. As we've seen, this is not necessarily the case, and I think the key point here is trying to understand from the retailer's perspective what exactly they require in terms of face-to-face interaction.

A senior retail director told me *'we are as keen as ever to have productive discussions with suppliers, but we have so little time or resource .... please just make communications easy for us'*.

In addition, it is very difficult to put a monetary value on this level of relational value creation and capture. The value is determined by the customer, so my proposal is that for collaborative strategic customers, it's vital to understand what exactly they require in terms of communication and interaction. What level should be face-to-face? What should be done through other methods?

With transactional value, the challenges we saw in the research were the lack of valuation of the activities, be they strategies or tactical business initiatives. This was true, particularly in the area of category management activities. In category management, as discussed previously, there is an enormous amount of work going on, but little in the way of quantifying and measuring the transactional value of creation and capture.

I propose we change this. It is easy to forecast the value of most activities that exist in a joint business plan with the customer. For either category management activities or other activities, it is possible to predict and measure the impact on both sides.

Further, with new technologies and automation in data and insights, this measurement can happen relatively quickly and also without a great deal of work. This area needs to transform if we are to move ahead on being much more transparent, open, and able to manage the area of transactional value creation. In addition, these activities and their value must be embedded in business plans, joint or otherwise. This will make clear their contribution to achieving value growth, but also indicate the value lost if they are not implemented (a behaviour we often saw with category management activities in the research).

There is a real danger here that if we don't do this and we carry on with the current ways of working. Retailers and suppliers will eventually call into question the vast amount of work they are doing in the name of collaboration, if its value is unknown and unmeasured. Where else in business would we tolerate this? If a supplier is looking to build a new factory, or buy a new IT system, there are rigorous analyses on its ROI. Based on my research and experience, that rigour is often missing in customer business planning and collaboration, where the investments involved are often one of the most significant expenditure areas for the business.

In Summary

1. Relational and transactional values are equally important in collaboration between the retailer and supplier.
2. Relational value is difficult to measure but can be better managed through greater understanding between each side's objectives and timescales.

3. Transactional value needs much greater emphasis placed on valuation of activities and embedding these in business plans.
4. New technology and automation can help simplify and streamline the measurement and management of value creation activities.

7. Customer Business Planning

When looking at the area of customer business planning, it was clear from the research that the first major issue to be resolved was around the plans being used with different customers. In virtually all the research cases, the evidence was of the supplier producing what they were calling joint business plans, when, in fact, the vast majority of them were developed by the supplier alone.

There was very little evidence of an actual business plan being developed jointly with the customer where the customer co-created the activities, strategies, tactics, and so on. There was some evidence of alignment between retailers and suppliers on the targets that were to be set, but no linkage of those targets to the activity that needed to take place to deliver them.

So why is that important? First, it's important for the supplier to be crystal clear with their business that what they're developing is a business plan alone. It's a plan that they would *like* to achieve with the customer, based on the suppliers' own desires, target strategies, and so on. However, by calling it a joint business plan, there is the danger that the wider business believes that this is a plan that the customers themselves co-created, and therefore have a greater support and endorsement from the customer. Clearly, in those examples, that is not the case.

The concept of joint business planning is one that's used extensively in other industries and has proved to be of real value. We can create value when we develop JBPs with a very selective number of strategic customers that are willing and able to collaborate. As highlighted in the discussion of customer prioritisation, my belief is that some challenges we've seen in terms of value creation and value capture started out as problems in this area of business planning.

Why do I say this? When suppliers believe they are developing a joint business plan but aren't, they develop a greater sense of confidence and security in the plan. This is because they believe the customer is fully committed to delivering it with them, when in fact that is not the case. Working as a consultant, I could see that it is vital to achieve the customer's commitment as soon as possible in any planning with a retailer in order to ensure success. This needs to happen, even if it stalls the process and timings. I have seen suppliers realise they need commitment, make a half-hearted attempt to gain it, and then carry on regardless. The plan starts with an inbuilt issue that they did not commit the retailer to the plan to start with.

I'm proposing that we use joint business plans incredibly sparingly, only with those customers who have shown the commitment and willingness and ability to want to collaborate deeply with the supplier. That means that they will not just develop an alignment on the targets between the two businesses in whatever areas are important but will also collaborate in the development of the strategies, tactics, and initiatives to deliver the plan.

Embedding Category Management in Customer Business Planning

The second area I want to cover in business planning is the area of value creation and capture. We have already discussed and highlighted that, in the research, there was little to no evidence of initiatives having the actual value attached to them, or of that value then cascading into a set of targets with the retailer. This was a particular issue in terms of category management activities.

The problem with this is that without this linkage, customers can see category management activities and other collaboration activities as 'nice to haves' or activities the supplier themselves are keener on driving than the retailer. As we saw in the research, typically what happens when there is a conflict is the retailer then shuts down these activities, believing that to be a punitive action against the supplier.

If we are to move forward as an industry, the valuation of these activities and embedding these in the business planning process and in the targets that are jointly agreed with the retailer is one way to ensure that they see their value. This should then mitigate against them being used as levers in negotiations when the retail makes short-term demands.

The purpose of category management activities such as range, review, space management activities (merchandising reviews, promotional planning and pricing approaches, new item introduction, etc.) is that they build value for the category, and they build value for the retailer, and they build value for the supplier. If the retailer doesn't believe that to be the case, then we have a major issue with a large part of the work that is being undertaken by suppliers in the name of collaboration and in the name of value creation.

This needs to be addressed. It's a fundamental issue to be overcome, and one way of overcoming it is to ensure that we forecast the value of these activities and embed them in the business plan. The benefit of doing this also extends to improving the implementation of these activities. In my consulting experience and in my research, although there is an absolute wealth of category management activity taking place in a supplier, the actual review of its effectiveness is very weak.

Embedding these initiatives and activities in the business plan means both sides will not win unless we implement them to their fullest effect. Said differently, unless we implement our business plan activities, we won't achieve our scorecard. Allied to that, there is the actual realisation then that if the retailer takes short-term punitive action and removes those activities, this will actually reduce the achievement of the scorecard and the targets that both sides have set.

So, it would be madness to remove an activity that is, in fact, in place to increase the business between the two parties. Taking this approach will mean that category management is not a stick with which to beat suppliers in a negotiation, but more of a core activity through which joint value can be created between both sides.

Customer Business Plan Review

The last area of change proposed in customer business planning is related to reviewing the plan. My experience and the research showed that there is a lack of focus on the review of the business plan. Was it on track? Are the targets achievable? Are there any corrective actions needed? Suppliers did this work poorly and infrequently. There are many reasons that were cited for this. For some, this was around the idea that the business plan is a one-off event and then filed away. Others talked about them not wanting to discuss the targets with the retailer, fearing that it would just start discussions on demands and short-term actions they didn't want to get into. For us to move ahead on this and build on the foundations of trust that we talked about earlier, this needs to change.

If we are in a position where we develop in a joint business plan, then it's logical that it needs to be reviewed. This review is not just about whether the plan is on track or not? But also, how close, or not, we are to achieving the targets that we had both agreed upon. And if we are not close and there is corrective action needed, this is a discussion that can happen frequently and throughout the year.

The point for me is that if this plan is truly joint, then both sides have a commitment to delivering on it; otherwise both sides will not receive the benefit that they are hoping to achieve. We've seen from the research and other evidence elsewhere that without this, the retailer is more tempted to move into a behaviour that says they still want the target delivered, regardless of what was outlined in the plan regarding the hoped-for achievement, and to use short-term actions to achieve it.

As we've discussed throughout the book, this must change. Otherwise, we will continue to move into the doom loop of further short-term activity and demands, which then really questions 'why plan at all' and indeed why do joint business plans, if all that's going to happen is that the minute the plan goes off track, the retailer shuts the plan down and just demands the money, anyway.

What I haven't proposed here is a detailed process or set of tools for KAM planning. If you do want to review that area in detail, I recommend 'Key Account Plans' by Ryals and McDonald (2007). If you want to look more deeply at co-creating value as a concept, I recommend 'From Selling to Co Creating' by Lemmens et al. (2014).

In Summary

1. Suppliers need to be clear when they are developing CBPs versus JBPs and why.
2. JBPs are a powerful mechanism to enable collaboration with a few, carefully selected partners.
3. Category management activities need to be clearly valued and embedded in CBPs and JBPs.
4. Scorecard and the review of plans are frequently the missing elements that need to be included and used in collaboration—enabled by new technologies as much as possible.

Chapter Summary

- The foundation principles of trust, partner choice, and honesty and transparency are the basis for the new model of collaboration.
- There are three high levels of opportunity areas that have informed the model: value creation and capture, category management transformation, and mastering power.
- Omni-channel mindset involves mapping our target customers and their shopper journeys to inform all the planning we do as a commercial organisation.

- Collaborative partner selection is focused on who we choose to work with and how.
- Mastering power analyses, the status of power in our relationship, and what does it mean for collaboration?
- Relational and transactional value asks us to identify the value we seek and how we capture it.
- Commercial work and skills identify the work and skills to enable the new future.
- Data and insights optimisation shows how we can transform the way we develop and use insights in our collaboration with partners.
- Customer business planning identifies the enhancements to how we plan and activate together in collaboration.

References

Bersin, J. (2018) A New Paradigm for Corporate Training: Learning in the Flow of Work. Accessed at: https://joshbersin.com/2018/06/a-new-paradigm-for-corporate-training-learning-in-the-flow-of-work/

Cowan, K., Paswan, A.K. and Van Steenburg, E. (2015) When inter-firm relationship benefits mitigate power asymmetry. *Industrial Marketing Management*, 48, pp. 140–148.

Dapiran, G.P. and Hogarth-Scott, S. (2003) Are co-operation and trust being confused with power? An analysis of food retailing in Australia and the UK. *International Journal of Retail and Distribution Management*, 31(5), pp. 256–267.

ECR Europe (1997) Category management best practice report. Brussels: ECR Europe.

ECR Europe (2011) Consumer and Shopper Journey Framework. Accessed at: https://www.ecr-community.org/the-consumer-and-shopper-journey-framework/

Kamel, M., de Montgolfier, J., Caine, S., Ringer, J. and Puzio, S. (2020). How to Ramp Up Online Grocery—without Breaking the Bank. Accessed at: https://www.bain.com/insights/how-to-ramp-up-online-grocery-without-breaking-the-bank/

Neff, J. (2021) Wal Mart has some data they would like to sell you. *Ad Age*. Accessed at: https://adage.com/article/marketing-news-strategy/walmart-has-some-data-theyd-sell-you/2342911

Shepherd, G. (2014) The Importance of Triple Win Thinking. Accessed at: https://www.thepartneringgroup.com/categorymanagement/the-importance-triple-win-thinking/

Szahun, T. and Dalton, R. (2021) The state of ecommerce 2021. Accessed at: https://www.kantar.com/inspiration/retail/the-state-of-ecommerce-2021-cn

Verhoef, P., Kannan P. and Inman, J. (2015) From Multi-Channel Retailing to Omni-Channel Retailing: Introduction to the Special Issue on Multi-Channel Retailing. *Journal of Retailing*, 91(2), pp. 174–181.

Walmart Corporate Website. Accessed at: https://corporate.walmart.com/our-story/history/10-rules-for-building-a-business

Further Reading

Lemmens, R., Donaldson, B. and Marcos, J. (2014) From selling to co-creating. Amsterdam: Bis Publishers.

Ryals, L. and McDonald, M. (2007) Key Account Plans (1st ed.). Routledge.

7

Summary and Conclusions: Making the Move Towards Real Collaboration

What we will cover in this chapter:

- A conclusion to the book, what we have discussed, and what I am proposing.
- A set of questions to assess where your organisation is now, and what your areas of focus for improvement could be.

When I started my career in this industry, I—like most people—had no idea how it would turn out, or where I would be in it after 20+ years. I have to say it's an industry that has me hooked, and I have enjoyed most of what I have done. For me, it has become more than enjoyment. It's been a passion, and that passion was been a big drive behind writing this book.

Another significant drive was my desire to share ideas, prompt new thoughts, and work to start a debate on where our industry could go in future. Putting to one side the size and scale of the firms involved, it's an industry that provides a vital role in society, and literally has the ability to change people's lives, along with their health, and wellness. I think this places a great responsibility on those involved. I believe we are called to do their best for the consumers and shoppers we serve and doing so in a way that is good for everyone.

Real Collaboration Must Be Our Default Position

This can only be achieved with collaboration. No one party can do this alone. Regardless of the different power dynamics between retailers and suppliers, no one has a monopoly on great ideas, the right resources and skills, or the ability to deliver fantastic products to consumers and shoppers.

It's only in the collaboration between these two groups that great solutions can be developed and delivered. Now is the time for us all to truly recognise this fact and put aside the adversarial and confrontation approaches that have characterised many so-called collaborations in our industry.

At the most fundamental level, we always want to do the best for our business, our customers, and our shareholders. But working in a way that has us perpetually engaged in actions at the expense of others and involved in often fraught relationships is going to end badly for all of us. Under the current conditions, we can't help but lose our sense of perspective, lose sight of where we are heading, and, more often than not, lose sight of the most important group of people we are here to serve—consumers and shoppers.

Time to Re-set the Way We Collaborate

In the introduction to this book, I characterised the dilemma we face as the danger of moving from the 'Triple Win to the Triple Loss'. We are now at a moment of decision. Are we going to come together as an industry to re-focus on what's important, re-set the way we collaborate, and re-boot our organisations to deliver the triple win? Or will we postpone or fail to take informed action and leave the future to be guided by the current, more destructive patterns?

As we have discussed, collaboration is a very complex and challenging dynamic to manage. There are multiple different factors impacting what collaboration is, who to partner with, and the work and skills we need to make it happen. But there are solutions, and there are some incredible people across the industry with the skills and capability to deliver it.

More than that, we are now in the right moment for new technologies to step change how we work. Already available and being used are transformative approaches to data and analytics, planning tools, and more, that can streamline, simplify, and speed up work that often required months and armies of people. Now is the time for us as an industry to grab these opportunities and the benefits they can bring.

What Have We Covered?

In Chap. 2 we discussed the history of collaboration in our industry and the retailer and supplier challenges as they exist today. We have seen the pressures both sides are facing, as well as the massively shifting consumer and shopper landscape which we need to address.

Chapter 3 gave a brief overview of some of the theories behind collaboration, including those related to power dynamics, and value creation and capture. These theories provide a meaningful contents and a strong foundation from which we can learn; other industries have faced similar challenges and we can gain insights from those experiences as well.

The case studies presented in Chap. 4 and analysed in Chap. 5 provided examples of how supplier businesses are operating and how they collaborate. The examples focused on different types of company, but all showed common themes that we can learn from, both good and bad.

In my final chapter (Chap. 6) I have brought all of the themes together to propose a new model of collaboration. This model proposes areas we can focus on and are designed to start new ways of thinking about how we can improve and develop our collaborative capabilities.

What's Next?

My model is intended to start the debate and to offer ideas to prompt deeper thinking on how they could be applied to your business. Some ideas will apply more than others; others will not have meaning for you in your current situation. Regardless, my hope is that, at the least, the model offered here starts a debate in your business on 'where next' when it comes to collaboration.

To help that process, I have developed some questions that may help start the discussion. Taking the themes and solutions we have covered, there are two or three questions per areas that can help you begin to identify your areas of focus and interest. Intentionally these are not detailed capability questions; rather, they are more intended to point you in a direction of improvement and help focus in on what is most important to you (Table 7.1).

As I mentioned, my hope is that you find use in these questions to start your own journey on how you can improve collaboration. I don't underestimate the challenge, I have been there as a supplier, retailer, and now as a consultant, I know how challenging transformation in these areas can be.

Table 7.1 Organisational assessment—questions to start your own thinking

Area	Question
Foundation principles	
• Triple Win needs	• Do we understand the needs of the three areas as they relate to our business?
	• Are we embedding this knowledge across all of our planning process?
• Partner choice	• Are we being selective in making choices on who to partner with?
	• Do we live the choices we make day to day?
• Trust	• Do we operate to the highest standards of trust with our partners?
	• Do we know if our partners trust us in our collaborative work?
• Honesty and transparency	• Do our partners recognise our honesty and transparency in the collaborative work we do?
Opportunities for growth	
• Value creation and capture	• Are we able to forecast and measure the value we create and capture in collaboration?
• Category management transformation	• Is our category management organisation fit for purpose with all our chosen partners?
• Mastering power	• Do we understand the power dynamic in our collaborative relationships?
New model of collaboration	
• Omni-channel mindset	• Do we understand all of the channels we are operating in—both in selling and communication?
	• Can we identify our most important customers in each channel, their shopping journey, and barriers and trigger to purchase?
	• Are we clear on our strategy for each channel, how we will collaborate with partners in each channel?
• Collaborative partner selection	• Is our partner selection model based on more than just size/scale measures—does it include commitment and capability measures?
	• Have we identified the collaborative work we will and will not do in each area of the segmentation?
• Mastering power	• Are we accounting for and managing the influence of power in our collaborative work?

(continued)

Table 7.1 (continued)

Area	Question
• Commercial work and skills	• Have we identified the future work and skills for our organisation across all areas involved in collaboration? • Have we reviewed the opportunity for one-demand team, and re-setting our commercial structure for the future? • Have we considered whether the category management organisation is fit for purpose to manage the omni-channel world? • Are we effectively integrating our RGM approach across the commercial organisation, in particular with category management? • Is our skills development programme focussed on a blended approach and founded on being always available in terms of high-quality digital support?
• Data and insights optimisation	• Have we identified and are we implementing new technologies and solutions where appropriate to streamline and better manage our insights work? • Are we identifying the value created from insights and reflecting this in our collaborative work? • Are we combining our insights capability with our partners as a key part of our collaboration work?
• Relational and transactional value	• Are we clear on our partner's relational and transaction value needs, and do we have this as a clear focus in our collaboration planning and work? What does 'good value' look like to them? • Can we clearly identify the relational transactional value we create and capture in our collaborative work?
• Customer business planning	• Is our business planning process able to work in an omni-channel environment? • Are we clear when we are using JBP versus CBP, and what that means practically for our collaboration? • Do we embed our category management initiatives clearly and accurately in our business plans? • Are our plans reviewed and revised regularly with the customer in order to develop joint corrective actions?

However, I also know that it's possible to bring about a transformation and often a number of small changes can have a huge impact.

I found this myself when I was working in a supplier earlier in my career. I was the newly appointed key account manager for our largest customer. It was my first 'KAM' role. I made the leap from leading the category management team, a big responsibility given that nearly a quarter of the company's business was in my hands!

I was daunted, but also excited. I approached my first customer meeting really having no reference points on how to best 'manage' a customer. At that first meeting, I was asked for a view on how the customer should change their category range. They were losing market share, and wanted to make a big change, and quickly. I went away and did my analysis, as any good category manager would do.

The following week, I was there in front of the customer. I made my presentation. In essence, I said, if I were in your seat, this is what I would do, and why, to address your market share issue and close the gap. I showed proposals for all the major parts of the category. How many of my own business's products did I recommend as part of the solution? Zero.

They had all of our major products, that wasn't their issue. Their issue was with our competitor products—they needed more of them, and I told them so. I demonstrated that this is what they should do in order to build their business.

I think some may have seen this as madness, aren't you as a salesperson supposed to be selling your products? Well, yes when those products provide a clear solution to the customer's own needs. I know that one meeting demonstrated to the customer how my company had changed approach and that we were there to help them grow. It transformed the relationship between us and built a joint business that grew well above market levels.

Life isn't always that simple, and there are often deeper and complex issues to solve, but what I know for sure is that small steps can make a difference. The important thing is to take that step. I wish you well in your endeavours.

Index

B

Business-to-Business exchange, 47–49, 57, 59

C

Case Studies, 47, 76, 78
    Alpha, 166, 168–174
    Beta, 166, 169, 170, 174–177
    Delta, 166–170, 180–182, 185
    Gamma, 166, 169, 170, 176–179
Category Captain, 96, 136–139, 142, 144
Category centred selling, 215, 218
Category management (CM), 13–20, 26–30, 38, 43, 44
Collaboration, 1–9
    barriers, 99, 101, 120–121, 123, 143, 144, 158–160
    purpose and choices, 90–92, 94, 132–133, 135, 152
    work, 95, 103, 106, 116–118, 123, 128, 135, 155
Consumers, 1–5, 7–9
Customer business planning, 198, 219, 225–230

D

Data and insights, 4, 5
Direct to consumer (DTC), 24–25, 42
Discounters, 25–26, 32, 34–36, 40

E

Efficient Consumer Response (ECR), 7

G

Global Organisations, 20–22, 30

H

Honesty and transparency, 192, 207, 229

J

Joint Business Plans (JBP), 93, 95, 105, 108, 109, 114, 121, 124, 127, 128, 138, 139, 147–149, 153–155, 158, 161, 162

K

Key Account Management (KAM), 47, 49, 50, 52–55, 64–77, 80

M

Margins, 16, 22, 24, 27, 35, 37

N

Non-collaboration work, 98–99, 120, 142–143, 158

O

Omni-Channel, 18, 22–24, 34–35
Organisation, 195–197, 199, 205, 208–211, 214, 216, 219, 220, 229
Organisational Assessment, 236–237
Own-brand, 128, 129, 133, 135, 136, 139–145, 147–149, 152–162

P

Partner choice, 191–192, 229
Power, 47, 52–57, 64, 65, 70, 71, 74, 76, 78

R

Relational quality (RQ), 47, 49–52, 67, 74

Relationship Marketing (RM), 47, 49, 55, 65, 68
Revenue growth management (RGM), 29–30

S

Segmentation, 191, 192, 202–206
Shoppers, 1–4, 7, 8
Structure, 200, 208, 210, 214, 216–221

T

Triple Win, 2, 8
Trust, 92, 100–101, 103, 113–114, 136, 155, 157, 159–161, 190, 192–193, 205, 228, 229

V

Value, 1, 4, 6–7, 9
  capture, 57, 63–64, 75, 89, 105–107, 109, 111, 126–128, 147, 161
  creation, 47, 49, 57–80, 89, 103–105, 109, 111, 124–126, 128, 130, 145–147, 152, 160–161, 163

W

Work and Skills, 198, 208–220, 230

GPSR Compliance

The European Union's (EU) General Product Safety Regulation (GPSR) is a set of rules that requires consumer products to be safe and our obligations to ensure this.

If you have any concerns about our products, you can contact us on

ProductSafety@springernature.com

In case Publisher is established outside the EU, the EU authorized representative is:

Springer Nature Customer Service Center GmbH
Europaplatz 3
69115 Heidelberg, Germany

www.ingramcontent.com/pod-product-compliance
Lightning Source LLC
LaVergne TN
LVHW021339080526
838202LV00004B/240